WHY YOUR CEC

'A truly remarkable exposé of doing business in China, told through compelling war stories! Since 1989, Jack Leblanc has witnessed first-hand China's breathtaking economic development. He offers insights into how the Chinese do business through anecdotes rich with humour. His provocative and practical lessons about negotiating with the Chinese, and understanding the Chinese psyche, culture, and business mores, entertain and stimulate. This book is a "must read" for anyone who wishes to achieve business success in China.'
— Dr. Huiping Li, Anisfield School of Business, Ramapo College of New Jersey

'There are people who understand business in China, and there are people who understand business in Europe. And then there is Jack Leblanc, who offers a unique insight into the fast-moving business worlds of both China and Europe.'
— Dr Sean Xiang, President & CEO, Bloombase Group

Jack Leblanc 先生是我多年的好友，也是我所见过的对中国商业社会、经济文化最有切身体会和深刻研究的外国友人。本书是作者将其在中国多年的亲身经历、敏锐观察和深刻思考进行精心提炼之后完成的，全书的叙述方式轻松易读，但内中隐藏的道理却十分深刻、发人深思。我个人认为，对计划进入中国的外国人和外国企业来说，此书是不可多得的学习读本。更加难得的是，本书作者特有的"中国通"和"外国人"的双重身份，决定了其对中国商业社会的观察和思考具有更加独特的角度和深度。因此，本书对中国读者，尤其是国内的商务人士、涉外的政府官员来说也具有相当的参考价值。
— Simon Huang, President, GREEN Bio-technology Co., Ltd, Executive President Zhongguancun Science and Technology Entrepreneurs Association

'Jack Leblanc arrived in Chongqing in 1989 a China virgin. After nearly two decades of trying everything from selling plate glass to engineering dotcom dreams, he now qualifies as a fully fledged "China Hand". I enjoyed this book – laughed out loud a few times – and some good memories of my own disasters and triumphs came back to me.'
— Paul French, Access Asia Shanghai; author of *Carl Crow: A Tough Old China Hand* and *Midnight in Peking*

'Jack's stories make it crystal clear that in entering the Chinese market, or any new market for that matter, even the best business plan is worthless unless one takes into consideration the cultures and unique business ethics of the region. This book is a wise investment for anyone working in China and a good hedge against having one's venture going down the drain.'
— Rizal Wijono, Managing Director, Sun Hung Kai Financial

'Jack Leblanc captured the essence of the China business scene by describing the real-life situations he experienced over the past 20 years as a barbarian entrepreneur struggling to get a piece of the alluring cake. China changed at an incredible velocity over the period and he portrays how this affected the Chinese business climate and people.'
— Frederic Montier, Director, Service Delivery Centres Program, Bull Information Systems

'Through its easy-to-read stories, *Why Your CEO Failed in China* shows a few unexpected situations this fast-growing economy can generate.'
— Alfredo Parres, Group Senior Vice President, ABB Group

'Jack Leblanc has been a serial entrepreneur in China since 1989. In addition to being highly amusing, his stories provide great insight into the changes in the business environment and the cultural challenges of doing business in China.'
— Jeremy Perks, Director, Mindset Matter Group Ltd

'Jack really gets into the guts of China. These are up-close and personal tales from 19 years of brokering deals, all the way from the western industrial heartlands of Sichuan to across the Taiwan Strait. This book goes beyond regular seminar fare and reveals the real pitfalls posed by the cultural divide. I highly recommend this entertaining and instructive read.'
— Josh Green, CEO, Southern Rock Seafood Ltd, SHUCKED Oyster bars; Former Chief Representative China Britain Business Council

'I have been teaching in China since 1993, and a book about China would have to be pretty darn good to get my attention. This is that book! It has information that only a real veteran can impart. Businesspeople planning a China project will ignore this book at their peril.'
— Prof. Farrokh Langdana, PhD Director, Rutgers EMBA, & Professor, Finance/Economics, Rutgers Business School

'We are fortunate to witness the unprecedented transformation of the PRC from a socialist to capitalist society, and more so, to deal with the changes in its people's mindsets. Jack Leblanc's lively tales will resonate with all those who have come from other parts of the world to live and work in China.'
— Martin Lin, Former Managing Director, China, Rockwell Collins

'After 16 years working in China I would recommend this book to anybody starting or having a business here. It will cut short your learning process and prevent many frustrations, but most of all it will help you sidestep major cultural misunderstandings.'
— Jean-Luc Cran, CEO Asia, Veolia Water Technologies

WHY YOUR CEO FAILED IN CHINA

True tales of how not to do business

in the People's Republic

Jack Leblanc

BLACKSMITH BOOKS

Why Your CEO Failed in China:
True tales of how not to do business in the People's Republic
Previously published, in shorter format, as *Business Republic of China*

ISBN 978-988-79638-1-3 (paperback)
© 2020 Jack Leblanc

Published by Blacksmith Books
Unit 26, 19/F, Block B, Wah Lok Industrial Centre,
31–35 Shan Mei St, Fo Tan, Hong Kong
www.blacksmithbooks.com

Typeset in Adobe Garamond by Alan Sargent
Printed and bound in Hong Kong
First printing 2020

Contents

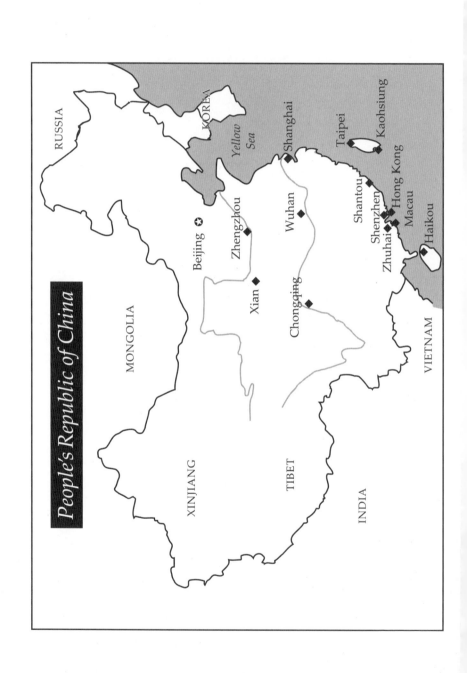

People's Republic of China

ACKNOWLEDGEMENTS

Below you will find, in no particular order, some of the remarkable people who gave me a chance to make things happen.

First and foremost I'd like to thank Xiao Han, my soul mate, partner and wife, who has always stood strong like a rock during life's storms and sunshine moments. She is always there, unwavering and dedicated to guiding me to the shelters of a sometimes-chaotic lifestyle. Her deep well of patience is an invaluable resource to counter my occasional erratic behaviour. Without her steady support this book would never have seen the light of day.

Alex P., your unbridled friendship and quiet dedication to assisting me with this project, has been and is immeasurable. Most importantly your stern comments were a gust of fresh air, which made sure this book became something of a more friendly read. Indeed, what a barbarian can do to the English language and the art of writing must often have felt painful and hilarious at best. At the same time your massive China insight, your enormous feel for what makes us barbarians love the China we experience every day, was an inspiration. Thank you so much!

Magda, you are a truly good friend. After this experience, I am sure our tribes have come a lot closer to understanding each other. Having an unexpected heap of papers to read through, while juggling your husband's desires, your kids' attention and at the same time managing your studies, must have been a struggle. Your attention to detail was phenomenal. You can rest assured I won't complain.

S. Lebon, my very good friend and partner, you are probably much too busy buying properties and selling shares on the stock market to fully realise the impact you have had on my business experience in China. Your selfless generosity during times I needed it most is unforgettable. The nuggets of inside information, the tidbits of legal fodder you've fed this barbarian brain over the years, are diamonds of wisdom twinkling against a stark black heaven of China's unknowns.

Sean X., your insights, your wit and lateral thinking on Chinese politics, history and society are fascinating as ever. Whenever our busy schedules allow, I always look forward to a meal of Shanxi food and a good conversation with you.

Also a special 3Q goes out to the Rutgers' Beijing and Shanghai EMBA alumni who have always been available to me to tap into their rich resources and to exchange ideas and made doing China business a piece of cake.

Irina V. for her passionate sharing of the sub-atomic world and steadfast belief that only good can come from challenging the status quo.

My appreciation certainly also goes to Eric A., my talented Beijing-based editor who rummaged through the string of sentences I collected over the years. Watching you turn my crippled and cryptic English into a regular text was magic!

This book was forged on the digital anvil of my dynamic publisher Pete Spurrier. A big thanks for tackling this project head on.

My neighbours Hein and Bea opened a world beyond the limited imagination of a ten-year-old. The road to the outside borders would certainly have been much more difficult without having them share their travel stories.

Finally I also would like to thank my parents Moethi and Tönke who give me a zest for life and adventure. At no time, despite how painful it sometimes must have been for your personal serenity, did you ever try to stop me from experimenting and unearthing the world's many undiscovered spoils. Only now do I realise the many sleepless nights this must have entailed for both of you. Rest assured your philosophical approach gave me more than is required to successfully conquer the daily obstacles along the way.

My lovely Ceravnjetsky, without your presence and complaints, how could we have made all this happen?

Also I'd like to show my appreciation to Max Vuijlvjel, Dania S., Ms Gao, Wim V., Peter V., T3, Graeme, Mr Zhu, Li Q., Marianne C., Michael P., Feng B., Kat, J. Lenoir, a flock of Chinese lawyers and my customers for their support, advice, spiritual input or eccentric thoughts.

Foreword

It is said that a foreigner who has had the opportunity to live in China for a period of two years might write a thick tome about the ins and outs of the country, its rich history, brazenly lifting the haze surrounding the political elite or demystifying the secrets of running a business here; while someone who has been residing six years in this rather complex society might settle for a brief exposé, realising that not all is truly understood, leaving much of the written word open for interpretation, afraid not to be able to catch the essence of what makes Chinese society tick.

Those who have had the privilege to spend a good part of their lives in the country take a deep breath, look back and appreciate the fact that nothing is as it seems. Scratching their heads in despair, they apprehend that nothing in black and white can genuinely grasp the 5,000 years of subtleties that run through the veins of this vast culture.

As such I sinned against this very axiom.

I apologise to you, the reader, if the contents in this book don't reflect your reality, your experiences and your facts on the ground. It merely echoes my business experiences in China. All errors, misinterpretations, omissions, inaccuracies or blunders are an unfortunate by-product of a steep learning curve.

March 2008

Nothing has changed since March 2008, though everything gained in complexity.

Jack Leblanc
Beijing
June 2020

不打无准备之仗,不打无把握之仗

Fight no battle unprepared,
fight no battle you are not sure of winning.
— Mao Zedong

$$\int_{0}^{1.4\,\text{billion souls}} \int_{0}^{+\infty} \frac{f_1\left(\text{Western business logic}\right)}{f_2\left(\text{5000 years of Chinese history}\right)} \partial_{2,1}\left(\text{Chinese mind}\right)\partial_{1,2}(\$\$\$) \approx \sum \left(\text{all misunderstanding}\right)$$

CHAPTER I

Barbarian roots

On his appointment to the position of Canton Commissioner in 1839, Lin Zexu declared that he would eradicate the opium trade: 'The barbarians all in all are a nuisance and it were better they returned to where they came from.' Unfortunately he never succeeded in getting rid of this particular variety of pest.

Rain or shine, the barbarians have continued coming to China, in search of adventure.

Within days of my arrival in the Middle Kingdom I got my first taste of some Sinofied Cartesian rules of thumb:

'The shortest path from A to B is almost never straight.'

'While travelling from A to B, most often B will not be stationary.'

'It doesn't matter how slow you go so long as you eventually reach B.'

Brussels, Monday June 5th, 1989, 8:37 AM

'The tanks are rolling over Tiananmen! The tanks are rolling over Tiananmen! The tanks are rolling over Tiananmen!' Zhang's voice grew louder with each repetition.

Standing in the doorway, I stared at him, still half-groggy from a long night renting out cars at the airport.

Zhang had a chili-red face and wild psychopathic gaze. He seemed like an apparition from a scary dream, and for a fraction of a second I seriously thought of slamming the door clean shut.

What was wrong with the guy? Zhang normally had a quiet, soft and sensible personality and would never raise his voice. But here he was completely out of himself.

'What do you mean, "tanks rolling over Tiananmen"?'

Zhang pushed me back into my apartment. 'It was on Voice of America! Let's watch the news!'

More asleep than awake, I sheepishly shuffled behind him, wondering what all the fuss was about. Setting some water to boil for a cup of jasmine tea, he plunked onto the sofa and switched the TV on.

There it was, smack in our face: The major news channels – CNN, BBC World – were chewing it over twenty-four hours a day. Every snippet of video analysed, scrutinised, and evaluated over and over again. The other TV channels wasted no time in following suit, and primetime was full of discussion of events on the other side of the world.

I remembered the Chinese students had been having a 'sit-in' on Tiananmen, but to me it seemed they were having the time of their lives. China was opening up, after all, and many thought it was perfectly normal for the Chinese authorities to allow all of this to happen. It was part of the ritual of growing up, to go against the establishment.

So what? Every twenty-something held idealistic beliefs, and protesting was just a way to provide relief while having a bit of fun. From the reports on TV over the past weeks it all looked cool and innocent. It even had a touch of Woodstock but with Chinese characteristics, on a big square, in the middle of a city. There was *perestroika* in the USSR, so there should be space for more of the same in China. How naïve these thoughts were, in retrospect.

Zhang and I were zapped for a couple of hours, not really accepting as genuine the words and images beamed into the living room. We couldn't take all the alarming reports coming from the journalists at face value. During the breaks Zhang tried on several occasions to call family members, but it seemed as if the rest of the world had already taken over the telephone trunk lines heading for the Middle Kingdom. That day he would not hear their hopeful, reassuring voices, or get fresh news from an independent source.

As the testimonies of reporters flowed out, Zhang couldn't stop reading the slogans the students had written on their banners. He explained the politics, the leaders, their history and the factions within the Communist Party. He almost simplified it to 'An Idiot's Guide to the Tiananmen Sit In'. I tried hard to take it all in, but much of it was not really comprehensible to me. While doing his best to enlighten me, Zhang jumped feverishly from channel to channel to catch the newest images. My friend sometimes stopped for several minutes on some international network where the anchor was speaking Italian, Spanish or German that neither of us could understand, but he didn't care any longer what language was coming over the waves. He simply soaked up every pixel displayed on the screen, and as time ticked by he became completely absorbed in his own world.

What was going through his mind, what was he thinking? He was suddenly so reserved. Even in these moments of horror he wouldn't show his inner feelings. From time to time he spoke in a detached manner about what he was witnessing, as if the pictures had had a sedating effect on him. But deep inside I knew his neurons were going berserk, and his thoughts were with his family, his friends, his country.

I tried on several occasions to kick-start a discussion of what we had seen, but it didn't go smoothly. Zhang was completely disconnected from his surroundings. Between sips of jasmine tea and an exchange of words I strove to grasp what it meant for China, and for his fellow students here in Europe. But I truly felt like an outsider, as if a shadowy Great Wall of China was separating our minds. We quietly sat there for a couple more hours, watching the same reports over and over again.

While staring at the TV, it also slowly dawned upon me that my dream of working in China was little by little turning into a 'no go'.

Two weeks earlier I had received the go ahead to teach Quantum Physics in a university in Xi'an and was actively preparing for my departure at the end of July. It was all I'd aspired to do since beginning my university studies six years earlier. I just wanted to go to China, work there, live in another culture, make friends, absorb their way of life and discover that part of the world. A couple of years earlier I'd been bitten by the China bug and slowly turned into a China freak, studying some Chinese, reading everything about the PRC that passed through my hands, attending receptions at the Chinese Embassy, even attending Chinese New Year celebrations in godforsaken parts of Antwerp to soak up the culture. . . . I was so looking forward to the big unknown, and now it was all ending abruptly as I sat on the sofa watching the news.

Sure enough, a couple of days later a call came. It was from the organisation that had hired me for the teaching job: 'Sir, due to recent events we're temporarily calling a halt to all our Chinese projects. But we still have open positions in Thailand or Brazil. Would you be interested in working in any of those countries?'

'Does this mean China is completely off limits?' That was the only question I could stutter through the phone.

'Most probably we'll suspend our China programme for a year, or longer if necessary.'

I just stared, blank and disappointed in everything. Why was nothing going my way?

Zhang, in the meantime, joined up with the rest of the Chinese students residing in Belgium and protested on a daily basis in the streets of the capital. I attended a couple of times, but things got even more confusing when scuffles broke out with Taiwanese students also present during those marches. That Taiwanese students were denouncing the events in China was unacceptable to the Mainland students. I truly felt as though this wasn't my fight. I certainly couldn't get to the bottom of their arguments, and anyway the discussions were mostly conducted in high-velocity Chinese . . . far beyond what my limited textbook knowledge could handle.

Roughly a year earlier I had graduated with an engineering degree in Nuclear Physics and could easily have walked into a secure nine-to-five job, buy a house with a cat and garden and live a nightmare. This mould was definitely not made for me. The motto 'Born to be wild, forced to work' seemed to be tattooed on every cell in my body. Adventure, discovering the unknown, challenging myself, and learning what was happening beyond the realm of my present world: these were my driving forces. Years earlier I had already set my thoughts on working in China.

Why? Probably because China had just reemerged on the scene, it was the world's biggest unknown, mysterious and misunderstood. My dream certainly wasn't to protest on the wet cobbled streets of Brussels.

My first attempt to control my destiny was not very encouraging either. After graduation, I ended up with a temp job washing and renting out cars at the airport. . . . But at least it gave me the freedom to continue hunting down my simple dream.

In the meantime all my friends picked up plush jobs and got company cars. 'You're a madman, you're squandering potential career opportunities. What the heck do you care about China? There's nothing there,' one would say. Another would snicker at the thought alone. 'China? A communist country! Are you indifferent to what just happened there?'

No argument was strong enough; the inexorable urge to go to China never left me.

'What to do now?' were the words that kept banging in my head. The China virus had contaminated me, and was slowly but surely eating into my sanity.

'In which direction can I steer my life now that working in China is all but out of the question?' I became rudderless for a while. I was lost but too stubborn to admit defeat.

How was it possible that events so far from my homely surroundings could affect me? Was I really cursed to continue wasting my time renting out cars at the airport?

'Maybe you should try Taiwan or Hong Kong?' proposed a whisper in my head.

But that would mean starting all over again. At that time there was no Google that would, at the flick of a finger, give you a whole list of organisations to contact by e-mail. No, it was the old typewriter that had to be pulled out of the cabinet to do all the work. The daily tasks were set on replay, like an old record player with a needle stuck somewhere in the middle of a melancholy song.

Rummage through the professional magazines in libraries to find contact addresses, type letters between my two shifts, mail them around to companies or organisations that might assist fresh graduates in starting a career abroad. And then an excruciating wait for answers. The rush to the mailbox became a daily ritual.

It took weeks to get replies, which most always started with: *'We've read your letter with great interest. . . .'* and ended with *'. . . but unfortunately there's presently no vacancy for someone with your background. Please allow us to keep your profile in our data base* and *blah blah blah. . . .'*

Every letter, before I opened it, drove my mood to the highest of peaks, and then brought it crashing down with the opening sentence. And so it went for several months. I spent hour after hour looking for opportunities that were closely or even remotely related to China. It even got so bad that the staff in the libraries already knew me by name. Sometimes my steadfast determination would be jolted by a mischievous thought that flashed through my brain: 'It's so hard to find a job in the Far East. Is this really worth all the hassle? How long would I search? How many more rental cars would I race from point A to B? How many more grumpy customers? How many more pranks could we pull over the airport loudspeakers, before the information desk discovered that the person I was paging – 'Mr Aihait Maisdu Pitjab' – was only imaginary, and that they were declaring over the PA: 'Attention! Attention! Mister I hate my stupid job. Please come to the information desk!'

Seeing the flow of businessmen coming and going from behind my rental desk I often thought that taking a real job in my familiar surroundings might be the easiest way out of my purgatory. But this nasty temptation quickly dissolved, as if some inner compass refused to lose track of that 'simple' dream: to work in China.

Sometime in September, out of the blue, a telephone call came: 'Sir, would you still be interested in working with our organisation in China? The previous position in Xi'an is already filled, so we're not sure yet to which university you'll be posted. But we have a job opening for you with the Chinese Ministry of Education. It's quite urgent, as classes will start beginning of next month. Could you please give us a reply in the next couple of days?'

I gave a firm yes on the spot.

On a cold morning in October, together with eight other pilgrims, I stood in the departure hall of Brussels Airport – not to rent out cars, but to make a great leap forward in my life. Everyone was excited about our bold journey into the unknown. Like any airport, this huge chemical reactor, which boiled up a roller coaster of emotional peaks and valleys at both the Arrivals and Departure levels, didn't disappoint either. Behind me a lot of people were left in tears, but I couldn't help but think that my China obsession would work out. I told everybody, 'This will be a great opportunity to open a new gateway for all of us to reunite in unfamiliar territory.'

The trip, with a couple of changeovers, crisscrossed through a string of cities: Brussels, Amsterdam, Rome, Bangkok, Singapore, Shanghai and at long last Beijing. At the time China was still considered a backwater, and no airline worth the name would fly on a regular basis directly from any Western-European airport into Beijing Capital Airport. Unless you were flying with Pakistan Airlines or the East German Interflug, the voyage into the Middle Kingdom would snake the intrepid traveller around the globe.

'Ladies and gentlemen, we'll be landing at Beijing Capital Airport in around thirty minutes, at 6:20 PM local time,' the pilot's voice crackled over the loudspeakers.

I had left my familiar environment roughly forty-eight hours previously. Looking outside, everything was pitch black, there was no way to perceive how high the plane was flying or where the airport was located. There was nothing that remotely looked like a city. None of the highway lights and cars we'd seen at the other airport approaches, no lit buildings in the distance. Zilch, only obscurity as far as the eye could see, with sometimes a faint flickering light in the distance, nothing more.

Then out of nowhere the runway lights appeared twenty metres beneath the plane. The pilot gave the usual welcome, and commented sarcastically that control tower had just informed him that 'There's no weather in Beijing today.'

Still looking into the pitch black, trying to detect some kind of life out there, all of a sudden I saw, in the plane's light beam, a Chinese man on a bicycle, pedalling like mad, trying to overtake the plane. Maybe this guy on the bike was the *Follow Me* to escort the plane to its designated disembarking gate?

Watching this scene unfold in front of my eyes, it instantly hit me: I was entering another world. Meanwhile, the plane was taxiing to a portal which led to a place where actions and events weren't processed in the way Westerners were imprinted with from birth.

At long last my feet were firmly on Chinese soil. The place I had endlessly fantasised about, and discussed with Zhang and friends for nights on end. Walking out of the airport even the air smelled different, it had something exotic, something unique. Even now, whenever this delicate mixture of scents reaches me, I experience an instant flashback to my first day in Beijing. Unforgettable. Forever grafted in the back of my brain.

The road from the airport to the city was a dark, narrow stretch of fissured concrete slabs. At both sides, white-painted trees glimmered up in the headlights of the bus before receding back into the night. For long patches the bus would get stuck behind a cart pulled by a donkey. Invariably this was a clear-cut signal for the driver to sound the horn as if his life depended on it, while the farmer on his cart remained transfixed by his daily business, indifferent to the commotion taking place behind him, as if two civilisations, centuries apart, happened to have crossed each other's paths for a brief moment. Only when the road temporarily widened could the bus pull away into the inky darkness. Barely at speed again . . . and now the driver had to handle yet another *crisis situation*. A time warp brought a flock of sheep across the road, into earshot of a klaxon blast. The animals momentarily surrounded the bus for an inspection before we could move again into the present day. Entering the Third Ring Road scarcely any car shared the road with us. Dark gloomy buildings stared down on the unlit streets, contrasted against the black sky. Some traffic lights in the distance brought welcome colour to a scene of shadowy contoured concrete structures on the roadside. No one walked on the streets, as if a curfew had been declared after sunset. 'How strange. Where is everybody?

A country with a billion people and not a living soul in sight,' I thought to myself.

The stately Friendship Hotel, located at the then-outskirts of the city, had definitely been designed by an architect with Stalinist tendencies. The place looked as if each structure had come from one and the same blueprint, copy-pasted one after the other into a rigid maze of low-rise buildings. In this place lived long-term foreign residents who were teaching language or working for the Chinese foreign press, 'Friends of China', and businessmen.

Driving through the hotel's gates a large red banner hanging above the entrance greeted our bus and exclaimed in white letters: CHINA WARMLY WELCOMES THE EUROPEAN FOREIGN TEACHERS. Apparently a committee of officials from the Ministry of Education had patiently waited several hours for our arrival and on seeing our bus enter the premises they thronged the bus door. In the initial chaos heavy handshakes and bright smiles were exchanged. 'Welcome you to China! You must be very tired from such a long journey. Warm greetings to our China friends!'

Next to me an embassy employee confided in a soft voice, 'Don't you worry. This is the inevitable Chinese welcome toast to show their consideration for the *honoured* guests coming in from far-away places.'

Not really expecting this kind of attention we grimaced nervously, doubting if this circus was really intended for our group. It felt totally over the top. 'What the hell is happening? This can't be right. Probably there's confusion with another more important group. Definitely a mistake.' Another of my co-travellers was nervously shaking hands, and he also seemed ill at ease. Sneaking up on him from behind I whispered to him half-seriously, 'The only thing missing is a big band playing along. Very soon you'll be expected to make a speech, so prepare yourself.' To which he replied, throwing me a wink, 'Really? Freedom of speech in China? Wow, that'll be my one-way ticket out of here. I'll have to keep that trump card close to my chest and use it wisely.'

Over the years this style of hospitality repeated itself on many more occasions.

Although it was eight in the evening, late night for Beijing people at that time, the whole crowd of officials gracefully invited the *honoured guests* to a banquet dinner.

'The kitchen normally closes at seven, but has remained open especially for you, so the cooks may be tired and we sincerely apologise if the dishes are not that tasty,' one of the hosts declared in a very heartfelt voice. The food was nothing like what was normally defined as Chinese cuisine in certain parts of Europe. Indonesian Chinese, who had escaped President Suharto's brutal communist witch-hunt in the sixties, ran most of the Chinese restaurants in Holland and Belgium. The menu invariably consisted of Indonesian delicacies like *bamigoring, nasigoreng, lumpia* and *krupuk* with a Chinese twist. For all these years the innocent patrons had wrongly assumed they were being served authentic Chinese dishes at 'The Golden Dragon' restaurant around the corner. Little did we know till the food at the Friendship Hotel came rolling in.

Only then did I come to understand Zhang's predictable and invariable rants about the food quality in the so-called Chinese restaurants in Europe. I had always thought that he was being vain when he claimed that 'at home' the dishes were heavenly. That night my taste buds confirmed his position once and for all.

The customary treatment for *honoured guests* arriving from distant horizons was also lavished on us. We ticked off the obligatory list of stopovers every tourist hoped to see in Beijing, starting with the Great Wall and ending at the Forbidden City. Having entered from the northern gate of the palace, the walk went through the whole length of what once was home to Chinese emperors, and finally exited through the southern gate.

A five-minute walk from there, the majestic Tiananmen was basking in the autumn sun. We took the pedestrian tunnel underneath Chang An Avenue towards the square and found hundreds of soldiers still camping in this dark alley, sitting on their bunk beds, smoking cigarettes, greasing their AK-47s, basically bored to death. A couple of long-noses strolling past their encampment was the only attraction of the day. Climbing back up into daylight, we found the place eerily quiet and empty, nobody on the grandiose

Square of the Gate of Heavenly Peace but for armed soldiers who stood guard every ten metres. A lone public bus in the distance was the single sign of life.

That very moment it struck me: 'Hey, we're standing at the very heart of the events Zhang and I watched on TV a couple of months ago.' One of the guides carried a letter to the soldier guarding the entrance to the square, and they went into protracted discussions. He pointed in our direction, where we were keeping our distance, and finally cleared the last hurdle to walk around the square. From afar the great gate looked just like the eternal Tiananmen: Radiating the country's self confidence, a testimony to its rich and glorious past, embodying all that the New China stood for. Close up, though, it became a painful trial to walk on that immense open place, where tank tracks had carved up the stones and the steps to the Monument of the People's Heroes were broken to bits and pieces. In several places around the square, soot-permeated stones showed up like black circles against the grey concrete backdrop. Soldiers followed our every move a couple of footsteps behind. The guide next to me looked straight ahead and murmured through his teeth: 'These are the remnants of the bonfires students made in the evenings.' In my mind I could vividly see and hear the students gathered there, playing music, talking politics, discussing the hopes and dreams of a nation. Till the moment the iron tracks came waltzing in.

All was quiet now, all was peaceful again at the political centre of the New China.

Thinking back to the words of a Brit, an Old China Hand who said 'China today is more certain of what it doesn't want than of what it does want', we all walked off the square, humbled by the experience.

Our departure date from Beijing finally arrived, marking the end of the sightseeing journey. The group of people I had travelled with from Europe split up into their designated work units, scattered to the four corners of the country. Some were heading for Wuhan, Shanghai, and Xi'an, while I was told that Chongqing was my final destination. Nobody in our group had ever heard of that particular city before, myself included.

'What city is this? Funny name. It doesn't ring a bell. This place certainly can't be that big. Maybe it's located somewhere in the countryside?' One of the guys in the group spoke hesitantly, not sure if that would be taken as a compliment.

'You're so lucky to be able to take the train. You'll probably be based a short ride out of the capital', another one congratulated me. 'So you can come to the capital on the weekends.'

However, Mr Li who accompanied me explained in broken English that 'we travelling for three days and three nights.' Still, in my mind there had to be some sort of misunderstanding, he had to mean three or four hours at most.

Coming from a place where driving two hours in any direction would entail at least one international border crossing, the idea of sitting in a train for days on end sounded totally absurd. Once the train had travelled over eight hours however, I got the message. This didn't look like a picnic into the countryside.

The views through the window were an exotic amalgam of scenery. Everything looked different from the familiar European landscape: As the train puffed its way to Chongqing, flat plains slowly moved by, arid areas where nothing seemed to grow, mountainous regions, luscious terraced hills, tropical trees waving in the wind, kids along the track who screamed *'Laowai! Laowai!'* 'Barbarian, Barbarian!' when they saw the *honoured guest* staring out of the window. News that a barbarian was sitting on the train must have spread like wildfire. Passengers from all over the soft-sleeper carriages came over for a chat, hesitantly at first, but quickly producing a torrent of questions. That first night I must have answered a hundred times 'Where do you come from?' 'Do you like China?' 'Do you like Chinese food?'

As the train carved through the uneven terrain the temperature got warmer and warmer with every stop. When leaving Beijing it was close to zero, but every twelve hours of travel along the rails seemed to add at least three degrees Celsius to the outside temperature. Three days later, as we entered Chongqing railway station at nightfall, the weather was a balmy twenty-two degrees Celsius.

A small metal case full of science books and clothes, containing my only belongings that linked me with the outside world, was plunked at my feet. Mr Li, wanting to make sure I'd stay put, pointed to me – 'You' – and then to my luggage – 'Here' – making it clear that I should wait on the platform and not wander around. When he felt sure the message had gotten through and the barbarian wouldn't escape, off he went to look for his contact.

During the wait, some thirty people surrounded Mr Li's *honoured guest,* gazing with extreme interest on this strange alien creature. Each and every one of them carried a bamboo pole in one hand and a rope in the other. They pointed at my case, trying to convey with gesticulations that they could lend a hand in carrying it away. In the meantime, it seemed that my presence was acting like a huge human magnet. The crowd swelled to a silent mob and hundreds were trying to get a peek at the alien, some touching my arms just to make sure the exhibit was for real. As the size of the crowd got out of control and the tumult surrounding me grew, the sea of people suddenly broke open. Mr Li, like a modern day Moses, got to his precious guest. At his side was Smile, of the university's Foreign Affairs Office, thus nicknamed because of the everlasting smile on his face. He was the kind of guy who was trusted by his superiors to keep an eye on the barbarian, to make sure he didn't stray too far from the beaten path of the curriculum. 'Why are people so interested in touching me?' I innocently asked.

'Don't worry, they were just curious why you didn't shave your arms this morning. Probably because of the long train ride you didn't have the opportunity to do so.' Smile informed me of this earnestly, without any further afterthought.

'The creature with the human features and animal heart that the old imperial scrolls referred to had just landed in their midst,' I giggled to myself.

Meanwhile Mr Li shook my hand as if to say *'Honoured guest* safely transferred to Chongqing University authorities. Mission successfully accomplished', before disappearing into the crowd, never to be seen again.

Over time Smile proved to be the one person a barbarian could always count on to provide solutions to the daily stream of Chinese problems. Nothing was bizarre enough that he wouldn't 'touch' it.

Chongqing University, with a campus consisting of a mix of traditional and new buildings, was surrounded by greenery and sat majestically on the outskirts of the city. The word *city* was a definite understatement. . . . With twenty million inhabitants at that time, Chongqing's concrete structures sprawled wide and far over the hills and occupied the Yangtze and Jialing river banks. It was more of a Mega-mega-metropolis than a city. But it was also a damp place where the sun never seemed to be able to pry its way through the dense clouds. It's said that all the dogs in Chongqing would start barking at the sudden, unfamiliar appearance of the sun.

The head of the Foreign Language Department, Professor Chen, together with the vice-head, Professor Zhen, were the first university lecturers to meet me. It was kind of an informal get-together to give an orientation to the place and provide the newcomer with a class schedule. Trying to distinguish the professors' names was hopeless, as in the local Sichuan dialect they sounded like 'Mr Tzen and Mr Tzen' to a barbarian's untrained ears. However, their English accents were the marker by which they could be differentiated. Professor Chen had a strong American pronunciation, as if the Bronx was just around the corner, while Professor Zhen had such an impeccable British pronunciation one had to wonder where he'd left his bowler and umbrella. Because they'd honed their English to perfection, my initial assumption was that both professors had been sent especially to meet the *honoured guest*. 'Certainly the university would want to avoid any miscommunication in the initial stage of my stay,' I thought. Expecting I'd be brought to the Engineering Department to meet my future colleagues very soon, I asked 'how many engineering students graduate every year from the university?'

No response. My question was simply passed over while the introduction to the university continued unabated.

'Probably they aren't that familiar with that department and so let the question slip by,' I thought to myself. 'Soon I'll know more and will be able to discuss in more detail the subjects I'm expected to teach.'

But things diverged dramatically from the original roadmap.

'You will start your classes in American Literature and British Culture on Monday next week'. After Professor Chen broke the news, there was an awkward moment of silence while I stared at them.

Hadn't they noticed my heavily-accented English? They must know that not all barbarians are native English speakers. Why would they expect me to teach literature or culture! For heaven's sake. . . . A subject I hadn't the faintest idea how to tackle, and had never studied in depth before. In middle school we'd had a brief course in literature, but to be honest it was something I'd always thought to be a waste of time. Perhaps this was how fate punishes those who look down upon the art of writing?

I couldn't assume this was a hoax as they were measuring me up very attentively, waiting for my initial reaction. As if I might suddenly and effortlessly start talking Shakespeare, while discoursing on all the historical convolutions that had led to present day English literature. It was definitely not going to be easy to get out of this one.

How on earth was I to explain that somewhere down the line, a 'mischievous' bureaucrat in either Europe or Beijing had perhaps mislaid my résumé, resulting in my being here? I was imagining some poor American or British language expert who was now facing a similar situation somewhere else in China, being kindly requested to teach the Dynamics of Schrödinger's Theory of Quantum Mechanics.

'Are you sure this is what you expect me to teach?' I was able to stammer out.

Both 'Tzens' looked at each other and in that fraction of a second I believe they understood the error that had been committed. But, relentless in their mission to keep the barbarian on the hook, one of the Tzens went on: 'Don't you worry, our students are all very eager to study from foreigners. You'll do all right!'

'Right!' There I was, in the middle of China, presented with a challenge I had neither the capabilities nor the materials to overcome.

Both professors left me behind in a daze. I needed to come up with a solution quickly, or I'd have a class mutiny on my hands the moment I opened my mouth on Monday. All night long I spun in bed, reflecting on why I'd come and what I should do. Hundreds of ideas came tumbling through my mind. I checked pros and cons one after the other, and immediately dismissed the scariest of them all: that I might return home. In a moment of lunacy, I even believed that American Literature and British Culture wouldn't be so hard to teach after all.

By early morning I hadn't made a single step of progress in my deliberations. But further delays in identifying a solution could have serious consequences, or so I thought. While finding the way to the language department, my mind kept on scanning my options for a practical way out. Hopefully they would accept a compromise that would make both parties happy. My heart had sunk to the bottom of my shoes by the time I walked into the meeting room.

'Professor Tzen, I think you're doing me too much honour by offering a position of such high responsibility. I believe there are much better-qualified teachers in your department, who just came back from overseas and know the latest British education techniques in teaching English as a second language. They must dearly want to exchange their knowledge of English Literature with the best and brightest of your students. I just arrived in China and don't understand your culture or local teaching methods yet. It would not be fair towards your students if I could not communicate properly. I'm really afraid the students will complain to you, and I'm sure you wouldn't want this to happen. I think students majoring in literature deserve to have a teacher who can also explain complex language concepts in Chinese.'

By now the professor understood that discussing prose and analysing dead or living writers was not my strong suit, and he took his time in evaluating the situation. There was another long uneasy moment of silence. But this time I wasn't prepared to break it because I knew the ball had slowly rolled into his court. The professor rigorously assessed me, his eyes piercing into my brain. Finally he cleared his throat and asked curiously, 'What do you suggest we do?'

'Wouldn't it be better if I first take on students whose English level is not that high? I would be able to teach them the basics extremely well.'

Again silence. I was staring at the tealeaves floating in my cup, not really daring to look him straight in the eyes.

'We could consider this situation. What about first-year English major students?' he responded.

'Sounds like a plan, but don't you think that students from the Engineering Department might also be interested? As I'm quite familiar with technical subjects, I could teach them Scientific English. They would be able to read and write scientific articles in English.' Hearing this proposal his face cleared up; the idea definitely struck him as attractive. 'I'll consider this suggestion, come back tomorrow afternoon, three o'clock.'

Ecstatic that my plan had worked, I spent the afternoon recovering from my sleepless night.

The following day I was right on time to hear Professor Chen's decision, only to be informed by the secretary that he would not be coming that afternoon. 'Could I reach him by phone?' I asked. 'Professor Tzen no phone' was the simple reply. It was Friday afternoon and still no decision. Now I was getting both nervous and uncomfortable with the fact that classes were only one weekend away and there was still no solution in sight for my awkward situation.

Another sleepless night followed. I didn't know if I had done wrong or right. Why wasn't Professor Chen present for our meeting as promised? I knew that teaching literature would be equivalent to throwing myself into a lions' den. I'd never come out of this alive and my ego might be bruised for the rest of my 'teaching' career. . . .

That Saturday I tried to forget the whole situation by strolling through some of the more picturesque locations close to our university: Ciqikou, built on a hill, with a small Buddhist temple at the top surrounded by houses made of bamboo, straw and clay. The place, one hundred and fifty metres above street level, could only be reached by climbing a long series of steep steps carved in rock. The little village overlooked the Jialing River, where in late spring dragon boat races were held. Having stood there for centuries, the area hadn't yet adapted to the present. It was impossible for cars to enter this secluded area from the other side of the hill, as streets and alleys were too small for even the tiniest of cars to pass through.

Except for some of the black and white TVs that were humming Sichuan opera, time seemed to have stood still for the last two hundred years. Undisturbed kids were playing in the narrow passageways. Lining the streets were small shops repairing shoes, stores selling daily necessities, a butcher's shop, small vegetable markets, and a couple of voluble ten-seat restaurants, while on the roadside farmers, patiently crouched for hours, sold their freshly harvested crop. In an open area two large stone wheels pulled by a donkey ground soybeans into tofu.

One week ago I was still breathing the air of greyish Brussels and now it felt as if I had walked into an Indiana Jones movie set. The vibes this place gave off were incredible. There and then I decided that nothing in the world would make me go back to Europe, even if it meant *teaching literature*.

As the evening settled in I couldn't let go of the place, and decided to soak up the colourful atmosphere a bit longer by taking a meal in one of the many restaurants bustling with noisy customers. Looking around for something familiar, I pointed my finger at a bowl of Chinese dumplings, or *jiaozi,* my neighbours were gobbling down. The waitress acknowledged with a shy smile and five minutes later my steaming plate of *jiaozi* were mixed with a fiery but lovely chilli pepper sauce. This was exactly the right dish to top off a perfect day before returning to reality.

When I entered the White House, as the building for long-term resident barbarians was mockingly known by university staff, Smile rushed to me. 'Where have you been? I've been looking all over for you. Professor Tzen wants to meet you.'

In the autumn drizzle that was coming down over Chongqing, I dashed to the Foreign Language Department, but all doors were locked and the lights switched off. Nobody was there. By the time I'd come halfway back, the drizzle had turned into a downpour, and I was completely soaked when I arrived at the White House. In the meantime Smile had left for home and I had no idea where or how to get in touch with Professor Chen. Returning to my room up a flight of stairs, I found the professor and a twenty-something lady waiting in front of my room. When he saw me completely wet, his serious expression turned into an embarrassed smile.

In his strong US accent he uttered, 'Come on, let's go to a restaurant and have some dinner.' Having just eaten a heavy dose of *jiaozi* I was not really hungry, but couldn't refuse as my career was at stake.

'By the way, this is my daughter Lily, she'll join us. You don't mind, do you?' Lily was timid, hiding every smile behind the palm of her hands.

The three of us ended up in a *huoguo* – aka Chongqing Hotpot – restaurant, just outside the main university gate. *Huoguo*, the number one Chongqing food speciality, consisted of a boiling cocktail of oils, fiery peppers, chillies, vegetables and other spices. A wide range of uncooked vegetables, noodles and raw chopped meat were placed to one side, ready to be boiled fondue-style. The tricky part: to plunge a piece of food into the brew and try to hold on to it with your chopsticks till the slippery portion was thoroughly cooked. This type of cooking would definitely kill any germ that had found its way onto the raw food, and was an ideal way to consume anything that hadn't seen a fridge for twenty-four hours. Unfortunately for the uninitiated, the spices also killed off the flora in the intestines ninja-quick, and it took me a couple of close calls to the bathroom before I'd returned to my normal self.

But this was beside the point, as Professor Chen was about to break the news:

'We've encountered quite some difficulties with the English courses in the Science and Engineering departments. Students seem not so engaged, and the subject doesn't seem to prick their curiosity as much as we'd like. After deliberation with the concerned departments we believe the idea of your teaching Scientific English is worth pursuing. We suggest you make your notes available for the coming week.'

On hearing those words, an immense weight was suddenly lifted from my shoulders.

The relief was immeasurable. No more stress about literature. As if heaven and earth had returned to their rightful places. Suddenly the food tasted even better. Chongqing could finally become my new adopted home. It was the first real hurdle I'd overcome in China, and I was very happy it had come to a good end. Throughout the rest of the meal we had some small talk about the professor's experiences in the States, and how life and culture there were so different from China. During the dinner Lily didn't say a word. She was content just to listen, giving a faint smile while she enjoyed the food.

While we dealt with the last bits and pieces on the plates, fishing slippery noodles out of the hotpot, Professor Chen asked me in a low voice: 'Do you think Lily can study in your country? She's a very bright student in Informatics and will graduate next year. We'd be very happy if you could give us any assistance, however small, in securing her the opportunity to study abroad!' I didn't see that one coming, and realised in a flash that one way or another I must have indebted myself pretty deeply by asking for a change in work schedule. Most probably Professor Chen had gone to great lengths to get the Engineering Department to cooperate, and the barbarian now owed him big. Refusing to help would probably sink this barbarian ever-deeper in a marsh of entanglements as the academic year wore on. 'Sure! I'll see what I can do,' I declared with newfound confidence.

Postscript

- For one year I taught Scientific English, Applied Physics and Computer Science at Chongqing University. The following year I moved to Tsinghua University in Beijing, where I taught similar subjects and got a salary raise from 400 RMB to 600 RMB/month.
- Professor Chen started a private school teaching English for scientists and engineers, initially based on the lecture notes I made.
- Lily ultimately went to study in New Zealand, two years after our first encounter, and is now happily married with two children in Auckland.
- Smile went twice to the States on a tourist visa. During his second trip he saw an opportunity to find work, and is now living his own dream.

- My good friend Zhang got accustomed to a Bohemian lifestyle, acting as a guest university lecturer in the UK and the USA teaching Chinese politics and economics.

CHAPTER 2

The great glass curtain walls of China

Successful negotiations in China require great reserves of the most precious commodity of all: Time. The ability to squander it as if you had a lifetime to wait will earn you the goodwill of your Chinese partners.

Extra credit points can be won by adapting to the some-times-unusual wishes of your host. When patience, perseverance and flexibility have become part of your China as-sets, success may finally be yours.

But sometimes – only sometimes – ignorance is bliss. . . .

Chongqing, Wednesday March 11th, 1990, 3:21 PM

Over the external loudspeakers near the White House a lady's voice, speaking in heavy Sichuanese, crackled through the cold soggy air: 'International phone call for Jieke. Hurry!' (Since my arrival in China, my name, Jack, had been transformed into Jieke.)

Inside the Middle Kingdom privacy became a precious com-modity, one you had never really appreciated until you left it behind at the border. Even when a telephone call came in, everyone within earshot of the loudspeakers knew who was being contacted and who was on the other end of the line. Most probably the operator had already conducted an exacting question-and-answer session regarding the reasons for the phone call before deciding it was worth passing on to the requested party.

It was a two-minute sprint to the operator's room. For whoever was footing the bill it must have felt like an eternity, listening to the background noises of the operator attending other calls while waiting for the recipient to walk into the telephone office. In terms of efficiency those telephone calls to the university must have been some of the most costly in the world.

No one ever called me from overseas, so I was worried that something bad had happened to a family member. 'Hello, who's this?' I asked.

'It's Jan here! How are you? Surprised to hear from me, right? Would you be interested in selling float glass in China? You know, six or seven years ago I sold a couple hundred thousand dollars worth of glass for the construction of the Great Wall Hotel in Beijing, glass curtains to be more precise. Since you're now in China would you be interested in being our eyes and ears in the country?'

Jan was an acquaintance of my mother's and I had met him on several occasions but we had never really talked business. I had heard of Jan's successful glass trade. Having him hunt me down all the way to Chongqing was already something special, but him surmounting the language barrier separating our two worlds was definitely a feat worth noting. He certainly was willing to walk outside his comfort zone and enter into the unknown. This was an opportunity I could not ignore, even though I had no idea what it would entail and couldn't imagine any demand for such material in Chongqing. But Jan was top of the league in this business and an exclusive agent for several American and European glass manufacturers. And anyway, why not? The teaching was only keeping me busy twelve hours a week and I had lots of free time on my hands, so I wouldn't mind taking a shot at filling up an order book from an eager crowd of Chongqing real estate barons. A little bit of extra cash definitely seemed like an enticing proposition, and I remembered the fun times I'd had as a student muddling with 'international trade'. . . .

During my student period Yani, a Hungarian friend of mine, would sell floppy disks, printers and PC boards in Budapest to computer geeks who couldn't get their hands on such equipment behind the Iron Curtain. Together with my neighbour we'd make monthly runs by car to Budapest to deliver the parts and return with a fistful of Forint to the Russian quarters close to Antwerp Harbour, where we'd exchange them for hard currency. The cash flow was mostly spent on racy cars with testosterone-heavy engines, and partying the nights away in Hungary. In any case a nice experience that had left only good memories, and which could easily be transposed to my current favourite town: Chongqing.

A couple of weeks later I received in the mail glass samples, slides, documentation and a price list. The only thing missing was a customer who'd be eager to fill the city with walls of glass as high as the sky.

My resourceful friend Smile had already put me in contact with Jackson Long, a trader in building material and, according to local rumour, a person very well connected to the inside gangways of the Chongqing political elite. Long had named himself after the 'most famous' of American singers, according to Long: 'The illustrious megastar, Michael Jackson.'

Our first contact was in the city centre, where he ran his building-materials empire. Most building contractors worth the name had to visit his offices to buy anything from bricks to bathroom appliances.

Sitting on the sixth floor of a white-tiled office building garnished with blue windows, Long's headquarters were something of a turn-off. The building had an elevator but due to weekly electricity rationing it generally sat lifeless on the ground floor. Each visit entailed a tiring walk up and down scores of dark concrete stairs.

His emporium occupied the whole floor and was shared with his younger brother, who dealt in hotel kitchen equipment.

A big aquarium with opaque, olive-coloured water welcomed customers in the tiny reception. Red blotches sporadically moving in the murky green signalled that there was still life in there. A rundown fake-leather couch, too low and too soft, would engulf anyone who dared settle on it. For the unsuspecting, it was always awkward to get out. Inside, staff were moving files, reading newspapers or just deep asleep with their heads cradled in their arms on the wooden desks. Jackson's office was at the back of the room, and consisted of a flimsy aluminium cage with glass windows all around so he could keep an eye on what took place in his emporium. His space consisted of a set of sofas similar to those at the entrance, a glass coffee table, a large mahogany desk with his black leather chair behind it, and a huge plastic-framed decoration with three-dimensional representations of black shrimps resting on light jade-coloured seaweed. His desk was always clear. It held only a telephone, a cup of tea and a little black stone horse prancing on its rear hooves. According to Smile he was the man, the one with the key to the front door of the illustrious palaces of *guanxi,* and all the extensive connections at the local government level.

Smile did the initial introductions. 'This is Jieke who I told you about – he's from Belgium and has some contacts in Europe for building materials, and is wondering if you'd like to do business with him.' Jackson was a forty-something guy whose face bore the obvious marks of some rough times in the past. Old J, as we started to call him, had made his fortune during the unexpected dynamism that hit Sichuan's major city beginning in the mid-eighties. He had left his position as building contractor in a construction company and leaped into the sea, or *xiahai* as the Chinese would say, to set up his own company, abandoning his iron rice bowl along the way. A chain smoker with heavily blackened teeth, he welcomed me with a huge smile. 'Sit down, have some tea.' A red metal thermos printed with chrysanthemums and plugged with a cork filled up three glasses, leaving tea leaves swirling around in the piping-hot water. From behind a waft of cigarette smoke he was assessing me, probably trying to figure out what the hell this barbarian could have to offer him. There was a moment of eerie silence broken only by the ringing of incoming telephone calls from behind the glass cage.

'Sorry, I can't speak a foreign language,' he said to Smile. 'No problem, no problem,' Smile repeated, 'Jieke is fluent in Chinese!'

I had spent the last couple of months brushing up my Chinese and had ended up with heavily Sichuan-accented Mandarin, but saying that I was fluent was complete hyperbole. I uttered something to the effect that I wasn't really as fluent as Smile pretended I was. Anyway that seemed to have broken the ice. A brief presentation on the glass samples followed, and I handed him some of the picture slides with completed buildings using the glass curtain. Up to that point I hadn't detected the slightest interest in the glass samples and how they might apply to his business. Holding the slides up to the light he peered at them, cigarette butt in the left corner of his mouth, but still appeared uninterested. Grabbing one of the samples he asked me how much it would cost. Explaining to him that it depended on the surface, the finishing, size and thickness seemed not to be the right answer. He wanted to hear a price, not all these questions from my side, so finally I threw out a dollar number.

'Too expensive. At least forty times more than the local make! Like this it will be impossible to sell here. You need to give me a much, much better price.' Old J mumbled something to Smile that didn't get translated. The meeting lasted a little less than thirty minutes. Soon we were back on ground level, amid the hustle and bustle of Chongqing city life.

'So? Will he buy? What's this all about? Why is he not interested in the technical questions? Does he have a project?' I asked Smile.

'He'll get back to us. He needs some time.'

Time in China is an unusual concept, a creature of quite different dimensions to what I was familiar with, and impossible to fit into a crisp Western model. 'Some time' was like aeons to me, but on other occasions 'China time' had already clocked in well ahead of schedule. Although I lamented to Smile that Jackson was letting us down as nothing had happened for weeks on end, Smile simply brushed off my complaints.

In the meantime the College of Architecture, which sits a ten-minute walk from Chongqing University, had somehow heard of the barbarian with slides of Western-style buildings. Over the course of three weeks I ended up giving four lectures, in front of an audience of specialists, about a subject I had only begun to grasp. In China, faith is definitely put through unexpected twists and turns. It so happened that among the audience were a couple of employees from the Chongqing Design and Architecture Research Institute, who seemed to have been inspired by what they saw.

In a planned economy those institutes can be likened to the R&D department of a company, except these guys worked on behalf of all the state-owned enterprises involved in the construction industry. They'd monitor all stages of building design and literally put their stamp of approval on blueprints. Some of the top-notch architecture institutes designed new housing estates, factory buildings and government complexes from scratch, which would then be copied and disseminated to state-owned construction companies all over the country. Even now, anyone wanting to build a concrete structure in China will one way or another have to get into the good graces of those institutes before a construction company will even want to get involved.

At last, Jackson gave a sign of life. 'If you want, you can come over again, because some important people want to meet you.'

Apparently the presentations at the Architecture College had struck a spark along some track of contacts, officials or other unknown channels, and had come around to the ear of our entrepreneur friend, who then shot into over-drive. Neither Smile nor myself had any idea of whom we were going to meet or what would be discussed. I assumed that a sale was close and prices needed to be discussed for a specific project.

Smile and I ended up in a nondescript government building in the city centre, where Jackson was nervously waiting for us. 'Quick, quick let's go upstairs, there's a load of city officials waiting for you!'

For some reason time never seemed to be in my favour, and could never be bent to conform to my Western concept of efficiency. In the eyes of my Chinese purveyors I was always either too late or wanted results too fast.

In a room the size of a small dance hall, with heavy curtains keeping the daylight out, the officials were seated on large dark sofas with oranges, peanuts and sunflower seeds piled in front of them. The waiting was endured with the help of the usual cups of tea, cigarettes, small talk and newspapers.

As we entered the room the chatter stopped. Jackson, who remained pretty nervous throughout the meeting, introduced me to those present, each of whom in turn handed over his business card and shook hands with me. Although the discussion was conducted in the Chongqing dialect, I could detect that I was being introduced to the group of officials as an expert in skyscrapers. As the discussions continued, I became more and more aware that, for one reason or another, Jackson was portraying me as a skyscraper construction specialist. Sitting next to me, Smile was, gauging from the heap of peanut shells on the ground, trying to keep himself busy while Jackson did all the talking. I whispered to him, 'Is Old J nuts? Does he really expect me to pretend to be a skyscraper specialist?'

'Don't worry, don't worry, he's just introducing you,' Smile muttered between two sunflower seeds.

While they listened to Jackson's story the officials smoked and made satisfied grunts of agreement, sometimes glanced at me while shaking their heads in unison. I felt trapped in a room with no safety exits, and was pretty tense by the time the officials started talking among themselves. I stared at Jackson and signalled with my eyes 'What are you doing?' He grinned back at me uneasily and gestured that I shouldn't be worried.

'Jieke, we think you should give a presentation of your slides to some of the Chongqing officials,' said a voice from the other side of the room. I felt ready to sink through the floor. 'Do they mean *now?*' I asked, looking at Smile. 'Yes, yes!' he said enthusiastically.

Within minutes a projector was installed and there I was with the shadow of my trembling hand magnified many times on the silver screen, giving the same show I had given in the Architecture College while glass samples were doing the rounds of the different sofas.

The officers gazed with much eagerness on what was displayed before their eyes, and with each passing slide depicting glass towers the humming in the meeting room cranked one notch higher. The slide of the Great Wall Hotel in Beijing seemed to be the highlight of the show. By the end of the slides, when the lights came back on, it seemed as if the room had filled with electricity. Jackson beamed at me, baring all his nicotine-stained teeth, and gave me the OK sign while Smile, indifferent to the commotion around him, continued piling up the peanut shells.

Our meeting concluded, as all good meetings should, in a typical private dining room of a restaurant: round table seating twelve, a trolley with orange juice, cans of coconut milk, soft drinks, *baijiu* (rice wine), a plastic sofa and TV *karaoke* machine. From the interactions of the restaurant staff with the officials one could definitely see that this was not the first time they'd eaten there. As the food started floating in, the dinner opened with a toast of scorching *baijiu* served in tiny glasses the size of eggcups. Then another one raised a cup to me, 'Jieke, you sold glass to a Beijing hotel, so you're an Old China Hand. Very good!' 'No, that was not me,' I objected repeatedly, but my denials seemed to be taken as further proof of my status as an 'Old China Hand'. . . .

As the Sichuan dishes entered in a well-orchestrated ballet of flavours, the waitresses started to take away the little cups and replace them with bigger glasses that could handle a more manly volume of rice wine. The drinking now took off in earnest, every toast demanding another, more bottles opened and circulated around the table. As the empty bottles started to clutter the little trolley, the heads of some at the table transformed into a wide spectrum of colours starting at cherry red, darkening into burgundy and finally dark purple.

To me the liquor tasted like fuel capable of powering a Long March rocket to the moon. The fifty-plus percent alcohol left an aggressive burning trace on the tongue and throat, but it seemed that the quicker you emptied your glass the easier it was to get rid of the heavy after-taste. It appeared better to empty the glass in one shot than shyly nibble at it; unfortunately this also meant that it would be refilled faster than one could shout '*ganbei!*': 'Bottoms up!'

Jackson was the worst, probably because in his eyes the meeting had gone well and in his relief he had imbibed enough to take him to the moon and back. Smile, a gentleman as ever, pretended he couldn't drink, faked doctor's orders, came down with a bad stomach ache. Like a pro, he had all his excuses lined up and pulled them one by one out of his hat as the evening progressed. I myself got trapped into toasting everyone at the table. As the rocket fuel slowly seeped into our brains and took its effect, the *karaoke* machine was put to good use. The drinking stopped and the singing began. I hadn't sung in public since elementary school and listening to our friends' voices climb into falsetto, I wondered if drinking was not the lesser of two evils. Hearing my voice resonate through the loudspeakers was painful for my ego, but in the end it was received with polite handclapping as I quickly handed over the microphone to the next in line. All ended with one last *ganbei,* and a drunken pledge to meet again soon.

Jackson swivelled a bit as he got off his chair to leave, but still seemed OK. However once outside in the fresh air, the oxygen boost got the better of him and knocked him straight out. The roads were wet and slippery from a brief drizzle, and Old J couldn't keep his balance on the cobbles. He wasn't even able to sit any longer; he mumbled something and went flat on the wet footpath. The others merrily left us behind while Smile and I got stuck with Jackson, who was rolling on the wet pavement, his reddish face staring into nirvana. By now it was dark and a taxi was still an unheard-of concept in Chongqing. The only way to move around in the city was to use small buses that seated eighteen or more depending on the amount of spare bamboo stools that could be put into the aisle. All begging and pleading went in vain as the drivers refused Jackson on grounds of his inebriation. So Smile and I ended up carrying him to his office three blocks away, one of us holding his upper body, the other holding his legs. The already ridiculous situation was made worse by my unsteady walk. The two of us tugging at a drunken buddy generated stares of disbelief, loud comments and laughs from the tables of the many outdoor street-side restaurants. The walk up the stairs to the office building was the worst – for Jackson at any rate – with parts of his body knocking the concrete with every step. We left him on the sofa, so I could tend to my own state of drunkenness.

The following day, with dictionary in hand, I deciphered the name cards, and found that I had been dining with the vice-mayor of Chongqing, the head of the City Planning Department, the director of the Architecture College, the vice-president of the Bank of China Chongqing branch, and the chief engineer of the Building Research and Design Institute. My newfound drinking pal hadn't disappointed. Two days later an embarrassed and apologetic Jackson came to visit me at the university.

'We need a price for thirty thousand square metres of float glass, and it has to be silver coloured. It's extremely urgent. I need to hand over the price by tomorrow.'

Again, my questions about construction timing, location, what type of building, glass type, thickness, double- or single-framed, environmental conditions, wind strength, who's the buyer, who's the designer, who will make the aluminium support frame, and, most importantly, whether I needed to include his commission, were all swiftly put aside.

'Make a price, I leave it up to you and will follow your proposal.' On the one hand I was thrilled at the opportunity, but the information given wasn't very encouraging. I had to create a quote out of thin air, with lots of 'ifs' hanging to which I had neither an answer, nor the expertise to guess at.

As communication with the outside world was always a tedious process that could take hours, there was no way I could waste time getting in touch with Jan for this extremely urgent quote based on inadequate technical details and shaky conditions. Knowing Jan, he wouldn't take me seriously anyway. Anything could be possible at Jackson's end, so I based my estimate on a couple of sample quotes Jan had given as a model to follow. Handwritten on a flimsy piece of university paper, my efforts resembled a real quote, albeit with lots of open questions. A scary margin of 100 percent topped it all off. After having handed over the prices to Jackson in person, communications went dead again.

What had initially seemed so pressing suddenly wasn't pressing at all. Weeks drifted by without any further news from Jackson. All my phone calls and protests were in vain: I had to wait. The Chinese time warp, where events would abruptly occur only after percolating for a certain time, had me in its grip.

Jan in the meantime informed me that the quantities of glass they wanted were huge, and he doubted they were for real. I didn't dare mention that most of the quote was based on technical presumptions that hadn't been checked with the architects or engineers. If he knew, he probably would have told me to sod off.

On a miserable drizzly Friday afternoon, a minibus from the Chongqing city government turned up at the university gate, blaring Michael Jackson's *Thriller* over the sound system. An import–export company had arranged the bus to drive us to their offices for a price discussion. Jackson and, surprisingly enough, several familiar and unknown faces greeted me from inside the bus. There were ten of us, including the driver. 'Come on, we've decided to bring you to the Northern Hot Springs!'

Yet another unexpected change: the official agenda had been transformed into an entertainment programme. The official goal was to 'get a vehicle to pick up the customer for price negotiations', while the unofficial goal was 'having fun for the weekend'. For any time-conscious Westerner, this was a stressful experience.

Unfortunately the unexpected move most often wins, and agendas change no matter how hard one holds on to them. Getting used to the 'mysterious forces' of intermingled relationships, interactions between government departments, and connections between people all looking out for their own interests, is probably the most frustrating and at the same time the most rewarding aspect of business negotiations in China. By now I had learned the hard way that going with the flow of events was the best way of avoiding unnecessary stress.

One thing I could already predict with 100 percent accuracy: Two days of rocket-fuel drenched meals, hot springs and *karaoke*-saturated nights. As expected, everything the first evening went according to plan B. After the *karaoke* session we all decided to rent bathing suits and take a night dip in the thirty-five-degree-Celsius hot springs. This was a major mistake! The hot water sent the alcohol into overdrive and our slightly tipsy feeling turned into a recipe for a killer hangover. That night closing my eyes made the room spin like a tumble dryer, and the bathroom was my new home. The next morning, most of us swore never to touch a drop of rocket fuel again, and even Old J committed. That was something new.

After a late breakfast we ended up in the conference room of the hotel where the discussions were to start in earnest. All the officials were present, with Jackson sitting next to me. Mr Zhang of the import-export company opened the discussions by claiming that the offered price was much too high, and that no one in Chongqing would pay such a horrendous price for glass. Sheepishly, I told the audience that I could offer a 20 percent discount if we could just establish some technical framework to work from. 'Not enough,' came from the other side of the room. 'We want a price that is much closer to our Chinese glass, which is at least thirty times cheaper'. All my protests led to nothing; I tried to explain to them that the quality of the glass was much better than any available on the local market, with uniform thickness, no air bubbles, and smooth colour.

All dragging on tar-heavy cigarettes, puffs of smoke slowly filling the room. All listening very attentively, but nothing but serene quietness in response. I tested the waters again with my mantra of technical questions, hoping that it would get some kind of reaction. Then, for the first time, Mr Yu of the Chongqing Building Research and Design Institute articulated something that resembled a technical question. 'What type of aluminium frame do we need to have? How do we install the glass?' After this initial timid foray a torrent of questions breached the wall of silence. Will you provide us with technical drawings of the aluminium frame? Can we receive a sample of the frame that holds the glass? Who will give us the structural details of the glass? Can you assist us with the calculations for the aluminium structure?... Most of the questions remained unanswered, as I was unable to respond without first receiving feedback from Jan. This in turn made some of the people in the room uneasy – now they started noticing that I wasn't at all the picture-perfect expert that Jackson had claimed I was during the previous meetings. But it didn't bother me any longer. Even the bus driver started grilling me about the price and quality of the glass, and if he could get in on the discussion too, I had to assume that the whole group was simply putting on a theatrical act. Even Jackson didn't mind that his storyline had fallen through. In the meantime our meeting was interrupted by the noises of a marching band outside, at least fifty people snaking through the streets waving colourful flags, beating drums and shouting: 'Long live birth control. One child is enough!' On this note the meeting was finally adjourned, after three hours of lengthy and, in my opinion, futile discussions. The only tangible result I could see of this meeting was two bulging ashtrays.

Next came a local delicacy: a very basic but nutritious bowl of cold noodles to wash the lingering traces of rocket fuel from our body, then we went off to a thousand-year-old Buddhist temple in the neighbourhood. During the short walk from the hotel to the road, the Bank of China director got the giggles, and all the others followed moments later.

'Jieke look, look: this is progress in Sichuan, this is a modern-day birth-control slogan.' He pointed at a red banner on the other side of the road, printed with white Chinese characters: BEAT IT OUT, KICK IT OUT, WHIP IT UP, LET IT FLOW, BUT DON'T MAKE CHILDREN! The desperate and frustrated bureaucrat who came up with that slogan had probably been in shock after receiving the latest birth statistics for his county. Quotas exceeded, fearing for his position, he must have felt drastic measures were called for.

Arriving at the temple, our remaining giggles stopped instantly when we witnessed Jackson go into a religious frenzy, burning large amounts of incense, offering hell bank notes – a kind of fake paper money to appease the ghosts of his ancestors – kneeling on one of the red cushions and praying next to the seventy-some-year-old grannies. For my part, I thought he'd been bitten by some sudden Buddhist beliefs, while the others just didn't know how to respond when faced with so much devotion.

This 'performance' was definitely the talk of the evening. After liberation, religion had been entirely marginalised and was only practised by the elderly. In the eighties, however, religion made a slow comeback as new uncertainties emerged in people's lives, and they sought new sources of comfort. The temples were finally recovering their role as places of consecration and contemplation, but to the officials, who saw them as nothing more than a tourist attraction, it was a great surprise to see Old J's sudden piety.

'I'm praying that our project is successful,' Old J afterwards whispered in my ears.

'Don't worry,' someone else interjected. 'We really want to do business with Jieke!'

The results of the prayers to Buddha were fast indeed. It was a relief to see how everyone considered me more as a distant friend than as a formal glass vendor.

The rest of the afternoon was spent in a huge swimming pool heated by the hot springs. It was full of visitors splashing around in the tepid water, no one able to swim as there were over six hundred guests soaking their bodies together. Around five, as if by an almighty decree from above, the bathers all ordered take-away boxes of steamy rice and spicy meat that was sold in the little shops beside the pool. To my astonishment, almost everyone consumed the contents of their meal while in the pool, discarding the inedible bits into the water. This was the signal for me to make a dash for the showers.

The evening was predictably spent eating hot and spicy Sichuan dishes and emptying glass after glass of rocket fuel.

In between *ganbei*s we celebrated all the changes swirling through the country. With the opening up of China to the outside world there were now plenty of opportunities to make money. Already a couple of Mr Zhang's friends had 'jumped into the sea' and were making a handsome profit along the way.

'Their wives remain safely in the confines of a state-owned work unit, providing a stable income and housing while my friends exercise their new-found freedom to make money by "feeling the stones to cross the river".'

Old J only grinned at the wisdom of his compatriots; probably he was recalling similar experiences from when he started off.

Over the years many Chinese had released themselves from the shackles of state-run enterprises and tried to live by Deng Xiaoping's statement 'To get rich is glorious'.

That night around the table everyone was dreaming of hitting it rich fast!

Finally the *karaoke* machine was taken out and we loudly chanted our favourite songs. Not once did anyone mention the glass business. We were just a bunch of buddies enjoying ourselves.

The following day the bus brought us back to Chongqing and after alighting at the university, everyone in the bus promised they'd get hold of me in the next few days.

Again, radio silence prevailed for several weeks. As I waited for Old J to resurface I was getting more acquainted with students and teachers in the university. But I quickly realised that the blunt openness with which I approached them was not being reciprocated. Although they were polite, friendly and extremely curious about the outside world, our discussions would end abruptly, or they would adopt government-approved points of view, whenever we touched on more sensitive issues of Chinese society. The aftermath of Tiananmen was still rippling through many minds. So my search for more meaningful conversation brought me to the Sichuan Fine Arts Institute. There the students were more creative in expressing their opinions while elegantly evading the political whirlwind still spinning through society. These were my kind of guys, ready to challenge the established powers in their own subtle way. Moreover, my newfound friends had a wonderful ability to turn any dull moment into a riot. A welcome change from the eternal waiting that had been imposed on me.

In the meantime I had talked to Jan, who was a bit upset with my big negotiation margin, and the fact that many of the unanswered questions were contradictory or irrelevant. All my arguments were shot down one after the other. He couldn't believe this was really serious, but the fact that we were talking big volume kept him hooked. Jan and I conducted a prehistoric version of Internet chatting via fax sessions at the Yangtze five-star hotel, thus discussing a wide range of technical questions and answers. At least now I had a much better grasp of the technical details, and what to look out for.

Then one afternoon while teaching I saw Smile's excited face through the small door window, signalling me to come out.

'I've just got a call from Old J, you need to rush over to him. Some large Hong Kong contractor and architecture company, involved in the design and construction of the building, is now in discussions with the Chongqing authorities. Jackson would like to have you there.'

This time, the meeting room of the now-familiar government building felt different. All the officials were dressed up, with flowers decorating their Western outfits. The Hong Kong company had arrived with all the big shots lined up. Again I was introduced as the expert who was to supply the high-quality glass. By now I gave my slide show presentation on autopilot, and threw in a bit of techno-lingo to demonstrate that I knew what I was talking about. The Hong Kong executives grilled me afterwards, but at least they had come prepared with specific technical questions. For the first time I heard what the building was all about: a luxury five-star hotel, annex conference and exhibition centre invested in by the Chongqing government. Jan was exhilarated. This was a dream come true, and the volume of glass required finally made sense.

No matter what I told the Hong Kong people it seemed they were still not satisfied with my answers, and tried to poke holes in my technical defences. I produced the required answer at every turn. To prevent us understanding them they'd talk in Cantonese, while Old J and the officials would hide behind their Sichuan dialect. There certainly was something bad brewing here. When I was asked for prices, Old J intervened on the spot and told me that those would be discussed at a later stage. As the meeting dragged on I felt tension growing between the contracting company and myself, as if I was an outsider spoiling their kill.

That evening was again spent around the dining table. Surprisingly enough everyone behaved, with only a couple of rice-wine bottles assaulted. *Karaoke* was sung in Cantonese, Sichuan Chinese, heavily accented Mandarin Chinese and Belgian English.

Two weeks later the Hong Kong company had flown back to Chongqing together with the representative of an American glass manufacturer. Apparently this was their long-term partner, and the favoured supplier for the job. The American sales team had already visited Chongqing several times for this project over the past year, and wanted this contract badly. Any interference with their plans had to be stopped at any cost, especially after all the courting they'd gone through. I knew nothing of the meeting or of the existing competition until two days afterwards, when Jackson told me that the Americans had come up with a killer price. In the meantime, I also had received feedback from Jan, who had made a quote based on the previous information gathered. Cautiously I put in a 40 percent margin and gave it to Old J. He would discuss it with the

Bank of China Director and Mr Zhang of the import-export company. Apparently Mr Yu of the Building Research and Design Institute and other local architects still preferred to go with the American glass. 'Don't worry too much about this, we still have a good chance of getting the deal, but your price is much too expensive. You really have to come down, otherwise you'll never get the order.'

'Do you have any suggestions where we should position ourselves?' I asked hesitantly. 'Much lower,' came the reply. This ambiguity in the Chinese language was certainly something that needed getting used to. Getting a precise 'Western' answer was like trying to simultaneously pick up two deep-fried peanuts with a pair of plastic chopsticks. On top of that, Old J never made it clear if he was 100 percent with me or just with whoever suited him according to the developing circumstances. I had assumed we were in it together and it had never even crossed my mind to look for another, maybe better-connected agent. Perhaps naïvely, I expected that Old J would respond with the same type of commitment.

But our ethical values were only compatible up to a certain point. In the end I had to accept the fact that all he wanted was to make money, and that I was only a tool in that strategy. Although this reality dawned slowly and uneasily on me, it shouldn't have come as a surprise. Implanted in Old J's DNA was five thousand years of Chinese history, constantly warning him that turmoil could come unexpectedly, and the best way to provide for the family on those rainy days was to make money when the opportunity arose. It was now or never.

Four weeks passed as we waited for the Building Design Institute to issue the bidding documents for the whole building. Anxiously flipping to the chapter about the glass, we discovered to our dismay that it leaned decisively towards the American type. It was 0–1 for the visiting HK-US team. This got Jackson a bit edgy, as he'd thought he had control over the whole project. He certainly had to whip up a new strategy soon.

The situation got worse when Jackson was informed that the HK company had arranged for all the officials to take an all-expenses-paid inspection tour to the States. This most probably had tipped the situation in their favour and the bidding document seemed to reflect this. 'Well, we could arrange a similar visit to Europe and show them around a couple of countries. I'm sure they'd like that,' I offered innocently. After I made this suggestion I could practically hear Old J's brain crunching the data, and the output was a huge smile on his face.

From there it went pretty fast: The bank director informed the Hong Kong company that, as this was the first time that any of them had travelled overseas, they would also need to visit Europe. Initially the HK company resisted any change to the programme, and then tried to get me to pay for the European leg of the trip, which I stonewalled by becoming unreachable. Ultimately the Chongqing officials got their way, and the HK company and the American glass manufacturer ending up paying for around-the-world tickets for ten people. We had the added tactical advantage that Jan would receive them after their US trip. We were back in business!

At last the home team had scored: it was 1–1.

In the meantime it was the middle of July and my stint at Chongqing University came to an end. A last farewell party was held with a gang of artists from the Sichuan Fine Arts Institute who I had befriended over the past year. The tide of rocket fuel that met us that particular summer evening was not one to consolidate a commercial transaction, but a lasting friendship.

My next base would be China's top engineering temple of knowledge: Tsinghua University in Beijing. The great thing about the prospect of working at Tsinghua was my 50 percent rise in salary: I was now running on a monthly budget of sixty dollars. The future couldn't be brighter.

From my Beijing HQ I continued the discussions by phone both with Jackson and Jan to make the final arrangements for the European leg of the trip.

At last, at the end of September, the whole Chongqing delegation arrived in Beijing with visas for the US, Benelux and Germany in their pockets. They were ready to fly out for the big unknown. Although Jackson was not part of the group, he knew how to play his cards and make his presence felt. Embedded in the group was

Smile, the group's personal interpreter. He would be able to give us useful feedback and inform Jan of possible actions to take after the US visit.

During the days the officials scattered to the four corners of Beijing, touching base with representatives of their respective *danwei* or work units: the Bank of China headquarters, the Chongqing municipality representative offices, the Chongqing Communist Party Beijing division, family or business acquaintances.... At night, however, the party animal in them would creep out. Their arrival spelled the end of the dry season. For the next few days I failed to give my all to my students as eating, drinking and – most sacred of all – *karaoke* blasted through my body and soul in one big blur till the delegation's 'timely' departure.

Jan's standing orders were not to talk price under any circumstances, but to make sure that the visit in Europe would be light on formal meetings and heavy on visits to exotic locales. It was best that he not join the group, but give Smile one week's travel money and let them enjoy the experience in their own way.

It was better this way because although Jan insisted on meeting the group, he quickly realised that they were out of his league. He arranged a memorable dinner in an expensive Japanese restaurant, probably thinking that the whole delegation would enjoy a hearty home-style meal away from home. Afterwards I got an ear-full about one of the delegates trying to sit on the tatami in a nicely decorated private room, losing his balance and accidentally smashing through the rice paper wall, disturbing a Japanese party in the adjacent room. Not to mention the countless jugs of expensive sake that were consumed in a noisy Sichuan drinking contest where two participants challenged each other in a word and hand-sign game. The losing party had to *ganbei* a glass, while the next participant readied for another bet. I could imagine Jan's unease and helplessness as the noisy celebrations unfolded in ever-louder screams and shouts. Thankfully Smile, as usual, acted as the perfect Chongqing ambassador, smoothing any bumps along the road.

On their return to Beijing, their Sichuan batteries were fully recharged at a well-known Sichuan filling station: the Sichuanese restaurant that was occasionally visited by Deng Xiaoping.

Hearing Smile's US story was a real relief. None of the HK company's employees had met them in the States and the Americans seemed to have treated them as any other customer. Apparently the group was shown an endless string of glass factories and glass towers, and fed on bleeding steak, hamburgers and mashed potatoes. Present score: 2–1 in favour of the home team!

Reporting back on the phone with Jackson I could hear he was more than satisfied with the present state of affairs. He would further stage-manage the situation on the return of the delegation to Chongqing.

Meanwhile, in November, as thunder rumbled through a sunshiny day, the Renminbi was devalued again. The last revaluation I remembered was December '89 when the USD/RMB rate plummeted overnight by over 20 percent. At that time the consequences of such change didn't filter through to daily life, as China tended to insulate you from the outside world. Now, however the outcome struck home at the speed of light: thanks to the new exchange rate of 5.2 RMB to the dollar, the prices of our glass in the local currency were bloated by 10 percent. This was definitely a bad omen, as I had noticed during discussions all prices were mentally converted to Renminbi. The gradual devaluations had been enacted to encourage more exports and earn the country foreign exchange. But for this ugly little capitalist it was a new situation to manage, and I feared that our prices would have to be devalued correspondingly.

As Beijing got colder and the daytime temperatures dipped below zero, I was asked to fly to Chongqing for final discussions with the import-export company. Apparently a large proportion of the various contracts had already been awarded to several suppliers, and one of the undecided parts was the purchase of the glass. Although the bidding documents could not be changed, Old J didn't disappoint. Memories of the delegation's cold reception in the US were still reverberating in the corridors of the Chongqing *karaoke* bars. As quickly as boiling water softens instant noodles he mollified the import-export company and Mr Yu's team from the

Building Design and Research Institute. Although officially the bidding documents would have to be followed, the European glass could be accepted under the condition that the price would be more attractive than that of any other party. A road towards 'price devaluation' was slowly opening.

Luckily for me the Tsinghua students were performing a military training session and I was able to free myself for a whole week. Heading for Chongqing was akin to returning to my Chinese roots. On approach to the airport, through the thick clouds, the rice fields suddenly popped up like contour lines on a topographic map. I was back home.

Though it wasn't raining, the humidity made itself known by drawing streaks of moisture on the airplane's windows. On the ground, at fourteen degrees Celsius, the cold damp air tackled my body head on. If not properly dressed for nature's persistent bite, one would get an eerie sensation as if one's bones were slowly cooling down inside the body. A far cry from the dry cold I was accustomed to in Beijing.

Jackson and Smile were at the airport, waiting for me in a rusty Russian Volga car on loan from Chongqing University. As the night settled in, we were on our way to my old *alma mater*. The road from the airport to the city wasn't yet the present-day three-lane highway, but a twisting road along a mountainous terrain of rice fields, rocks and the odd village. In the darkness, the car drove slowly through a reddish-brown landscape carved up by the headlights, until one of the front tyres suddenly gave out. Here we were in the middle of nowhere on a pitch-black cold damp night. Unprepared for the event, we had to feel our way into the back of the car for the spare tyre and carjack. The spare tyre seemed worn out but OK; the jack however called in absent. A spare, no jack, pitch dark, cold, we were quickly running out of options and the occasional car passing through refused to stop for a bunch of castaways. Desperate, Jackson walked up the road to see if he could discern anything on the other side of the hill. Not soon afterwards he returned back shouting that he had seen a dim light in the distance. The only problem that remained was deciding who would venture into the complete darkness through the fields to that place, avoid the hungry dogs that probably protected the property, knock on the door and face the wrath of the farmer who might think a thief was sneaking in to take away his belongings. Definitely not a mission for the faint-hearted. In the end we settled on the driver – as an ex-military man he would be able to deal with the situation.

Indeed, roughly two hours later, we heard the heavy 'tacketack tacketack tacketack' of a small farm vehicle coming our way. Sitting behind the farmer, our driver was waving triumphantly. We had been lucky, the tractor-owning farmer turned out to be a trader who collected rice from the surrounding villages. After roughly an hour, a hundred RMB, and thousands of thank yous, we were back on the road. . . . I went to sleep at 3 AM in the morning – the following day would be the big one.

At 9 AM I walked into the meeting room with yesterday's dirty jeans and sneakers full of reddish mud, and still feeling very tired. Not really the image I wanted to convey. Old J however had already explained the situation and most of the people in the room by now knew me pretty well from past meetings. As expected, the discussion went back and forth between technical explanations and price. Like the experts they were, the import-export people, headed by Mr Zhang, made junk out of the price structure I tried to maintain. I gave way too fast for nothing in return. I hadn't really learned my lesson. At the same time we were discussing an English-Chinese contract with many paragraphs written in lawyer's lingo that gave me dreadful headaches. Although Jan had given me the authorisation to sign, he had to agree to each and every line before he'd give me the go ahead. Here I was, the wannabe China businessman, sometimes lost on the commercial terms of the contract but having to keep up appearances. The negotiations had been pretty intimidating and I felt as if I couldn't really keep up. Luckily Jan was a good and patient man – he had to be, so near to closing the deal.

By noon we finalised that day's discussions and I was told that I'd be contacted again the following day. As I left the building the Americans passed by, all in their smart Wall Street striped suits, ready for the kill. The HK guys accompanying them sneered at my muddy shoes and dirty pants. I couldn't care less, although in my mind it was now 2–2 with the psychological advantage to the visitors.

The contract was faxed to Jan who would review it and give me his comments during the night, and the following day I would have to defend his sometimes-cryptic ideas. Old J was not really of any help either, as the only thing he wanted from me was a lower price, and furthermore was not at all concerned with the contract's contents. As the days crawled by, at least six versions of the contract went under review, a kaleidoscope of possible payment terms were proposed and rejected by both parties, quantities of glass per container shrank and grew, delivery terms were stretched or squeezed as was seen fit, and damages on faulty payments, non-timely delivery or bad product quality took on psychedelic proportions. When Jan realised that no shipping company in Europe was willing to insure the goods to this 'unknown' inland destination of Chongqing, even the port of delivery changed several times, moving from Chongqing to Shanghai, Guangzhou, Ningbo and back again. Not to mention the fact that I had to navigate my way through paragraphs of Chinese that also changed on a daily basis, trying to match the English version. At that time the Internet was unknown, a laptop a rich man's gadget, and a PC word processor an archaic unfriendly creature. All this resulted in contract proposals that were literally cut and glued together with strips of fax paper, slivers of typewriter printouts and handwritten sections. A real work of art that each afternoon was duly retyped by a pretty secretary on the import-export company's two mechanical typing machines: One for the Chinese text and one for the English version.

As the import-export people kept us on edge about their choice of partner for the glass deal, the Americans were becoming restless, nervous and fed up. They threatened to leave Chongqing by Saturday if no decision had been made. As if to call their bluff on this artificial deadline, Saturday went by without any meeting. On Sunday, when asked to come over for final discussions, I saw the American team still present, obviously back-tracking on their threat to leave beautiful Chongqing. Apparently it was not that easy to walk away from a million-dollar contract.

In the meantime, eight thousand kilometres away, Jan was also getting a bit edgy, having to work over the weekend and unaccustomed to such lengthy and – in his words – miserable discussions. Myself, I stopped keeping track of my mental score of the home team versus the visitors. It might well have been 15–19 for all I knew. That Sunday, we still couldn't close the gap that was separating Jan's idea of the contract's contents and those of the import-export company. Price-wise, we were already 12 percent below the initial price Jan had given me.

Mr Zhang & Co. undeniably knew how to play hardball, and it was certainly not the first time they had squeezed the last drop out of a price negotiation. They were pros, working all the levers at their disposal. We just had to dance along to their daily melody while invisible strings pulled us to the beat. I had to be back in Beijing on Monday evening, but could always feign a stomach ache to stretch my time. Jackson meanwhile informed me that the bank director, vice-mayor, and import-export people had been invited by the HK-US team to one of the top restaurants in town. All this followed by a super-deluxe *karaoke* bash and more. . . . All three services rendered for the sake of building a better society. I couldn't compete with such extravagance; I'd have to work another year in Tsinghua to cover the expense.

Time quietly ticked by. The only activity that could be detected in the daily discussions was the emptying of overloaded ashtrays; nothing indicated any preferential leaning towards either group. Jackson, meanwhile, was working behind the scenes and already had arranged several private dinners with key individuals. For obvious reasons I was *persona non grata* at the dining table. Then on Thursday morning, thirteen days after arriving in the Pearl of Sichuan, Old J took me aside and gave me clear instructions to give way on the following points: In case of discrepancies in the contract the Chinese version prevails, and the L/C [Letter of Credit] would be opened with 20 percent down payment, 55 percent against shipping documents and 25 percent on arrival of goods. We would also need to have a bank guarantee valid for one year for a value of 20 percent of the goods, and we had to give another 5 percent discount.

'No problem. I think this is acceptable', I said, faking it. Entering the meeting room, everyone seemed to be gearing up for the final sprint, the cigarettes all lit, the teacups chock-full of chrysanthemum flowers – this meeting had another aura to it, it was somehow different.

'Jieke, we think we can trust you, I hope you won't disappoint us. We need you to agree on the following and the contract is yours,' and up came all of Old J's points.

My speech in response could be distilled into the following: 'We've gone a long way, we've been talking about this glass for over a year and honestly speaking I'd love to give you what you want, but I simply can't. You've dragged the price to the bottom of the Yangtze River; you've requested so many concessions and Jan has gone (hesitantly) along, I'm worn out working the fax at night and waking up early to prepare for the meetings, I can't give you anything more but a lunch.'

Silence in the meeting room, you could almost hear the tea ooze from the tealeaves and the smoke rising from the cigarettes; the bank director stared at Mr Yu and Mr Zhang, basically saying: 'It's your call, I'm fed up too, I have other things that need tending to.'

Mr Zhang finally spoke up. 'Well if that's the case, let's go and have lunch, there's nothing more we can accomplish in this meeting room.'

During the meal, the room filled with rocket-fuel fumes, everyone remembered the good times they'd had in Europe, and no business issues were brought up until the very end, when I initiated a final push: 'We can deliver the goods you want, but you're asking for the impossible. We've become close friends, it's a pity we couldn't ink this into a contract'.

At this, the bank director hinted to Mr Zhang that he should speak a few words. 'Yes we are old friends, but you have to know that China is very poor, we need to be very careful how we spend our country's money. We can't just go with every proposal that might suck money out of the motherland.'

'I understand, but I believe that none of us want to cheat the Chinese government. If that were the case I wouldn't be able to sleep at night.'

'Jieke, you know the devaluation has forced us to be more careful with the hard currency that is allocated to us, we need to make sure we comply with the government's regulations on how the resources are used.' On this final note, we decided that there was still some room for discussion and moved back to the meeting room, filling the afternoon with smoke and jugs of tea.

Finally, after four more hours of discussions touching on almost everything in the contract, we came to the following conclusion: 'The L/C would be opened with 20 percent down payment and 80 percent against shipping documents. A bank guarantee for a value of 10 percent of the contract remaining valid for three months after shipment and a 2 percent discount on the price'. From the import-export company offices I called Jan to ask him if this would be acceptable.

Crackling in from the other side of the line came: 'I'm tired of this haggling, we're selling glass here, not camels. They can have the glass on those payment terms, but *no more* discounts. Don't call me unless you've signed the contract!' Off I went to the meeting room, to tell them that Jan was about to call off the deal, and conveyed to Mr Zhang that basically all contract points could be agreed upon, but a further discount would be impossible.

At that Jackson asked me to leave the room for ten minutes for some internal discussions. An hour later, a beaming Jackson came out: 'Mr Zhang is ready to sign the contract!'

Later I understood that Jackson purchased the glass with the help of the Bank of China, which loaned him the money. Jackson then made a handsome profit selling it to the Hong Kong construction company, whose overall profit margin was seriously dented in the process. This transaction helped many people live a more comfortable life.

Postscript

- After the delegation's inspirational trip to Europe, where they saw the pedestrian-only shopping area of Frankfurt, Chongqing's city centre, Jie Fang Bei, got a revamp with a no-car look-alike.
- Mr Zhang of the import-export company is now head of the import-export department of a Chinese conglomerate listed on the Shanghai Stock Exchange.
- In November 1991, I moved on to work for a small trading company in Hong Kong, while Jackson set up office in Shenzhen just across the border. Over the course of many weekends I became a regular in Shenzhen's crazy, wacky night scene, which resulted in Jan's glass being fitted on three more skyscrapers.
- Jan died in a road accident during the summer of 1994. He only visited China once.
- In 1995 I decided that the time had come to set up my own trading company and moved to Beijing.
- Years later I worked together with the Hong Kong construction company on the building projects of two European factories in the Shanghai area.
- Einstein and his theories that the universe might be contracting and time is a relative concept were severely criticised during the Cultural Revolution, because they clashed with Marx's proclamations that the universe was absolute and infinite. Remnants of this clash of intellectual models can still be observed on a daily basis whenever time is a pressing issue in Chinese business.
- In the last couple of years the Renminbi has gained in prominence on the international market. It went on a controlled revaluation by more than 26 percent against the US Dollar. Whispers go around that one day the Renminbi will become a reserve currency.

CHAPTER 3

The fluttering flag

Having powerful connections in China will enable you to avoid many of the frustrating – sometimes maddening – business ambushes that litter the road to a successful deal.

The path to signing a juicy contract can be child's play, but that's not taking into account the baggage some Western managers unwittingly carry around: cultural indifference, ignorance, arrogance and most annoying of all, internal company politics. Those are liabilities that can derail even the most straightforward of discussions.

Therefore damage control and encouraging sensitivity on both sides of the negotiation table is often part of the intermediary's job. But sometimes events unfurl faster than one can handle.

Tuesday, March 6th, 1996, 11 AM

'Incoming, ten metres, with the red jacket!' I screamed.

We were a total of seven people on the windy Great Wall in Jinshanling, enjoying a view of the symbol of China meandering its way over the mountain range in front of us. Some other tourists, however, seemed more interested in cleansing their inner bodies by scraping their throats. Hanging their heads over the side of the Great Wall, they were letting fly into the cold air. Phlegm was picked up on the wind and coming in from all sides. The only alarm bell was a hawking sound from the human launch path, before the missile was released. A couple of unwary travellers in our group had already been hit and an early warning system was the only defence.

Among our group was James, an equipment expert from FET, producer of vegetable oil extraction and refining equipment; Roger, head of Project Management Ltd, a subsidiary of FET; Etienne, a project engineer working for Roger; Mike Yeoh, a BBC (British-born Chinese) and private banker/investor; and Mr Xie and Mr Mang who each had a grandfather who had experienced first-hand the nine-thousand-kilometre Long March with Mao in 1934 while on the run from the Kuomintang.

After my trial by fire with Old J, and the surprise success with the glass business, I decided that it might be time to start my own trading company in Beijing in 1995. Having mailed over 1,500 letters to different corporations around the world, the first serious response to my call to do business in China was FET.

FET had big plans to conquer the Chinese market. In 1995 China's annual per-capita consumption of vegetable oil was only three and a half litres, compared to an average of sixteen litres in Europe. In that year China's National Bureau of Statistics claimed that the country was the world's largest producer of peanuts, second-largest producer of rapeseed, and third-largest producer of soybeans. On paper, definitely, a dream market too tantalising to avoid. Demand for refined oil was booming due to the change in diets and the need for a healthier lifestyle, but also the cumulative effect of other industries pouring their money into the coastal areas and requiring more and higher-quality oil, meal and oil derivatives. Manufacturers of instant noodles, cookies, ice cream, animal feed, cosmetics and other heavy users of oil seed extracts were all vying for a part of the Chinese market. Anyone dealing directly or indirectly with the vegetable seed, oil or animal feed markets simply needed to be in China. Large-scale projects were popping up in seed-rich areas or along the Chinese coast, mostly spearheaded by investment from overseas Chinese based in Indonesia, Malaysia, Singapore, Hong Kong, Taiwan or Thailand. Those investors had already built reputations in their own markets by processing palm oil and South American soybeans. Now they were bringing their expertise back home.

It had all started roughly six months previously when James contacted me regarding a huge turnkey project in China. The information at that time was still sketchy but it would be one of the bigger projects FET would realise in the coming years. A Chinese customer required a factory complex capable of processing seven thousand tons of soybeans on a daily basis. At that time it all sounded too good to be true. The plant would be an industrial complex at least eight times larger than the largest existing soybean-processing factory in China. All to be financed by Mike Yeoh, who'd put up the funds and syndicated loans through his extensive banking contacts in the UK, Singapore and Hong Kong.

A couple of days after our initial telephone call, James informed me that Mike Yeoh had asked us to make a company presentation and we were urgently requested to go to southern China to meet 'his' contacts.

Urgency: a lovely concept from a Chinese perspective, but often misunderstood in the West.

Twenty-four hours later James landed in Hong Kong. Together we took the short boat trip to Macau and walked across the border into Zhuhai. On the Chinese side, some guy was waving a plate with our names and quickly huddled us into a black Lexus with military licence plates. The right-hand drive, probably 'borrowed' from the streets of Hong Kong, raced us with blazing sirens and flashing lights to a top-class Cantonese restaurant. Already sitting at the table and drinking XO Cognac with five other guests were Mr Mang and Mr Xie. In their late twenties, they emanated a sense of self-confidence and power I had seldom seen in China. In their designer clothes, with the latest mobile phones and expensive watches, they definitely weren't Mister Average.

Mike Yeoh was nowhere to be seen.

Having introduced ourselves and exchanged name cards, the next natural step was a glass of cognac and a welcome *ganbei*. Which was followed by uneasy silence. Trying to get the conversation into gear again, we mumbled a bit about FET and how great this company really was.

Although they listened to our introduction speech politely at first, the Chinese party was not genuinely interested in our stories about vegetable oil or soybeans. James and I were a bit intimidated by the whole situation.

'What the heck are we doing here? Who are these guys?' James muttered while trying to chopstick a peanut.

At the same time our hosts went to great lengths to reassure us that we should relax and enjoy the evening out. During the day we'd have ample opportunity to enlighten or bore their engineers to death with our sophisticated sets of pots, pans and pipes. Like a fine-tuned clockwork mechanism the food came flowing in. Caviar, lobster, garoupa, scallops, turtle, shrimps, shark fin soup. . . . Basically anything expensive that lived in the water came to us through the chef's hands.

Also sitting at our table and keeping to themselves were two tall Caucasians with military crew cuts, sharing a bottle of xo. The Caucasians turned out to be two Russian pilots, who were in town to demonstrate the Russian Sukhoi-27 fighter jets to the Chinese military brass during the Zhuhai air show. As the bottles were opened and emptied one by one the conversation became decidedly livelier. Sitting next to one of the pilots, we started to discuss airplanes. Being interested in anything moving faster than 200 kilometres per hour, I got Vagram to loosen up a bit.

'The Americans have a problem on their hands, the F-15 is like a sitting duck in a dog fight.' Meanwhile he moved his hands in the air to demonstrate how the F-15 would crash and burn at the hands of a Sukhoi-27. The others were also eager to hear more fighter-jet stories and his colleague, Nickolai, certainly didn't disappoint. Having already consumed three times the quantity of alcohol I had, the stories they dug up got more and more entertaining. Both had flown missions in Afghanistan during the eighties and they got pretty animated going on about the rough terrain and the difficulties of operating a fast-moving fighter jet in that region of the world. Their pronouncements ranged from 'I like to fly behind some mountain range, suddenly appear in the open and surprise the enemy on the ground' to 'many young Russians died far away from home thinking they were doing the right thing, but this is a place impossible to control, this was a stupid mistake to invade this country'. Amid all the discussions taking place I couldn't help but ask Mr Xie's other guests if China was interested in buying any additional Sukhoi, thinking my question would get bounced off into abstraction.

'I can tell you even more than that. An agreement was recently signed for a technology transfer to China to manufacture 200 Sukhois in the coming years.' Whoops, there went the veil of secrecy. Whoever thought that China was mired in mystery probably never asked the right questions of the right people. . . .

While the dinner party was being wrapped up, Vagram asked Mr Xie where we were staying for the evening. 'They'll be housed in the villa right next to the one where you're staying.' At this Vagram gave me a faint smile and whispered in a heavy Russian accent, 'Tomorrrow I vill be yourrr vake-up call.'

The villas were strategically located next to the airport and mostly rented out for top dollars to the companies attending the show. In the very early morning, a thundering roar followed by the vibration of all the windows in my room got me straight out of bed. My very lethal hangover disappeared on the spot.

'Vagram's wake up call!' James yelled as he rushed out onto the rooftop balcony.

Seconds later, the next wall of sound hit us dead on. One of the jets, tipping its wings, screamed by tens of metres above us and disappeared behind the hills surrounding the villa compound, leaving in its wake complete silence, heat, a reek of burned kerosene and the air displacement of the engines. James and myself were totally mesmerised by this private show and continued to scan the sky for more. Then, out of the blue and from both sides of the hills, the jets reappeared with a spine-chilling growl. Having decelerated dramatically, they looked as if they were hanging in the air, almost falling out of the sky. While making sharp curves they suddenly accelerated to mind-boggling speed, twisted above our heads and thundered straight up into the heavens with a deafening howl. With the roar of the engines still rumbling in the depths of our stomachs, the jets returned side by side at low speed. To our amazement, while one of the jets continued straight on, the other Sukhoi abruptly pulled up its nose. The aircraft pitched up to a 110-degree angle of attack and looked as if it would stop in midair. Tipping forward, the nose fell back to horizontal and it continued on its original path as though nothing had happened.

After this the Sukhois, decorated in the colours of the Russian flag, gracefully ploughed through the clouds and took off for the heavens once again.

Best wake-up call ever! Unfortunately once the show was over, our feet were firmly anchored on terra firma once more, in the 'exciting world' of soybeans. . . .

The main broker, Mr Yeoh, had promised James that they would be flying into Hong Kong at roughly the same time. Twenty-four hours later, however, there was still no sign of Mr Yeoh. I could sense that neither of the 'Long March grandsons' were willing to have any kind of meaningful discussion with us without their buddy Yeoh being present.

Around 10 AM we got a telephone call from Mr Mang saying that the driver would pick us up for a meeting in town. Hoping for the best, we were all turned out in black business suits, ready for the kill, spick and span for our first business appointment – or so we thought.

But when the car stopped in front of a massage parlour, I knew better. The place was apparently owned by Mr Liu, a friend of Mr Mang's, and was bustling with women taking care of customers. Mr Mang, dressed in green slippers and a wrinkled blue bathrobe, met us with a huge grin: 'Welcome to Mr Liu's massage parlour.'

A rather villainous looking Mr Liu welcomed us in the hoarse, raspy voice of a heavy smoker. James was pretty reluctant to enter a massage parlour, thinking something unpleasant might happen as soon as he walked in. His nerves had got the better of him and he was probably as anxious as the first time he kissed a girl. In the reception area, all worked up, he frantically started pushing the numbers on his mobile phone in a last-ditch attempt to get in touch with Mr Yeoh. As usual, Mr Yeoh's UK number was never reachable, except when he wanted you to reach him.

Initially I stood there in the reception area trying to calm him down. Not wanting to offend our guests, it fell to me to lure him into the pleasure dome. Once I explained to him that all the sanitary conditions would be met and . . . what was to be expected behind the reception area, he 'reluctantly' agreed. Without a stitch on we went for a body scrub and afterwards soaked ourselves in a communal hot pool. Floating next to me, Mr Mang seemed to enjoy the moment intensely, his eyes closed, his breathing deep; he absorbed the energy in the air. Also James seemed to have pulled himself together and had relaxed entirely, happily enjoying the fringe benefits of this trip. Asking Mr Mang for some news about Mr Yeoh's whereabouts, he was met with: 'He has promised to be in Zhuhai in the next few days. In the meantime we take care of you.' This was the only direct business-related discussion that day. After roughly an hour of drifting aimlessly in and out of sleep in the hot pool, we moved to the second floor (this time in bathrobes) and seated ourselves in a room full of deckchairs. Ladies immediately tended to our needs, manicuring our fingernails, cutting our toenails and serving tea. The rest of the day was spent eating, drinking, resting and singing songs in Mr Mang's favourite *karaoke* haunt.

The next morning when we heard that today it was Mr Xie who'd arranged the extra-curricular activities James got into a temper.

'Don't these people ever work? Don't they realise I've got to be back in Europe by the end of the week? We've already wasted two days doing nothing. Where's the urgency Mike Yeoh was talking about? He's not even here. We really need to tell them that we're not here for pleasure!'

If I told him that we actually were working, and that saunas, massage parlours, restaurants, and *karaoke* parlours were extended offices for many Chinese businessmen, I would only make matters worse. I decided it would be wise to keep quiet and feign ignorance. The unknown factor for me was Mike Yeoh, whom I'd not yet met, but I could already deduce that he was not your Mr Average either.

And indeed he was not. Arriving a full four days late, he had left me and our Chinese hosts with no doubt that he was important and worth waiting for. James, when ushered into the private room of a restaurant, was extremely relieved to see him sitting between the princelings Mr Mang and Mr Xie. Stressed by having to cancel his departure out of Hong Kong, he forgot all the bad feelings that had built up during the massage sessions. The dollar signs were back on!

James probably still believed that Mike Yeoh was *the* key to selling the equipment, and had not yet understood the power at the disposal of Mr Mang and Mr Xie. The fact that their grand-parents had been on the Long March was enough to secure their families a place in the political hierarchy for generations to come. Those two were actually carrying out the commercial activities of their family members who held high positions in the government. They decided who would participate in the deal, but more impor-tantly they had all the connections in place to procure the right facilities and necessary permits, fast and hassle-free. Mike's con-tribution of finances and the credibility of a trustworthy overseas Chinese banker was relatively minor compared to this political clout.

The following morning we were driven to the centre of the city where a meeting was held with some specialists in vegetable oil and fat from a research centre based in Xi'an. The meeting reiterated once again that the capacity of the plant would be seven thousand tons per day and that it would entail harbour facilities to load and off-load the soybeans, process them into vegetable oil and meal, and arrange for storage, bottling and packing.

During the three-day sessions with the engineers, Mr Yeoh, Mr Mang and Mr Xie were nowhere to be seen, and we were too busy and excited about the magnitude of the project to bother inquiring as to their whereabouts. They were probably floating around in Mr Liu's pool, soaking up the good life.

Having discussed at length the technical outlines of the project, James wanted to see the site on which the project was expected to be built, as it called for some specific requirements: a huge piece of land, at least 600 by 250 metres, more than half of which would be used for storage of raw and finished materials. In addition it was mandatory to have a berth to accept Panamax vessels – in other words, a parking space for gigantic ocean freighters able to carry around fifty thousand tons of beans and requiring a water depth of at least fifteen metres. On top of this, such a colossal plant needed spacious access roads for the massive numbers of large trucks which would carry out the vegetable oil and soy meal.

The following day, as if the heavens had heard our wishes, Mr Yeoh's entire crew showed up and we were shuttled to a seaside location where the plant was to be erected. The place was a flat area of grasslands, inundated by wind and ending with steep rocks dropping into the sea. In the distance we could see Zhuhai city but within a radius of five kilometres there wasn't a single living soul, no electricity grid, nothing but some seagulls hanging in the air.

The ever-optimistic Mr Yeoh explained, 'the Zhuhai government has appointed this area as a new industrial zone and given us priority to choose a plot of land of one and a half square kilometres that we'll be able to operate for fifty years.' Pointing into the distance he added, 'over there we plan to build one of the largest instant noodle factories in China, and over there we'll be installing an animal feeding plant to provide fodder for farmers in Guangdong Province and beyond.'

From James's and my expressions he could read our scepticism. James only saw a pie in the sky, and couldn't believe he had wasted more than ten days in China for nothing but a view of some rocks and a dark grey-green sea. He whispered to me, 'this area is nice but would require massive infrastructure before the customer could even think of starting to run such a plant. They should realise that at full capacity around three hundred huge trucks would drive in and out of the factory on a daily basis. Without the necessary road infrastructure this place would get clogged in no time.'

Mike Yeoh intervened: 'James, what do you think? Isn't this the perfect site for the soybean processing plant?'

'Well, it certainly could be, but there's a lot of work that needs to be done: Electricity, fresh water, wide roads, and a fifteen-metre-deep sea channel all the way from the open sea to a berth to accommodate Panamax vessels, just to name a few points that I see are still missing.' At this, Mr Yeoh took a walk with Mr Mang and Mr Xie, returning five minutes later with a simple 'Done!'

James and I laughed nervously. Was he kidding?

During the evening meal James touched on the subject of the site again. 'Mike, do you really mean that the piece of land we saw today can be turned into a first-class industrial site within a year?'

'Without a doubt. If Mr Mang and Mr Xie tell me it can be done, it can be done.'

James continued undeterred. 'But is there no other site we could visit where we could build such a plant?'

Mr Yeoh turned to Mr Mang and asked in the most casual of manners whether we could go to see another piece of land. Mr Mang thought for a moment whilst sipping on his mixture of XO and lemonade. 'Shouldn't be a problem. Let's drive tomorrow to Shantou. My uncle is in charge of a new industrial development along the coast, that could certainly also be worth visiting.'

For James the trip to Shantou was one trip too many, as it would take more than five hours to reach our destination. He needed to be back in the UK and so was dropped off at the Macau border at 6 AM. Mr Yeoh, Mr Xie, Mr Mang, Mr Liu (of the massage parlour) and myself continued our quest to Shantou.

Mr Xie and Mr Mang were both driving their own cars, and together with Mr Liu in his Lexus they all agreed to race to Shantou. I was seated in Mr Xie's Saab and Mr Yeoh was buckled into the racing seat of Mr Mang's BMW M3. Apparently this car had been tuned in Hong Kong for the previous year's Macau Grand Prix and was later sold to him. In the early morning on the deserted highways of Zhuhai, dust was quickly blown up and within minutes the speedometer hit 180 kilometres per hour. The place was desolate – luckily, because the three cars were dashing through only metres from each other, any steering error a potentially deadly hazard. It wasn't their first street race, as the drivers were all smiles, gesturing to each other and chattering on their mobile phones about the performance of their cars.

Unfortunately as the early sun rays broke through the dawn more trucks hit the road, and those lumbering mastodons weren't expecting us to be sprinting by at such speed. Worse, the overloaded trucks were puffing through at a snail's pace, taking up all available lanes and unmindful of their surroundings. For Mr Xie & Co. this didn't mean reducing their speed, but instead trying to anticipate the truck drivers' next moves as they slalomed past, using the road shoulder as an additional space for overtaking. Racing the concrete slabs was definitely fun, except for the one sitting in the passenger seat. Getting stuck in the co-pilot's seat of a Sukhoi-27, at the mercy of those Russians, would have been a joy ride compared to what we went through. After staring death in the eyes on several occasions, both Mr Yeoh and myself were more than happy to arrive in Shantou and get out of the car. We reached our destination unscathed but for the adrenaline burning in our veins.

In those days Shantou was known as a smuggler's paradise. Anyone wanting to bring goods into China whilst avoiding paying taxes pushed it through this port. Many 'smart' government-owned import-export companies went through this route to save a buck or two for their customers. The city itself was brimming with luxury compounds, exclusive cars and hotels. Even the massage and sauna parlours were a notch above average. Needless to say the crew was known in town and an extensive exploration of those parlours had been planned long in advance. More booze, more women, more *karaoke*, more hangovers, more seafood, more saunas, more than my body could take.

Sitting down with Mr Liu during one of those sessions I started to realise that he, with the backing of the Xie and Mang Clan, was a major importer of vegetable oil originating from North and South America, opening letters of credit in the millions of dollars and chartering whole Panamax vessels into . . . Shantou harbour. During one of those conversations he bragged repeatedly that he'd cancelled 'irrevocable' L/Cs while the freighters were in the middle of the Pacific Ocean because soybean prices on the international market had dropped below a certain level. For him it was a perfectly normal practice, and he found it entirely justifiable to kill a deal if no money could be made. Querying him on how he was able to withdraw irrevocable L/Cs, the answer was simple, to him anyway. 'In small cities or towns we receive backing from the branch offices of major Chinese banks who'd do anything to get our business. If we say don't pay, well, they just don't pay the advising bank. The barbarians have no idea that the L/C is opened in an insignificant branch office. They only see the bank's name and trust that all is OK. See, it's easy to make money in China!' He smirked at me while blasting a puff of unfiltered smoke into my face.

As far as the Shantou site was concerned, it was not what FET had in mind. The existing Shantou port was over-crowded and the new industrial area was a hilly green field with a muddy path linked to a provincial road twenty kilometres away from the nearest highway. So in the blink of an eye it was (re-)decided that Zhuhai was to be the location of the processing plant.

Not yet able to support myself in a life of *karaoke* and saunas, I had to leave behind the joyous crew and go back to the 'real' world, giving my liver a welcome reprieve from working overtime.

Mr Liu also decided that he had learned enough from his competitors and offered to drop me off at the Shenzhen-Hong Kong border.

To satisfy his need for speed, we were soon flying low over the highway at 170 kilometres per hour. All went fine till a huge cloud broke and quickly coated the road with a thick film of water. On several occasions already the car had slightly fish-tailed but Mr Liu, deaf to the signals his vehicle was giving him, pushed on at relentless speed. Finally we went into one skid too many and the car started spinning uncontrollably over the concrete at high speed. After hitting the kerb at least twice, the car came to a full stop in the middle of the highway, only to be hit by another car in the flank. Although I was wearing a seatbelt I was still pretty well bruised above my left eyebrow, and blood started gushing out like from a freshly slaughtered pig. Mr Liu himself was OK, the airbag had done its job. He hobbled his car onto the shoulder, got out in the rain and started a cursing match with the driver who'd hit us. Roughly fifty kilometres from Shenzhen, in the middle of a storm, blood all over my clothes, how much worse could it get?

But it did: the moment Mr Liu suggested getting me to a local hospital.

The idea of having to go to an unknown hospital to get patched up cleared my pain in an instant. Nightmarish memories of the Chongqing hospital where, many years ago, I had had a health checkup before getting my working licence came bubbling up again. It was a dark, cold and damp place, cavernous corridors with paint peeling off the walls. A morbid smell of medicine and cleaning products was always hanging in the sultry air. Bare twenty-Watt light bulbs dangling on live wires from the ceiling created a gloomy atmosphere just bright enough to get you from one end of the hall to the other. On the unadorned cold concrete floor, patients in light-blue pyjamas were moving around in wheelchairs, lying on stretchers or pushing IV drips under their own power. As I waited my turn in the sitting area, a three-year-old girl squatted in front of me and did her thing while her parents chatted on. When my turn came, thirty minutes later, the excrement was still cooling on the cold concrete floor. This flash-back sent a cold shiver through my body. No way would I risk my health by walking into some unknown place like that. I was bleeding heavily from my head, but would pay whatever it took to get to a Hong Kong hospital. Luckily other drivers slowed down to have a good look at the wrecked cars and I was able to flag down a taxi, bringing me to the Hong Kong cross-over.

While standing in the queue waiting for my passport to be stamped everyone stared at me, probably thinking: another victim of a business deal gone bad.

A couple of weeks later the project started to take shape, at least on the Chinese side. Having met several 'behind the scenes' officials in Beijing who supported the project, I could feel that the decision to go ahead had already been made. The light was green. Money for the plant was available, Hong Kong and Singaporean bankers were fighting to finance the deal with Mr Yeoh, and permits for starting the general infrastructure work were all given the go ahead.

Regrettably, the more reports I sent back indicating that this project was for real, the less convinced the people on the other side of the world were that China needed such a plant. It was the business world turned upside down: the customer having to beg to be allowed to buy. With a juicy project in hand, the FET people were reluctant to trust it, and so technical quotes stayed out of reach. Although their subsidiary company certainly had experience with plants in South America and the Middle East, they stubbornly refused to accept the idea that such a plant would be viable in China.

So for weeks on end James and I had to beg, urge, woo, supplicate, pray and plead to be given something to offer our customer, all to no avail. It seemed top management had decided it was impossible that China would buy such a plant, and therefore no resources had to be spent on it. Mr Yeoh started to get angry at the lack of feedback on plant designs and cost structures. After our meeting in Zhuhai roughly two months before nothing concrete had been proposed by FET. Finally James, fed up with all the delays and lost time, got Roger, head of Project Management Ltd, to agree to look into it, with the condition that the Chinese side would wire US$350,000 to the company's accounts to start the preliminary study.

Within days Mr Yeoh sent the wire, and the money landed safely in the company's bank accounts. For Project Management Ltd, this was the first time a customer had ever paid so much money for a preliminary study. And what did the Chinese customer get in return? A copy of the plans for an existing plant in the Middle East, with the name changed to Zhuhai Vegetable Oil project. As if this could not have been done eight weeks earlier for free. . . .

At any rate, it got us rolling again. Extensive technical discussions were held with the Xi'an Oils and Fats Research Centre. The thick bundle of equipment and project management proposals finally boiled down to around 109 million dollars. 'Bingo!' we were all thinking to ourselves. This was to be my largest contract to date in China. The end-user, a commercial arm of the military, was extremely efficient and had already gotten the Zhuhai government to start building the basic infrastructure while the port authorities were finalising a dredging analysis.

Still, during my project-status presentation at FET headquarters, Roger was suspicious about the whole thing. He didn't want to believe that this could be for real. The road was wide open: for once annoying competitors were kept at bay, and the Chinese buyers were not vying for more time but pushing hard to get it done ASAP. We had only an internal stumbling block to overcome. Although money had been paid for the design phase, the top guy of Project

Management Ltd refused to believe in it. To him, it wasn't even faintly possible that a Chinese company would want to invest in this type of plant. Even after the charming Mike Yeoh drove over in his Rolls and explained all of the financing involved; in his mind the word 'impossible' was still flashing in bold red. In the end, the CEO of FET told him to fly over and see for himself.

So here I was, with Roger and his most loyal project manager Etienne, sitting on a flight bound for Hong Kong. Nothing much was said during that flight because his ego was a bit bruised after being ordered to go. Although he may not have thought of it that way, his pride had taken a dent or, to put it in Chinese, he had 'lost face'.

When the duty free cart passed by, I realised I didn't have any token presents to give to the 'crew', so I decided on the spot to purchase the trendy elixir of the day and acquired the plane's entire inventory of XO, six bottles in total. On seeing this, I got four wide-open eyes staring at me in disbelief, followed by: 'Don't you dare put this on the company expense accounts.' A pleasure trip with those two it certainly was not, so I was quite relieved to see that James was already in Hong Kong after meeting with another Southeast Asian customer.

Surprisingly enough, Mike Yeoh turned up in the lobby to meet us all as we checked into our hotel.

'Welcome to Hong Kong, Roger. Tonight you'll meet the key players of the project.'

Not only was gentlemanly Mike Yeoh on time, he had also invited to the party: two Singaporean bankers, the three top managers of a huge Chinese import-export company, the general manager of the company purchasing the plant, Mr Xie and Mr Mang. The dinner as usual was top-notch and to top off the evening it was decided we would visit one of the best *karaoke* bars Hong Kong had to offer.

Although James was by now accustomed to the trade, both Roger and Etienne felt pretty uneasy. When twenty-five ladies in micro skirts walked into our private *karaoke* box and the mama-san asked us each to choose one as a companion, both men cringed in their seats. Having enjoyed a good Catholic education, they were not at all comfortable having to select an escort lady. What might the wife at home say if she ever found out. . . . James, for his part, didn't hesitate but picked out a gorgeous long-legged southern beauty.

On seeing this Roger nearly hyperventilated: 'James, this is like a livestock market. I can't be part of this. This, this is prostitution. . . .' To which James pungently retorted, 'Not choosing a lady at *karaoke* is like saying you smoked marijuana but didn't inhale.'

Trying to break the tension, Mike quickly told them to only take a lady if they were really interested in women. With these fine words, they were given a choice to be with the boys, or not. Reluctantly, eyes almost closed, they each randomly pointed at one of the girls. Sitting stiffly in the sofa, both men did their best to avoid noticing or talking to those exquisite female specimens. There were no further difficulties during that *karaoke* session, unless you count one of the bankers' beauties, who drank a tad too much and ended up vomiting.

At the very end of the evening Mr Yeoh decided to reciprocate for all the bottles of XO we had brought for the Chinese party by offering each of us a lady for the night. Not wanting to refuse such a generous offer in front of all the other Chinese guests, James and I willingly obliged and took 'our' girls back to the hotel room. For Roger and Etienne however, the situation only sank in as we were outside hailing taxis. Holding Roger's hand, one of the ladies wanted to lead him into the car. There and then all of Roger's fuses blew. Looking straight at me, he started screaming that it was a scandal that he had flown all the way to Hong Kong to be humiliated, and that company resources were spent on lewd, decadent activities. His shouting certainly attracted the attention of the other night-time revellers, who thronged around us, enjoying the scene and making comments about out-of-control barbarians. By now it had become a pretty embarrassing situation for Mr Yeoh who couldn't understand what all the fuss was about. These were top-class ladies after all. . . .

The only solution I could think of which might defuse the situation while leaving Mr Yeoh's face intact was to kindly propose to both of the rejected ladies that they join me in the taxi, and disappear into the night.

The following day at breakfast, Mr Yeoh walked up to me with radiant eyes. 'Jack you really impress me: Three ladies in one night. I wish I could still handle that sort of thing. What about Roger? Is he OK? Is he gay or something?' Which only made us chuckle later when both gentlemen joined the table.

As if some mysterious disease had tainted us, Roger and Etienne segregated themselves from James and myself by only talking if absolutely necessary.

By the time we arrived in Zhuhai the internal bickering had taken its toll, and the stress in our team was clearly visible. When Mr Yeoh wanted to start the evening by heading for Mr Liu's sauna, James reacted with lightning speed to call it a day, saying we needed to prepare for the coming contract discussions. If it weren't for Mr Liu's presence, his massage parlour would have caused the whole soup of bad feelings to boil over again. The project was now dangling by a thread because we couldn't present ourselves as a cohesive team.

Certainly this was bad news for me as I saw my commission blown away into tatters. James and I therefore decided to keep up appearances and only joined in the nightly follies when the other members were sound asleep.

The following day's contract discussions went into full swing and required our full attention. For me this was one of the easiest technical and commercial discussions I could imagine. We had backing from several banks who were eager to get into the deal. There was Mr Yeoh himself, who had set his heart on the well-known capabilities of FET, and thus there were no competitors sitting in a room next door, waiting their turn to undercut our price.

Roger saw it differently, however. He didn't like nitty-gritty discussions about every aspect of the equipment. It was as if the Chinese engineers were challenging his company's technical integrity at every turn. But the Chinese from the local building department and the Oils and Fats Research Centre needed to do their due diligence because they were responsible for making sure that FET delivered on its technical promises. At the same time there was no doubt that they wanted to improve their know-how in order to be able to design something similar in the not-so-distant future.

But for those who were not yet up to speed with Chinese negotiation antics, it was irritating when the Chinese either repeated yesterday's discussions in another format, or suggested that certain parts be manufactured in China, or challenged FET's production processes, or requested FET to redesign the lay-out of the factory, or wanted to know in (too much) detail how certain equipment was designed and manufactured. But commercially it made sense to manufacture certain non-critical parts locally, as it would lower the cost of the contract by roughly 5 percent, give the research centre a stake in the manufacturing process, and on top of that certainly buy us the goodwill necessary to get all the permits to build and run the plant.

While in the evening, around the dining table, Mr Yeoh discussed with us the commercial terms laid out by members of the import-export corporation, the daytime technical discussions had already dragged on for over a week. The longer those discussions lasted, the longer the Chinese engineers could enjoy the Zhuhai weather and Cantonese cuisine. So why bother to hurry back to their dreary office building far away from the lights and glitter? The discussions full of Chinese platitudes were tedious, exhausting, nerve-wracking and put even the most tolerant on edge. But since there was a multi-million dollar project at stake, self-restraint and the prospect of an eventual end to negotiations should have given us the hope and courage to put up with the Chinese negotiation tactics.

During one of those memorable discussions, a Chinese engineer in all his vagueness launched into an 'I assume we could. . . .' upon which Roger, who had already dug too deep into his reserve of patience, promptly interrupted him and snapped: 'If you assume, you make an ASS out of U and ME!'

Everyone got quiet while the Chinese fellow, now wide-eyed, laughed nervously, clearly missing the pun. The ones that spoke English misunderstood Roger completely, and from the discussions that followed with the other Chinese they apparently thought that Roger was afraid that they wanted to assault him. The confusion then persisted as the Chinese staff kindly informed Roger 'No, we don't want to assault you, we want to be friends.'

At this Roger lost it all, stood up, roundly cursed everyone present and went into a tirade against James and myself. In response Etienne sheepishly shrugged his shoulders, while James dryly exclaimed: 'Too much stress, I assume.' The Chinese certainly were flabbergasted by Roger's reaction, and now thought that he, and therefore FET, didn't want to be friends. . . . This was one of those moments when you recoil within yourself as all the caricatures of the insensitive, obnoxious barbarian who loathes the Chinese culture come to life before your eyes. Although it definitely led the discussions nowhere, Roger thought that this confrontation was the answer to all the 'miseries' he had faced so far. This turned the already strenuous discussions into a protracted war of words where our Chinese counterparts stonewalled on technical and commercial issues. Normal dialogue became practically impossible as discussion topics that had been settled much earlier now again became points of contention.

Thinking that a change of environment might help settle the tensions, Mr Yeoh decided to continue the discussions in Beijing at the import-export company's headquarters, combining this with visits to the wealth of culture that surrounded the city. And that's how we ended up on the Great Wall on a Sunday afternoon, dodging incoming phlegm.

In the end the discussions limped on for a few more days but we couldn't get Etienne and Roger's full commitment to get it all back on track in a manner that gave everyone face and a sense of accomplishment. Luckily, in the evenings Mr Yeoh would spoil the Chinese team on *karaoke* sessions and saunas, making sure they were taken care of in the best possible terms. Whenever possible James and myself would sneak out and enjoy the bonding sessions. The engineers were just as intent on enjoying themselves at night as they were on appearing professional during the daytime. After lingering for a couple of days in the capital, our pleasure tour came to an end when Roger decided that the two weeks he'd spent in China were more than enough. There were more important things to take care of at home.

Personally I was not sure what could be more important than this mega-contract, but having lost so much of Roger's trust already, I was in no position to convince him to stay any longer.

James and myself remained to finalise whatever technical and commercial issues had been left unresolved. Interestingly enough, Mr Mang's and Mr Xie's senior relatives were always present during the evening dinners, giving a show of their power and decision-making that made doing business in China a child's game. Mr Yeoh was among equals here.

As projects above US$30 million required the blessing of the central government, the whole project was split up into four parts and so remained under the radar in terms of political scrutiny. Once the whole factory was built, Beijing would be unable to meddle in the local government's decision-making process or, what would be worse, kill the contract entirely.

In addition some top military brass, the Mang and Xie descendants and import-export company managers would visit FET's offices in Europe to clinch the deal. I was in seventh heaven, all the agony, drinking sessions and saunas had come to a good end. As for James, who had swallowed more Imodium pills in the last couple of weeks than he had in his entire life, he only wished for a good steak and fries on his return home.

The next month was taken up by bickering with Roger over having the project split into four parts. He wouldn't accept the Chinese logic and thought the move must be ill-intentioned. As I was trying to assuage his fears that negotiations with competitors might be going on concurrently, another bombshell landed in the form of a telephone call from Mr Yeoh directly to the CEO of FET and Project Management Ltd.

'The Chinese government is in the process of setting up a couple of large conglomerates, some targeting the food industry, among others. For this strategy certain core technologies might be of interest to support those industries. Would FET be interested in selling a controlling share to a large Chinese state-owned investment company?'

Within hours of the news trickling through, Roger's interest in China had turned around a hundred and eighty degrees. Suddenly

China was his darling, the land of plenty. Having an excellent relationship with the owners of the company he was definitely the right man to broker such a deal.

Unfortunately, having refused in the past to receive gifts from Mike Yeoh, Roger had put himself in an awkward position, where Mike was unwilling to consider him FET's real spokesperson. I could see Mike thinking 'How would Roger be able to handle acquisition negotiations if even women are such a volatile issue? Where's the pleasure in doing business?'

As was to be expected, Mike became unreachable. For extended periods of time, both Roger and the FET owners desperately tried to contact him. As time slipped by communications didn't improve and I became the target of their desperate telephone calls – at all hours of the day. As if I would be able to magically reach Mike. . . .

For my part I was more focused on drawing the Zhuhai project to a good conclusion. I already had enough on my plate, arranging all the technical and commercial discussions into four contracts that would please both the Chinese import-export corporation, FET and the bankers. On top of that I had to arrange a trip to Europe for eleven people who were expecting to be entertained with an eight-days-eight-countries extravaganza.

Discovering the whereabouts of Mike Yeoh, or learning which state-owned company might be interested in buying the shares, were the least of my worries.

Mike for his part was kept in the loop on the contract details and made furtive phone calls whenever financial terms needed to be revised. When he phoned, I dutifully told him that Roger and the company owners were looking for him. This too fell on deaf ears and he kept himself inaccessible. Probably a good negotiation strategy, as I noticed their eagerness to sell the shares becoming more acute.

Finally, Mike decided to reappear on the scene and a meeting was scheduled at FET headquarters with the various shareholders. These discussions were held the week preceding the visit of the Chinese delegation and I assume Yeoh wanted to have an initial feeling for the terms and conditions under which the shares would exchange hands.

One week later, I landed together with the eleven-man throng at Amsterdam Airport, where a bus was waiting for us. The fabled European trip everyone was looking forward to went into full swing. Along the way a signing ceremony would be arranged at FET offices for the Zhuhai contract, and one Singapore banker had even made the effort to be present. Definitely one guy who knew how to revitalise his relationship at every possible opportunity.

The day we were to visit FET headquarters everyone was in a great mood. A day earlier Mike Yeoh had joined us, the Chinese food that had been served in a local restaurant was authentic; the striptease following the meal was to their liking. I couldn't imagine anything that could possibly go wrong on this beautiful late summer morning. But when the bus drove up to the main FET building ... my eyes beheld the impossible. Fixed on a pole next to the FET flag, the Taiwanese flag was fluttering against the perfect blue sky. In the back of the bus there were Chinese military, there were people whose family had experienced the Long March. . . . I thought of asking the bus driver to turn around but it would have been too odd as the top brass of FET were already outside to meet us and anyway, manoeuvring space for the bus was limited. This couldn't be real. Once everyone got off the bus, they'd see this offensive symbol. There was no way they'd miss it. Indeed the cheery atmosphere that had marked the start of the day turned funereal. The FET people at first didn't realise the blunder that was literally hanging above their heads. Outside the bus, while the Chinese group 'pretended' not to have seen the flag, furtive handshakes were given to the shareholders, Roger and the CEO. Mike Yeoh stared at me, his eyes asking me what this was all about, before being quietly questioned by Mr Mang and Mr Xie. I took the FET CEO aside, explaining to him about the provocation the flag represented. The seriousness of the situation became apparent to him pretty quickly when the whole group toured the facilities out of politeness, but ten minutes later walked back on the bus without another handshake, never to set foot at FET again.

No apology could induce them to change their mind. They had been offended to the core and that was the abrupt end of it all. No

$100 million contract, and certainly no purchasing of company shares. Loyalty comes at a price!

Apparently a secretary had mixed up the flags. Nobody at FET had noticed the bungle and they're probably still wondering what all the fuss was about. In the bus everyone was quiet but in the hotel lobby all bad feelings were given vent. I was loathed, cursed and asked not to join the rest of the journey. It was the lowest I had ever felt. People with whom we were building a relationship of friendship dropped me without hesitation.

A couple of years later I read in a Hong Kong newspaper the following:

> A former Hong Kong trader working in Shenzhen and running a smuggling ring in edible oils was sentenced to death recently, with a possible two-year reprieve for good behaviour. The Guangzhou Provincial Higher People's Court sentenced Mr Yang, formerly the legal representative and GM of a large trading company in Shenzhen.
>
> He was convicted of coordinating a smuggling ring and bribing officials. The ruling put an end to the marathon trial of Yang's smuggling clique, which has taken six years of investigation and litigation.
>
> Liu, a principal accomplice, was found guilty of smuggling and was also sentenced to death with two years probation.
>
> The remaining ten members of the ring were all convicted of smuggling and sentenced to jail terms ranging from three to ten years, the court said.
>
> The court said Yang, fifty, a Hong Kong resident, collaborated in the trading of special import permits for edible oils and importing permit-required edible oils, such as olive oil, soybean oil and rape seed oil, between 1996 and 1998.
>
> Yang smuggled 827,500 tons of edible oil into the Mainland and evaded over 2.4 billion yuan (US$296 million) in tariffs. Yang gave 10 million yuan in bribes to custom officials in order to facilitate the smuggling. He was detained in

2000 and sentenced to death in the first trial by the Intermediate People's Court of Shenzhen in 2004.

Although I'd never met this Mr Yang, there was no doubt in my mind as to the identity of Mr Liu.

Postscript

- China's air force now has close to 400 Sukhoi fighter jets. Since the first flew over China, about 250 additional Shenyang J-11 fighter jets, based on the Sukhoi-27 design, have left the Chinese factory floors. The Shenyang J-15 version is designed to operate from the *Liaoning* aircraft carrier.
- Since China opened its soybean market in 1995, soybean imports have risen from 800,000 tons to 66 million tons for 2013.
- Every year in November the Macau Grand Prix is held on the city's narrow streets. This race is considered the major jumping board towards the F1.
- I'm still in close contact with Mike Yeoh who now is a major wheeler-dealer for large Asian conglomerates, investing in Indonesian palm plantations and buying up the exploration rights of oil fields along that country's coast.
- Although the Zhuhai deal went wrong we succeeded in selling five (smaller) plants for FET over a four-year period. The score could have been better but the Asian financial crisis sapped the money flow out of the Asian investors.
- Years later FET shareholders found other overseas investors to offload their shares.
- As far as Mr Xie and Mr Mang are concerned, I met them years later while selling measurement equipment for steel mills. They're now filling up the Chinese countryside with power plants and steel plants. Their lifestyle hasn't changed a bit.

CHAPTER 4

The wheels of commerce

Intellectual property rights (IPR) infringements have been part of business relations between China and the West ever since paper, the seismograph, cast iron, porcelain, silk and gunpowder were duly copied by the West. Traditionally in China knowledge has been considered a common good and not something to protect for profit.

Taking this into account, Western lawyers have been screaming down the Great Wall to no avail, while many Chinese businessmen wonder what the fuss is all about.

Therefore, businessmen facing IPR issues might enlighten themselves with a George Bernard Shaw quote: 'Some men see things as they are and ask "why?"; I dare to dream of things that never were and ask "why not?"'

Ahead of China's entry into the World Trade Organisation (WTO), a farsighted Chinese businessman retained our services to prepare his business empire for the legal ambushes that might come his way.

Sometime during 1997, pre-Asian financial crisis

Just like any well-oiled relationship network, the *guanxi* system was simmering with information twenty-four hours a day. It's probably the only type of network in China that remains hard to monitor and censor. This time, one of the Chongqing *guanxi* networks I directly or indirectly belonged to had picked up that Jackson Long's barbarian business partner had moved to Beijing. Apparently the Westerner had set up a company some time ago together with a group of friends, and was looking to assist Chinese companies with their great leap forward into the international arena.

More *guanxi* antenna picked up the signal, and the information stream ended up reaching Mr Li, a motorbike tycoon who ran his manufacturing operation from beautiful Chongqing. From there, Mr Li's scouts in Beijing were asked to sniff out a few more facts and check if we were bona fide enough to deal with his company.

When the signal came back indicating our trustworthiness, my lawyer friend Adam's *guanxi* network was informally plugged into the loop, to see if we'd be interested to assist Mr Li.

Even from behind the cloud-shrouded mountains of Sichuan, Mr Li's name was already reverberating in Beijing's imperial corridors and business circles. His company manufactured over one million motorbikes a year, with roughly fifty production sites scattered over the country. With a couple of headliners on his hands about copyright infringement lawsuits involving Japanese manufacturers, he was considered *big* business. So when we heard of Mr Li's intent to ask for a business 'favour', it wasn't long before I was flying back into the eternal Chongqing fog.

Picked up at the airport, I was driven in a limo to visit our prospective customer. No more muddy-puddle roads, but a pristine three-lane highway that rolled out in front of us like a dragon twisting its way through the mountains. From behind the darkened glass I caught a glimpse of the economic miracle unfolding here. One more city trying hard to become the next Hong Kong.

Where once farmers worked the dark red earth, now apartment blocks towered, and majestic five-star hotels, private universities, office towers and cranes were filling up the skyline. Large brand-new factories scattered the landscape, all dressed out in blue or red rooftops under which workers and machines were toiling away to produce goods destined for the rest of the world. The highway roadside was still filled with the familiar tack-tack sound of small farm vehicles, but now they numbered in the hundreds, hauling vegetables in a swarm to the many marketplaces in the city. For the less fortunate the bamboo pole was still, as it had been for many generations before them, the only method to move vegetables and meat to their destination. Among all those new and familiar sights and sounds, the clutter of slogans welcoming the return of Hong Kong to the motherland couldn't be missed. A sign that the auspicious date was coming close for the long-lost son, who would finally return under the reassuring wing of a confident and rising China.

Mr Li's headquarters were no different from the many other factories in the neighbourhood. Huge front gates guarded an immense concrete courtyard with some badly-maintained hedge plants; in the back several blue-roofed factory buildings provided jobs for thousands of people.

Standing only 1.6 metres tall, Mr Li received us in his twenty-square-metre office. Of average build and casually dressed, he would never have been perceived in the West as head of such a large enterprise. This unpretentious, smart, down-to-earth guy had started his company less than a decade earlier with the equivalent of two thousand dollars. Then he'd built it out into an immense network of factories dispersed all over the Chinese continent, with over ten thousand employees.

He certainly wasn't a man who wasted too much time on niceties, and after tea was served he brought the discussion straight to the subject at hand.

'The WTO discussions will conclude soon, and China will become a member. We therefore may have some problems with some of our production sites. According to certain overseas manufacturers, we are infringing on their patents and production know-how. Pure rubbish! But with the WTO around the corner we need to understand what we may face in the short term, and how to make sure we can overcome legal disputes and at the same time start promoting our products overseas.'

His openness in talking about the key issues that were on his mind was a refreshing experience. Where reading tea leaves was normally part of the game of understanding what was really on the mind of a Chinese entrepreneur, for the visionary Mr Li time was money, and both needed to be spent with the utmost efficiency. Conquering the world from his Chongqing headquarters was a project that brooked no delay; every tick of the clock had to further his progress towards that goal.

Taking a sip of my tea, I responded to Mr Li's gut feelings. 'It's true that the WTO issue will give foreign manufacturers more leverage through their respective governments to push the Chinese government to make sure companies operating here clean up their acts. There's a real risk that the WTO will offer overseas corporations more leeway to pursue patent infringements, production methods and trademark violations.' After a pause I went on. 'We've all read in the newspapers that several Japanese corporations have been claiming that your company has used some of their engine designs, logos and brand names. A number of them even sound and look similar to existing brands. There's a good possibility that the only way to avoid further lawsuits is to regularise your products with Japanese companies either by creating a joint venture or paying royalties on a licensing agreement. Or developing your own designs and technology.'

Mr Li grinned, a bit surprised by my silly suggestion: 'But for me to be able to sell our product, initially we had to copy what the best in the business were manufacturing. How else do you expect to compete with them? Those companies have enough money to spend on research and development. But we had neither the resources nor the time to waste on such niceties. To survive we had to get our products onto the market fast and cheap. Now that our company has become respectable and is able to compete on quality, we can think about developing our own product range. Those lawsuits have been a bit of an annoyance but most in the meantime have been settled. What I'm looking into is moving my company into the next stage. At the moment there are over one hundred and twenty local competitors breathing down my neck trying to become as good as me. They've even started copying *my* business model. So I must be doing something right.'

Pausing to flash a million-dollar smile, he continued with a stern look borrowed from government officials breaking bad news to the people: 'Competition is too fierce on the Mainland. Everyone is vying for the same customers, and cutting prices, and I see my margins getting smaller by the month.' As he spoke he punched holes in the air with his finger.

Then his expression turned indignant while his voice went into a higher pitch: 'On top of that the government limits motorbike licences to avoid pollution in the cities, which in turn leads to oversupply and, as you can guess, even lower margins for me.'

Then, his theatrical act over, the CEO was back at the helm. 'With the enterprise we've developed I need to make sure I can continue to grow. I believe the only way out is to sell abroad. Over there I'll be facing the same international competitors but I certainly know how to tackle those guys. It's the Chinese competitors that worry me most. If I don't make a move, they certainly will.'

Having provided similar services for a Chinese pump manufacturer, I thought it wouldn't be too difficult to develop an initial strategy to enter into overseas markets where their motorbikes could sell well, and I told him 'I'm thinking Vietnam, Indonesia, Philippines, the African continent. . . . Those markets could be used as a jumping board to enter Europe and the States.'

Apparently Mr Li was expecting something more brazen that would mark his company as different. 'I already sell roughly 15,000 motorbikes a year in Vietnam and Cambodia. What do you think if I set up a factory in Germany and use German engineers to develop my products? Wouldn't it make things easier to enter the European Union? What about hiring a design company in France or Italy that will make my motorbikes look modern and trendy? That way I could make my name known to the rest of the world!'

My eyes almost popped out when I heard his high aspirations. It took some time to take stock of the situation before I was able to make a sensible comment.

I realised that if we wanted to get this contract we'd better adjust our thinking to the same *big* level as Mr Li. Apparently the time for Chinese companies to become an international concern had arrived. In the end, I only muttered that it would all be possible, so long as we had time to work on the legal and commercial framework.

At this Mr Li stood up excitedly and showed me around his factory. The gigantic plant was buzzing with activity, crisp and clean, well-lit and running like clockwork. The plant was split into different areas of functionality, and everyone in the various work areas was dressed in a specific coloured uniform. In one area, one could see workers dressed in blue operating a battery of Korean CNC (Computer Numerical Control) machines, chipping away at blocks of steel, making cylinders, crankshafts and other motor parts.

A bit further, workers in red were handling the quality control of parts and making statistical measurements to ferret out production discrepancies. Those parts ended up on long rows of tables where hundreds of ladies dressed in yellow were assembling the engine parts into complete motor blocks. In another area of the factory floor workers dressed in green did quality control tests on engine air tightness before adding a lick of lubrication oil.

In yet another area workers in grey were operating row after row of injection-moulding machines that pumped out colourful plastic parts used for bike lights and other trimmings.

Finally we entered the main assembly area where a conveyor belt was moving motorbike frames around at a constant speed, while workers in orange manually assembled the different parts into fully-fledged motorbikes. The whole place looked like a sleek Japanese factory I had once seen in Osaka, minus the battery of robots. Slogans placed in strategic locations reminded workers that production quality and employee safety were as important as keeping the customers smiling on their motorbikes.

At the end of the chain the motorbike got a bit of petrol and a worker in white revved the engine, testing the acceleration and speed before whisking it off to the storage area.

I was curious about the different-coloured overalls, and Mr Li's explanation was simple: 'Workers are not allowed to go into other sections of the factory without authorisation. If a blue worker is walking around in the red section he'll be picked out immediately! It makes it more difficult for employees in the factory to gain all the knowledge necessary to start up their own factory. In the past I've had at least five employees who set up their own company. Now they've all become my competitors because they were able to grab complete production information. I don't want this to happen again. There are now very clear and simple guidelines in the factory to avoid homegrown competitors. There are of course always ways to get the knowledge, but at least I've made it more difficult than in the past.'

While we walked back to the office he revealed the secret to his success: 'In all the key company positions I have close family members working for me. This way I can be sure no one runs off with the company's know-how: ranging from the sales network to the technology.'

While he munched on a hamburger and French fries for lunch, courtesy of Western efficiency, Mr Li remained focused on the subject at hand. Trying to get me up to speed on the exhilarating field of Chinese motorbikes, he continually emphasised the competitive environment he worked in. During that meal a picture began to emerge, showing that the only way forward was to turn his organisation upside down by designing his own products. He certainly wouldn't go into a joint venture or want to pay royalties. . . . He was probably thinking: 'Pay for what? A piece of paper? Now that's ridiculous!'

Although China is one of the largest motorcycle manufacturers in the world, many factory owners lack the will or the capability to initiate their own research and development. Mr Li had to take advantage of this window of opportunity before others put the same strategy in place. As a first mover he'd be able to have his company develop its own technology and image for overseas markets.

One key point would be to identify which overseas markets would welcome his motorbikes, so that his exports could take off and his brand could be positioned as innovative both in China and abroad. In our discussions he hammered at the idea of hiring an overseas design company that would develop a homegrown design for his motorbikes. Executing all his bold ideas, however, would be no walk in the park. Cost issues were certain to put a brake on many of his plans.

As the brainstorming session came to an end, I wanted to carefully broach the subject of compensation if we were to be retained for our services. The reply was 'We'll discuss it later in the day, but for now please go to my brother and visit the R&D department.' As I was led to the department, Mr Li's brother was already instructed to show me around and to let me see anything I'd requested.

'There should be no secrets, as he needs to understand our company thoroughly.' All this based on the trust he had placed in his informants, and only a couple hours of meetings.

I ended up in one of the 'top secret' parts of the company where only a few of Mr Li's acquaintances were allowed to work. For me, this was a definite sign that we were retained for the job.

The place was a spotless laboratory that could easily have been confused with the lab where Q thought up gadgets for James Bond. Everywhere engineers in crisp white overalls were busy with computers and high-tech gadgetry. Only the buzzing of small electric motors, the occasional beep and the sound of fingers tapping on keyboards broke the silence. Three-dimensional scanning machines of Japanese and German make were littered over the whole area. This equipment was used to digitally duplicate mechanical parts by moving a scanning probe over dismantled motor elements. The probe, like a mechanical finger, would 'feel' the shape and relay its movements to CAD software where a three-dimensional drawing was created in real time. This data would then ultimately be fed to the CNC machines in the production hall.

On other measuring machines, motor components coming from the production hall were placed side by side with the 'original' parts of an Italian motor brand, remeasured and compared for any imperfections. As those machines couldn't measure and copy with 100 percent accuracy, additional tests and fine-tuning were done on the CAD files so as to ensure that the different parts would fit with the best possible tolerances. In another part of the laboratory high-end spectrometers were conducting crucial material and hardness analyses on the originals. Those tests were done to get the best possible match with the steel and aluminium alloys available in China. It was something of vital importance, guaranteeing that the engines wouldn't start leaking or burn lubrication oil into a puff of blue-grey smoke: the hallmark of a badly-copied motor.

Trying to make sense of my earlier discussions with Mr Li about designing his own products, I asked Brother Li if he realised that what he was doing here was basically stealing the intellectual

property of another company. Without the slightest show of embarrassment he retorted, 'the motorbike we're making here was
purchased roughly two months ago in Italy by our company. We
paid for this motorbike, so it's our property and we are allowed to
do whatever we want with this sample. We're allowed to destroy it,
and we're allowed to copy it. This motorbike belongs to us, and I'm
very proud to say that we can prepare all parts for mass production
within six weeks of our tests. In the past, when we still worked more
closely with the Japanese, we got our hands on master copies which
were of excellent quality but now we've got to use what we can find
on the open market.'

It was hard to argue with the guy, as he didn't acknowledge any
of the abstract concepts of intellectual property.

The idea must have been alien to him, as after 1949 the majority
of product research and development was relegated to state-owned
research centres. The findings and know-how of those centres
would then be disseminated free of charge among state-owned
enterprises. Over several generations this became an idea that
remains stubbornly entrenched in all layers of Chinese society:
Intellectual property is a freebie that can be used in any way. This
systematic 'theft' continues to be a serious headache as it chips away
at the competitiveness of those companies that invest in research.

The reason why it was an Italian motor being copied this time
and not a Japanese one was fairly simple: 'The Italian manufacturers hadn't yet found their way to the Chinese courts.'

On the walk back to Mr Li's office music was coming out of the
loudspeakers in the courtyard. About eight hundred workers had
gathered outside. In chorus they were singing the company's theme
song while the company's flag was being slowly lowered and folded,
military-style. Finally the country's flag was lowered. Apparently in
the morning the same ritual was performed, with the raising of the
flags and ten minutes of physical exercise.

I couldn't help but think that this place was run like a prison, a
school, a home and factory all at the same time.

Entering the office, I'd hoped to sit down with Mr Li to finalise
our discussions and most importantly discuss our remuneration –
unfortunately he had already disappeared for other obligations. A

delegation from another province had come over to learn how his enterprise had become so successful and how they could duplicate his success (of course) in this delegation's own backyard. Apparently several delegations were coming into the factory on a monthly basis, pen and paper in hand to take notes. Although all this sapped quite a bit of his time, for him it was an important link to the local government officials who organised these visits. Most probably he'd be receiving 'most favoured' business treatment in return.

An old Chongqing University student of mine, who happened to be in charge of tax collection in the district of Mr Li's factory, told me that only a minuscule amount of taxes were collected every year. This formed an attractive cocktail of 'tax incentives' and 'IPR theft' that made his rags-to-riches story all the more credible.

From his secretary I received a quick debriefing, and was expected back in Chongqing two weeks from then, with a proposal for his company. Having experienced the way customers sometimes decide to forget to compensate us, it was a situation that had me a bit on edge. 'We haven't talked about compensation and since this will absorb most of our time I'd like to know your opinion. How does Mr Li compensate for our services?' To which the secretary gave a dry reply: 'I don't know, you should discuss that with him.'

This was the chance we had been looking for, a chunk of business that could keep the company busy for a long time. So it wasn't too much of a struggle to decide to go for broke, without a clear financial incentive.

The idea went as follows: sell Mr Li a strategy that would enable him to break away from his competitors by conquering overseas markets, while executing it within the best possible legal framework and in such a way that he could accept as financially sustainable. Huddled up in our office we brainstormed, argued, doubted and convinced each other, discussing and altering our 'Li strategy' until we had something executable and attractive to present to him. Before we knew it our time was up, and I was again watching the plane's wings stir up Chongqing's perpetual fog as we flew in.

The following day Adam and I got Mr Li to stay put until late at night, while we threw our ideas at him and he twisted and contorted them into his own unfamiliar business views. Let's say they received a Sichuan variant of the notorious 'business with Chinese characteristics' treatment. Subsequently we further fine-tuned our initial proposals in light of Mr Li's reactions. We could see him ponder the pros and cons of every idea we fed him, while challenging us at every turn on the costs involved and what benefits would come out of it. Nothing was lost on him, even in the wee small hours; while Adam's and my own concentration was flagging, Mr Li's focus never faltered. He hammered away until the 'Li strategy' really was his own. Past midnight, Mr Li finally accepted the framework.

The short version of the final strategy went as follows:

Set up a trading company to avoid involvement with state-owned import-export corporations.

Initially, the existing factory would continue manufacturing the present line of 'copycat' motorbikes and start selling them *en masse* in Southeast Asia and South America through a network of financially strong distributors that could place minimum orders.

In the mid term, he would establish joint ventures (JVs) with overseas distributors to provide after-sales and maintenance services.

Factories would be set up in countries close to China with loose legal frameworks, which would not be part of the WTO for years to come. The shortlist was Russia, Vietnam, Cambodia and Indonesia. The R&D centre would remain in Chongqing and the data stream for the 'copy machines' would be sent over by CD-ROM.

In China Mr Li would continue selling the 'copycat' bikes under an independent label until the WTO accession was imminent.

Snatch away capable R&D engineers from existing Japanese JV-manufacturers in China, and start up an original engine design and motorbike range.

All original designs coming out of the R&D centre would be patented in China and in certain Western countries.

The image of Mr Li's company was to be elevated by hiring a European design company to develop new types of motorbikes.

A Beijing office would be set up to execute the overseas marketing and sales strategy.

A European or American company would be found that was willing to partner up with him to manufacture parts in those areas of the world.

During the whole day the taste of Sichuan food continued to elude us, as we were served the same boring fast food from around the corner. My only consolation was that the following day there would be no rocket-fuel-inflated burps. Ultimately it was a good thing, as we needed clear heads to discuss compensation for our efforts with Mr Li.

We had never seen him so serious as when we asked him for a payment for the work delivered. 'You know those are just ideas that anyone could come up with. How can I pay for those? What I'm more interested in are people who can execute the strategy. Therefore I would like both of you to become my employees!' I shuddered at the thought of sweating away for someone else. Having worked a long time ago in a small Hong Kong company with someone who ran a tyrannical show, I was wary of walking into a similar scenario. For Adam, too, a Chinese boss was not something he wanted to face again. We both cherished our freedom too much to let someone push us around. Taking a gamble that we might be rejected and all our efforts be ruined in a moment, we told him that we couldn't work for him.

'We can't work for you as we have our own business to take care of. However you can buy our time to implement the whole or partial strategy.'

Unfortunately, Mr Li suddenly became old school – the idea of an outsider working at the core of his expansion plan was unacceptable. We discussed the issue at length, and even resorted to an extensive Sichuan dinner drenched in rocket fuel, but finally we were sent back to the airport with no financial reward, only the burning aftertaste of rice wine. Returning to the airport empty-handed was not the highlight of our business experience.

At the airport the mood wasn't cheerful either. The airplane had been delayed due to bad weather in Beijing. After two hours of waiting in the hot, humid terminal some passengers worked up a grumbling temper. 'We're hungry, we're thirsty. We want the airline to provide us with some amenities!' a couple of them shouted at the two hostesses tending the gates. Then some other joined the quarrel: 'This is a disgrace! We should be compensated for the loss of business we suffer!'

As their fury grew the two ladies couldn't handle the situation any longer and guards were called in. This show of authority didn't help either, but at least now the anger was vented at the men in uniform. 'My meetings have to be postponed!', 'Give us back our money. We want to change airlines!'

One hour later two buses arrived at the gates to pick up the passengers. The general mood had turned for the better once more. At long last we were on the move! But when we reached the plane on the tarmac, two airline employees signalled that the plane was still not ready to be boarded. So the bus doors remained closed while the Chongqing heat built up until the temperature inside was scorching. Five minutes into our ordeal one passenger fainted in the bus, and the others screamed at the top of their lungs to quickly open the doors. The two employees were unyielding; the doors on the bus would remain closed. Seeing this, one of the guys in the bus took the lead and ordered everyone to jump in unison. So we did. '*yi er san* – one two three' and the whole bus began wiggling and waggling. Outside, the airline employees pointed in the direction of the bus and laughed at the sight. Then a passenger used a small safety hammer to shatter two bus windows into a thousand pieces. By now the bus driver, in a panic, decided to open the doors of his vehicle independent of orders from outside. The whole busload was unleashed. Some of the passengers ran towards the two airline employees, by now terrified, while most of the others rushed for the staircase and onto the airplane. About fifteen minutes later the rowdy crowd had boarded and taken their designated seats. I never really saw what happened to the two staff on the tarmac, but have to assume things never turned into a full brawl.

Again the minutes passed by, and then suddenly a trembling, red-faced man got onto the plane and placed himself in the middle of the aisle. Over the loudspeakers an airhostess announced 'Ladies and gentlemen, the person presently standing in the plane is the driver of the damaged bus. He would like to recover the little safety hammer that is missing from his vehicle. Please hand it over to him so the plane can leave Chongqing.'

The previously rowdy crowd became extremely quiet. Everyone turning their heads, waiting to see who would stand up.

Nobody seemed inclined to return the hammer to its rightful owner. Again the airhostess pleaded with the passengers. Nothing helped.

Then it was the turn of the captain to speak over the intercom. 'Ladies and gentlemen, this is a serious matter. I will not take off if the hammer is not found.' Another five minutes passed by, the crowd now relatively docile.

Finally the hostess spoke again. 'Ladies and gentlemen, the captain has decided that everyone must disembark. The plane will be searched and all passengers will return to the terminal for a pass through the metal detector.'

As requested, we disembarked in a civilised manner. No one dared challenge the authority of the pilot. But once back in the terminal, the grumbling slowly resumed. Some passengers insisted that their rights had been violated and wanted a refund. Piece by piece our hand luggage was scanned and all passengers walked through the metal detectors. The entire exercise produced no little hammer; even an extensive search of the plane's cabin revealed nothing. In the end the pilot decided that it was safe to fly, and roughly an hour and a half later we were in the air.

During the flight a buzz of discussion about the bad service swirled through the cabin. Some passengers had organised them-selves into a syndicate and their self-proclaimed leaders went from row to row petitioning for other passengers' support. Finally the majority of travellers agreed that no one was to leave the plane until the airline came forth with compensation. Landing in Beijing, that's exactly how the drama unfolded. I for one wasn't willing to risk the wrath of a planeload of determined passengers. Another hour passed as the hostesses pleaded with the passengers to disem-bark. Nothing worked. Finally, after another hour of sitting in the plane, airline staff informed us over the intercom: 'Ladies and gentlemen, the general manager of the airline has agreed to com-pensate every passenger for their discomfort. You will receive a full cash refund of your ticket as you leave by the cabin door.' By the time we walked out of the plane, cash in hand, it was close to eleven o'clock at night. We had reached Beijing more than nine hours late. But at least the misery of our business loss was lightened a little, thanks to the compensation.

Roughly three months passed without any word from Mr Li. Then, out of the blue, we got a call to meet up ASAP. As could be expected from any good *guanxi* network, the constant tom-tom of information exchange once again produced results.

Apparently Mr Li had been invited by a Hong Kong–China friendship organisation to be part of a group of prominent Chinese businessmen who would witness the handover of the territory to China. During the ceremony, and for several days after, they were wined and dined by HK businessmen, bankers and government officials. Among those movers and shakers was my old friend, the generous Mike Yeoh. Although he was an Englishman born and bred, his allegiance was apparently with Mainland China and he took great pleasure in the fact that, in his words, 'a hundred of years of imperialism, colonialism and humiliation was finally coming to an end.'

On one of the occasions when Mr Li and Mike sat down to exchange small talk, my company's name came to the fore. This was enough to prompt Mr Li to get in touch with us again. In his eyes my company was famous. . . . In my eyes, Mike Yeoh putting in his best for us meant that all bridges had not been burned following the flag incident.

So with Mr Li on the phone and nothing to lose we decided to play hardball. First of all, we needed to be compensated for our past efforts, and on top of that any future activity would be partially funded in advance. When we left the bargaining table it felt as if Mike's words had acted like a magic potion. We had gone from pariah to trusted partner in the blink of an eye. Within days our bank account was bloated with cash.

Since our last encounter Mr Li hadn't been standing still either; like a busy bee he had continued construction on Fortress Li. The Beijing office was set up, the import-export company was in the final stages of approval and he had initiated his own sales network throughout Vietnam, Indonesia, and Cambodia.

In the process he bypassed local agents that had in the past developed part of the market for his motorbikes via a state-owned import-export company.

The new network consisted of descendants of an old branch of the Li family that left the Mainland half a century ago in search of better opportunities overseas. It was apparently here that the shoe didn't fit. Having bypassed the government controlled import-export company, he thought he could control prices and distribution through his family network.

He had entrusted those 'family members' with his company's money by providing them generous credit terms to develop the market and start selling motorbikes. To my astonishment, he had never met some of the people to whom the motorbikes and spare parts were shipped. By relying merely on telephone calls and the hearsay of intermediaries, he had come to the conclusion that trusting his extended family ties was enough to make the business go smoothly.

Going against a well-established *guanxi* rule, he went to the outer offshoots of his network where relationships tend to be blurred and complex. There was also the heightened risk of getting those connections to work in his favour. The result was a lesson in humility. Within days of the containers arriving in Vietnam via an overland smuggling route, the goods had mysteriously disappeared. The Vietnamese family members insisted they were not involved in the hijacking and requested another shipment.

The family link in Indonesia was big in the construction business but had no idea how to handle selling motorbikes. Having accepted the job half-heartedly, the Indo-Li link had actually hoped that Mr Li would be their gateway into large construction projects in China. As they were not geared toward selling motorbikes, Mr Li's assets languished in their vast warehouse outside Jakarta.

The news out of Cambodia had something of slapstick comedy. There the far-flung Li branch had established a Phnom-Penh-based trading business that included motorbikes. Apparently the blood of the Cambodian Li clan was no longer as pure as it used to be. A smart Li member there saw an opportunity to make a quick buck and returned two containers of motorbikes to Mr Li, stating that they had mechanical problems.

When those containers were opened they contained brand-new motorbikes of Chinese make. The only difference was that they were bikes made by a different company. Without the slightest remorse, Mr Li's motorbikes had been swapped for an inferior product. Quality-wise they were miles away from Mr Li's meticulously copied engines.

Despite all his shrewd business sense on the Mainland, the international arena seemed to be a ruthless jungle where his familiar rules no longer applied. His most recent 'tuition' payment consisted of lost inventory and a heap of scrap in his backyard. Not something he was particularly proud of.

His 'trusted relatives' had already given him a taste of the medicine that was indiscriminately dished up to outsiders doing business in this region, and he had to face the fact that another approach was required if he wanted to succeed.

Competitors were breathing down his neck and time was not on his side. Mr Li therefore didn't want to develop a new strategy from scratch, and hired our company for a six-month stint to establish a distribution network and possibly find places where he could set up assembly plants.

As we would often be working out of Mr Li's Beijing office, our first move was to get acquainted with the staff based there. The office was in a top-grade office building and consisted of two hundred square metres of space. In order to project an image of opulence, more than half the space was taken up by the lobby and a meeting room. Behind the lobby wall six people were crammed together at small office desks. The team, each with a Chongqing pedigree, consisted of Mr Wang and Mr Gao, ex-staff from a large import-export company, a secretary, an accountant and two office clerks.

Introducing ourselves to the team, we explained our reason for being there and the short-term goals we wanted to reach together. As our meeting was winding up we asked the secretary to have a copy of the entrance key made. One minute later she returned with a copy of the key duly printed on A4 paper from the copy machine. Apparently in a blend of panic and misunderstanding, the poor girl had got the message mixed up.

Initially everyone tried to keep a straight face, until Mr Wang quipped: 'Never forget that we're working for Mr Li. If you want to succeed make sure you copy in style!'

A couple of days later we got our key, and moved into overdrive to get the dealer network base up and running.

Another network that urgently needed to be up and running was a couple of computers and a printer. After struggling with the others in the office to get the hardware to communicate, we gave up. 'Plug and play' apparently wasn't our cup of tea. So I looked in my database of capable IT people, and the name of my good friend Kat popped up. In the early eighties he arrived from the Congo into China to study computer science. After he graduated from Tsinghua University he married a Chinese lady and picked up a job managing large computer networks in Beijing. He would be more than capable of starting up our poor-man's network.

When he walked into the office, the secretary goggled at him. She then quickly turned her head to stare at me in shock as if to say 'Do you see what's entering into our office? What should we do? Run for the exit?'

Trying to ignore the embarrassing moment, I introduced him to everyone in the office. Kat didn't bat an eye, he was probably used to it. Fluent in Chinese, he said hello to everyone, listened attentively to the problem and went on to make the computers talk with each other. The secretary, not yet over her reaction, whispered excitedly to Mr Gao, 'Hey. He . . . he can also speak,' as if Kat were part of a circus act she'd never seen before. The whole time Kat was there she kept 'politely' ogling him in total amazement. This was definitely the highlight of her day. Probably she was too confused to notice he was also talking in her mother tongue.

After roughly two months of digging in the commercial sections of several embassies and treasure hunting in the Hong Kong trade office, we had a grasp on the various Vietnamese, Cambodian and Indonesian companies that could make a difference for Mr Li. Initially the idea was also to enter the Russian market but this was quickly dropped after we realised how gruelling it was to deal with Russians.

In order to assess the quality of the potential overseas agents, several visits in person were required. But to back up those overseas trips hard currency was essential. At that time cash was a scarce commodity as we were in the midst of the Asian financial crisis and the RMB was under pressure to devalue. Therefore all Chinese banks were put on alert not to exchange any hard currency without the explicit approval of the government. The good thing about China is that it usually provides a solution to the inconveniences caused by its government, so we tapped into the parallel money circuit. Initially we wanted to change an RMB equivalent of US$8,000, but ended up changing much more as Mr Li needed money to send to his daughter who was studying in Australia. Mr Wang handed over wads of RMB to us, nicely wrapped in *People's Daily* newspapers and put in a plastic bag. The cash was to be exchanged on the now overheated black market, where we had to wait our turn in line. In the end we walked away with over 60,000 dollars, which the money dealer exchanged without raising an eyebrow. His daily limit? Over one million dollars. And all this monkey business was taking place in a small, wobbly shack surrounded by clothing hawkers.

In the end, several trips to the black market were required to conclude the several rounds of discussions we had with the importers. For the contract-signing ceremonies with each of the main importers, Mr Li flew over to ink the deal in person, and have his picture taken with his newfound partner. The most peculiar of these ceremonies was in Cambodia, where AK-47-wielding warriors provided security to and from the airport. I've never figured out if this was actually necessary or only a face-giving gimmick for Mr Li.

As the small network developed with sales of around twenty thousand bikes in the first year, we realised that to break through to a larger market advertising might be a good option. In accordance with Mr Li's decision-making process, everything had to be negotiated and renegotiated at length. Therefore, after a series of hard-wrenching talks, he finally gave in and agreed to provide a substantial budget to position his brand in Vietnam through road-side billboards. As was the case in China, the motorbike in Vietnam is a vehicle to move a family of three or more from home to a market, the rice fields and back. So we came up with the idea of the image of a young family of four sitting on Mr Li's motorbike, riding away from a market with a basket full of vegetables. Initially he didn't like it. For him the motorbike had to be the centre of attention in the ad. To please him we ended up mixing two images in one ad campaign. Whatever image was the right one didn't really matter any longer, sales soared in the second year to over seventy thousand bikes in Vietnam alone. Similar campaigns were later initiated with different levels of success.

Now the distribution of motorbikes has grown into a network of subagents oiling Mr Li's international trading machine, generating millions of euros in profit. Over time new countries and continents were added to his sales network. By the time China entered the WTO, overseas production and assembly lines were already part of his group of companies. Mr Li's copy bikes can still be admired at street corners in Hanoi, Yangon, Phnom Penh and other capitals in the world.

As the Chinese government took an excessive interest in taxing his overseas revenues, the wobbly money-changer's shack continued to play its role, until the volume of cash became too cumbersome to be carried around. For his overseas investments Mr Li was put in contact with a reliable underground bank often used by Taiwanese investors, which specialised in cross-border cash transactions between Hong Kong and the Mainland. Basically the money would be deposited in an underground branch at one side of the border and, a single telephone call later, would reappear on the other side squeaky clean, either in a regular bank account or at an underground branch in cash of the currency of one's choosing. All without leaving a bothersome paper trail.

As time went by lawyers have had a field day with the whole array of patents and trademarks that have been added to Mr Li's basket of assets. This time they weren't ensuring that what he did was legal, but rather protecting all the time, effort and money he'd put into developing proprietary designs and building a strong brand name. For Mr Li this was the pinnacle of international respect, and he was prepared to chase and sue anyone daring to copy even the smallest part of his motorbikes. Now he can claim that most of his factories are clean, in China at least. At the moment a small European design company develops efficient and trendy motorbikes for Li's emporium. Production has yet to materialise in the West as labour costs for blue-collar workers far exceeds the going rate in Asia.

Since then we've worked on and off for any of the projects where he deemed our input valuable to him.

Postscript

- Five years after our initial meeting, Chinese motorbike brands are omnipresent in Vietnam and Indonesia. As was to be expected, price wars have followed whenever new contenders tried to break into those markets.
- China entered the WTO in mid-2000.
- In 2005, over seven million Chinese motorcycles were exported worldwide. By 2012 this had grown to over 11 million.
- Although foreign companies sometimes think they're helpless to protect their IPR, it can be done by applying for patents in China and also by installing protection mechanisms against competitors wanting to get their hands on the know-how. While this costs money in the short run, a reluctance to do so will affect the bottom line faster than one can imagine.
- The underground banks have also moved into the digital age, and now make extensive use of the Internet for the sake of their customers' anonymity.
- The acronym CCC states that products conform to Chinese safety and quality standards. According to some disenchanted barbarians, the letters stand for China Certified Copy or China Copy Centre. It actually stands for China Compulsory Certification.

CHAPTER 5

Joint adventure

'China is a fiery dragon to its enemies, a puzzle to its friends.'
Many visitors to the Middle Kingdom are confused when friendship and business intermingle. Often the barbarian mind is trying to differentiate between commercial practices and acts of amity when dealing with a Chinese counterpart.
Unfortunately this road frequently leads to the incorrect business expectations, broken dreams and loss of potentially faithful allies.
Many foreigners and – let's not forget – Chinese businessmen have returned home disappointed and misunderstood, their faith in mutual trust completely quenched, blaming the other party for a missed opportunity.
Very high expectations, unfortunately, lead to disappointment more often than not.

Our Beijing offices, Friday, December 10th, 1998, 2:27 PM

'There are no joint ventures in China,' I told Marco, our visiting customer. He stared at us in disbelief, wondering if he had met a couple of madmen out of touch with reality.

'But our company has a JV in Hainan,' he replied, a little annoyed. 'What about this heap of contract agreements I brought over? Isn't that enough? Listen, I came here to solve a problem, if you can't help so be it, but don't waste my precious time. I've already squandered enough of it in China and I'm fed up with listening to rubbish! I was told you could help, but I can see that once again it's not going to turn out the way I'd expected in China. Bunch of amateurs.'

My Chinese partner Adam and I just kept quiet, looking at this hyperactive guy, venting his frustration inside our meeting room. He was a standard investor, one who had not only lost a lot of money, but whose sanity had also gone astray during his venture in China. The worst type to deal with. The room went silent just long enough for him to feel uncomfortable.

'There's no need to raise your voice. Keep it cool. On paper they all look like joint ventures, but in reality we've only seen joint adventures.'

On hearing this, it was as if sudden order had come to chaos. Reality flooded through his brain. In an instant all the mental pain, squabbles, misunderstandings, money matters, arguments, handshakes, misgivings, *karaoke* sessions, lost inventory, staff problems, Chinese accounting rules, sleepless nights and smiling partners started to make sense, so long as he perceived it through the coloured glass of an adventurous voyage.

For a short while, a lonely fly frenetically buzzing around the room was the only sound audible against the backdrop of silence.

Not much came from Marco. Only a blank desperate gaze at the heap of files he'd brought along. Marco was a forty-something manager appointed by his Italian employer to identify a Chinese partner to set up a factory producing and distributing 'Aqua Minerale' mineral water. As there were a growing number of Chinese city slickers who fancied something more than a cup of tepid water to lessen their thirst, the idea wasn't far-fetched. In a normal world, Marco's business acumen would have been spot-on, but here in China, with its different business frameworks and customs, it became obvious that he hadn't taken the time to understand what he was getting into.

Breaking the silence, I tried to get the shock therapy moving again. 'Listen Marco, we're always amazed to see how many business people want to torture themselves and risk shareholders' money by establishing a joint venture with a Chinese partner. There's definitely no disrespect intended towards the Chinese partner, he's probably doing all he can to make the deal work. The problem is that from the moment the JV is sealed on paper, expectations have already started diverging. Most often a Westerner's thinking is long-term, looking to recover their investment anywhere from five to ten years in the future. A Chinese partner, on the other hand, will be most happy if he can recover the majority of his investment ASAP, in let's say the next two to three years. This brings us to the second problem. You're probably eager to reinvest, expand the business before you've even recovered the initial investment, but the Chinese partner is probably keen to skim the JV for what it's worth, while avoiding any preventive maintenance, expensive equipment upgrades or expansion plans. Third, the purchase of raw materials and sales of products will more often than not utilise existing networks of family, friends, business connections and intertwined provincial politics. On top of that, cultural misunderstandings often turn a JV into a recipe for disaster. How frequently have we heard the Western partner claim that a *karaoke* entertainment room is a waste of money. But how can you expect local government dignitaries to solve all your electricity/ water/gas/fire/wastewater/staff problems without entertainment? Do the Westerners think they're the only company in the area competing for those commodities?

'Marco, do you realise that your Chinese partner might also be at a loss to understand what you want? Let me guess, but shoot me if I'm wrong. How often have you talked with your partner about the following Western gibberish: increasing shareholders' value, making sure the organisation is run according to good corporate governance, providing market forecasts for the next five years, conducting environmentally friendly production, the company's social responsibility towards its employees and society? Most probably you transmitted those ideas to your Chinese partner through an interpreter who had no clue what you were talking about and couldn't put those concepts into the right Chinese perspective. During those meetings, everyone will have nodded in agreement to avoid offending their guest from a far-flung country, and politely waited till it was time for a good meal to bond the friendship. Your partner wants to make money, make it fast and show off his newfound wealth by buying a luxury car. He doesn't need abstract principles or a pile of written reports to get the business done. Trust me.'

Again silence permeated the room.

'I think you're kind of right, that sounds a lot like the script I went through. We came in with high expectations. Only considering the upsides of the venture: cheap labour and the willingness of millions of eager customers to drink our bottled water. And we expected to run the place as if we were just outside Milan. Maybe Chinese managers run the place a bit differently from those in my home country after all.'

It seemed that our discussion had had an ameliorating effect on his depressed state of mind. The fact that he was not alone in this type of ordeal, and that many more before him had gone through the same agonising pain of a faltering JV, soothed his ego . . . a bit.

'But you know we built those expensive Western-style flats for the Chinese management, including imported kitchen equipment, we paid for all the food, flew several of them over to Europe at our expense, and their salaries are higher than any other factory in the area. Our engineering team stayed over for months on end to make the factory run. They could at least show us some respect for what we did!'

Deep down I was wondering if this last complaint had to be understood as a revisitation of his great-grand-father's colonial visions, a racist slur or a superiority complex towards those poor Chinese who he'd expected would accept his own pointers of culture and civilisation as their own guiding light.

In the end I settled on cultural ignorance caused by an impenetrable wall that prevented him from seeing beyond chopsticks, a difficult language, rags-to-riches tales and the urge to pull China into the 21st century.

Ignoring his last comments, Adam and I once again went over his myriad complaints about the joint venture, trying to put in sequence the torrent of information Marco had unleashed upon us over the past two hours.

'From what we understand, you feel that your partner has not been following the JV agreement to the letter, they've moved away from major commitments to the operational side of the factory, quality problems continue to plague the final products and have not been dealt with properly, the sales plan was not implemented, your company was cheated out of money which has caused serious friction and resulted in your partner playing the workers against you. Is there anything that is actually working out?'

Marco gave a deep sigh and looked over our heads. 'Besides the kitchen and the entertainment area, I don't see anything else functioning for the JV.'

Interrupting his thoughts, Adam went on. 'But you must certainly have realised early on that there was something wrong in the company operations. Your JV agreement was signed roughly four years ago, there must have been signals that indicated that you were losing control of your baby?'

'Well, the JV discussions lasted for over a year, you know, and didn't progress easily, to say the least. It was definitely a painful delivery, but pressure from headquarters forced us to go forward, as too much was already at stake. Probably we bulldozed through some critical points that we thought weren't major issues. Shareholders were getting nervous that they were missing out on the China market, as the whole world wanted to get a piece of the action in the new El Dorado of the East. Our CEO felt it was time to deliver, and that any bump along the road could be smoothed out as we went along. Already too much time and money had been spent on our pre-market study and in identifying which partner company would be most suitable to our needs in China. Since settling on our Hainan partner, we've had so many discussions with the Chinese team, and gone through such agonising negotiations over minute details, that our CEO began dreading to fly over. Fearing that he would be taken hostage for another round of drawn-out 'ping-pong' arguments, he often talked too much at the dinner table and then left us behind to work out the details of his rice-wine inflated promises. In the end the technical team and I started to get worn out by the Chinese negotiation strategies; we just wanted to be back with our families. We all thought that coming to an agreement, with the main points clearly written out in black and white, would give us peace of mind.'

In the end I had to interrupt, as the Italian predisposition to elaborate on a story was getting the better of him. He wasn't providing hard facts to help us better understand his earlier complaints. Most probably he was still in the denial phase. Deep inside him was a lingering spark of hope that whispered to his ego 'It's all just a bad dream. A miracle will still take place, and wipe out all perceived evil in this JV.'

I always wonder if this is what psychiatrists face with their patients. Pulling information out of them, one bit at a time, while trying to pick clues from the disordered rush of sentences. Slowly working open blocked mental doors, and peeking inside in search of objective reason, while guessing at the roots of the mental disarray of their 'couch victim'.

A dose of psychology would definitely be of use in pulling information from these battered businessmen. Maybe we should install a couch in our meeting rooms too, so as to get *all* the information faster, and get a clear picture of the heart of the JV.

Unfortunately our 'patient' often comes in too late, having spent too much money and human resources desperately trying to save the JV, tired of picking the wrong fights over and over, exhausted by the sleepless nights, disillusioned by the broken promises, made cynical by the ever-changing rules for accounting, tax-payment, banking, employment and financial reporting, depleted of mental strength, and misunderstood. He's basically ready to throw in the towel. They have just one little spark of hope, either for revenge (the battered manager on a payroll), or for a rescue mission to identify what can be salvaged (the investor), or for turning the place into a wholly-owned company (possibly a China lover who at long-last lost his virginity). All this should ideally be realisable in the next couple of days . . . please, and thank you very much.

I felt that Adam, wiring himself for corporate forensic evidence, was getting impatient. 'Marco you really need to get to the point. First and foremost, who controls the JV bank account, and who has the company chop?'

'The chop is in the hands of the Chinese investor. They've had it most of the time, because it's required to run the operations. Normally both partners have to sign for amounts in excess of two hundred thousand RMB, but for lower amounts this is not necessary. I'm not really worried about this point.' Thinking this was the right answer, Marco rested his case.

'Well Marco, you should be worried. Do you have any written bylaws that clearly state that purchasing contracts, employment contracts and lay-off agreements are only valid when both partners sign? What if one of the employees writes himself an employment agreement, properly stamped by the company, stating that if he's dismissed from the company he gets a severance package of two million RMB?'

'That's impossible, we'd sue them to the end of time and. . . .'

Without giving Marco the chance to continue, Adam went on: 'Well Marco, you need to realise that the person holding the chop can control the company. Unless there are clear markers written down in the JV agreements, you might find yourself in a pretty serious mess. In China the company chop is legally binding, and makes any document official. There's no need to identify who used the chop to indebt the company, now or in the future. Without clear bylaws a handwritten signature doesn't really count over here. The chop is master in its own right and no signature has the power to dethrone it. Give us some time so we can go through all those agreements you brought along. I'm sure we can find something useful. In the meantime I suggest we all have a bite and get back to you later, after our visit to the site.'

Walking with Marco through Wangfujing to the nearest Sichuan restaurant, the late afternoon Beijing traffic tango was already well underway. This was the most pleasing hour of the day to sit back and enjoy the road anarchy unfolding. Shoppers, retirees, police-men, salesmen on tricycles hawking their wares, moms with kids, backpackers with worn travel guides in hand, monks, news vendors, school-kids, a couple of soldiers, businessmen, beggars, an older couple in Mao suits and students all swamped the streets and took over the asphalt. Cars crawled over pedestrian crossings, bicycles swarmed left, right and centre, squeezing through any gap that opened in the wall of people, a waft of diesel fumes filled the air, taxis held up piles of cars while pimping for their next customer, a driver and bicyclist argued right of way, a dissonance of horns, toots, honks, rings and other blaring clatter begged for attention. An elderly lady walked backward, completely indifferent to her surroundings, an electric bus stuffed with people snaked through, a raw gutter stench came from the back alley, a police van with blaring sirens inched along the walkway, five spectators squatted on the roadside commenting on an ongoing game of Chinese chess, more honking, a broken-down heavy truck from a nearby construction site sat idle in the middle of the road, heavily tarred cigarette smoke drifted from passers-by, a 'big potato' sedan flashed its lights while crawling against the traffic flow, the cyclist and driver still arguing over right of way.

Looking beneath the surface, however, there was definitely order in the chaos of daily traffic. No better place to witness chaos theory in its full splendour. As long as pedestrians didn't look at the cars, the cars couldn't possibly be heading their way; as long as drivers knew their cars didn't actually exist, they'd avoid the pedestrians at all costs. Honking the horn to announce one's presence is futile if only the driver himself is listening. . . . Amid this beautiful picture, counter to all laws of barbarian logic, the blob of 'commotion' actually moves along. Order in chaos. . . . 'You know Marco, have you ever tried to cross a Chinese street with your eyes closed? You pay the tab if I survive this, OK?'

'Mmmm. . . . OK, it's a deal!' he replied enthusiastically, not realising he could never collect on the wager. 'Now just watch and enjoy.'

Closing my eyes I veered into the stream of traffic, passing safely through while all the other commuters of flesh and steel did their best to dodge me. In the background I could hear Marco shout at all the near hits that were coming my way. I arrived safely at the other side of the road, with my eyes still closed. 'As you can see, miracles do happen in China. Many thanks for the meal!'

Marco's eyes stared wide. He was trying to classify this as Russian roulette, stupidity, calculated risk, madness, Belgian folly, brilliance, the Old China Hand gone mad – his face told it all. He had never seen so many near accidents in such a short period of time. Anyway, since the customer is king, you've got to entertain him, even in the most depressing of circumstances.

'As long as you're willing to soak up some Chinese logic, you'll be able to survive, even the Beijing rush hour,' Adam teased him.

Two weeks later Adam and I were on the plane, destination Hainan Island. As we flew into Haikou Airport scores of half-finished buildings appeared through the clouds, testament to half-baked business plans, cheap loans, suicidal joint adventures and a slight pinch of Asian crisis Grand Cru '97. Coming from sub-zero Beijing, how better to start the day than being greeted by a warm breeze as you step out of the plane? A couple of days earlier, Mr Lei, head of the JV, told me that they'd be quite busy during this time of year and he wouldn't be able to send a car to pick us up. 'Not a problem, we'll take a taxi!'

Hainan Island was known for hundreds of years as a pirate hideout par excellence. Here a myriad buccaneer families cruised the South China seas in search of their next victim. On the way to Marco's JV, the taxi driver showed us some of his great-grandfather's gall by pulling off the highway and refusing to move any further unless we quadrupled the original price to our destination. There we were, trapped on a strip of concrete, luggage in the back of the car, nowhere to go, ignored by the cars rushing by. Refusing to accede to this unreasonable demand, we sat there quietly, neither side willing to talk, each hoping the other would crack. As time ticked by, he occasionally threatened us verbally, testing our deter-mination . . . till the cavalry arrived. A police car popped up, pulled the driver out, an empty taxi was flagged down and we were on our way again. Probably not the first time this type of 20th-century brigandage had taken place on the Hainan highways.

Arriving at the JV's gates, there was certainly no welcome com-mittee awaiting our appearance. The doors were tightly locked and the guards were instructed not to talk to outsiders. The place was surrounded and protected by four-metre high walls, finished off at the top with broken glass from beer bottles. In the meantime, all attempts to reach Mr Lei only produced a recorded 'mobile phone is switched off' message. Calling the fixed lines resulted either in the cryptic beeps of fax machines, or a secretary who hung up within seconds. We returned the next day but only got more of the same – while workers walked, cycled and drove in and out, we were stuck in our taxi outside the factory walls, going nowhere.

We ate at the scruffy food stall strategically located next to the gates. Made up of two wooden benches, a homemade table and worn overhead plastic sheets with an annex for a small gas-fired stove, this place was the truck drivers' favourite location for slurping up a meal in the dust of passing traffic. Nothing of any worth could be gotten out of talking to them. If anything, it caused us more trouble as the drivers reported to their supervisors that a foreigner was asking too many questions at the gate. After two days of waiting and trying to worm our way in, our taxi was surrounded by twenty-plus workers, who shook the car as if it was a toy and seemed ready to smash it into pieces. This was enough to send us packing – the driver to save his precious vehicle and us to save our limbs. Returning to our hotel, Adam suggested finding a local third party who might be able to help us reach Mr Lei. But who to approach? Who would be the key to open the gates? Without any local connections among the police, city officials or managers of the industrial development zone it would be hard to get Mr Lei's attention. From the pile of papers Marco had left behind we could identify two banks that had provided credit lines to the company. 'Maybe one of the JV's bank managers? They should have a vested interest,' Adam ventured. However, two strangers walking into a bank and asking the staff to spill the beans on one of their clients sounded like a mission impossible. 'Let's call Marco, he should be a able to give us an idea of who might help.'

At around noon Milan time, the phone rang at Marco's home. After several tries, a disgruntled wife picked up. Marco, too, seemed a bit upset, and complained that it was a most inappropriate time to call. I was thinking to myself, 'For days on end we've tried to get through to Mr Lei, wasting time in front of a closed gate, all with the ultimate aim of assisting him with the failed JV. And now *he's* annoyed that we're calling him? What's going on? Had he already forgotten his despondent state of mind last time he sat in our office?' In the background we could hear his wife giving him a taste of nasty Italian operetta.

While we were trying to get through the gates of the JV, most Italians were having a Christmas party, enjoying a fine meal in the presence of their families. We had crossed into a major no-go zone: 'Never ever disturb Barbarians when they're having holidays.' Christmas on our side had consisted of noodles, road dust and dreary waiting sessions.

Marco came up with a second mobile phone number for Mr Lei, the one he gave to close friends and the mama-sans of *karaoke* bars. According to Marco this number would most probably be available after seven in the evening.

It sure was. After a bit of haggling and pretending he was not the Mr Lei of the JV, he agreed to meet us on neutral ground.

A brief meeting was scheduled in the lobby of our hotel at eight in the evening the following day. As was to be expected, the meeting hour crawled by without Mr Lei appearing. Calling his phone, we were informed by a lady that he was still having a sauna and massage. Several hours and many conversations later, the master himself picked up, informing us that he'd soon be on his way. As time ticked by slowly, hotel staff began heading for bed, and only a lonesome guard remained to check the comings and goings of the hotel guests and their scantily clad companions.

A full hour after midnight, accompanied by his troupe, Mr Lei finally appeared in the lobby. Briefly apologising for the unexpected delay, he sat down in front of us. In his forties, overweight, with heavy gel keeping his dark hair in place, he was dressed in a smart black suit and open collared white shirt, his shoes the latest Milanese style. Gold rings encrusted with green jade garnished his fingers and he had the latest mobile phone in hand. He gave us something of a smile. His boys remained in the background, staring in our direction with suspicious eyes.

'Mr Lei, it's a great honour to finally be able to meet you in person. We've flown into Haikou to talk to you and do hope you can give us some of your precious time. We know you are a very busy person and certainly don't want to delay you excessively. As you know, Mr Marco has contacted us in the past month about assisting with your JV.'

The smile on his face briefly disappeared when he heard that name. Adam continued explaining our reason for being in Hainan Island, and how we could be of assistance in bringing the derailed business back on track. Mr Lei looked at me intently, wondering what this barbarian had to do with the JV. 'Mr Lei, don't worry, I'm Adam's colleague and only here to assist you in any way possible.'

'Where did you learn Chinese?'

'Eh, while working in Chongqing,' was my dry response.

'I thought I discerned a Sichuan accent. My wife is from Chongqing, so I should know.'

Having seen what he was dealing with, and realising that we were in no way about to harm him or, worse, kidnap him for ransom, the atmosphere turned a bit friendlier. Cigarettes were exchanged, small talk ensued and he proposed that we meet in the factory the next afternoon. With a cigarette still safely tucked behind my ear I went for a well-deserved rest. Finally we were making some headway.

We were parked in front of the gates, and one of the frosty guards came out of the security booth to nag the driver about our visit and slip in some specific queries. The guards were a crucial reception antenna for the wheeling and dealing of their work unit, and enjoyed gathering vital information. This would be used to provide regular updates to the staff on what was happening at their workplace. 'Why?', 'Who are you?' and 'Who are you meeting?' certainly weren't unwarranted questions in this context.

We definitely seemed to be expected, as the attitude of the guard had thawed to a more pleasant style of interaction. But neither did we receive the red-carpet treatment, as our work permits, passports and ID cards were copied. Also, the car and driver had to wait outside. Anyway, he probably preferred this arrangement after his close encounter with the local workers the other day.

The gates at last unlocked, we were finally getting our long-awaited, in-depth, face-to-face meeting.

It was a five-minute walk up a small hill to the main office building. Straight palm trees surrounded the whole compound, lush tropical greenery and a couple of large concrete fishponds enlivened the area. To the left, the sliding doors of the water-bottling plant were wide open, the equipment sitting idly, silvery stainless steel tanks full of treated water sparkling in the sunshine. The red chimney of the boiler plant was contrasted against a heavenly blue sky. It stood proudly, waiting in vain for some smoke to swirl out of its factory's guts. The only activity we could discern was a couple of people inside the bottling area, seemingly busy moving dust from side to side. On the bottling line, uncapped PET bottles waited to be filled. All this imported equipment was producing no drinkable water, much less generating the return on investment described by the many Excel sheets Marco had probably displayed in the Italian investors' boardrooms. The blue Aqua logo was already fading in the piercing Hainan sunshine.

To the right, a three-storey building twice the size of the bottling plant was buzzing with activity. With no windows, the fifty-metre-long concrete building looked more like a storage area than factory. Here empty trucks with the Aqua logo emblazoned on the doors were rushing in and rolling out full of cardboard boxes. At least some investment here was being put to profitable use.

When we reached the office building, Mr Lei was waiting for us with a bright smile. 'Come in, come in, sit down and let's have some tea.' Small talk ensued for twenty minutes, and ranged from Hainan food to how beautiful Belgium was.

'Have you been to Belgium? When was that?' I asked in faint amazement, never expecting him to have set foot in that rain-soaked corner of Europe.

'About three years ago, Mr Marco's company invited us over to Europe and we visited seven countries, including Belgium. Very nice place with good Chinese food, close to some big square that was kind of the Tiananmen of Brussels, but too cold.' Well if the Chinese food was good, then definitely the place must be beautiful and worth remembering to any Chinese visitor, I thought to myself.

More cups of tea were filled and cigarettes were exchanged. Mr Lei was able to blow more smoke than the chimney outside.

Marco's name had been dropped, and it seemed the discussion was slowly gravitating to the subject of our visit.

'When was the last time you met Marco?' Adam asked. 'Mmm, Marco?' he said, while slowly sucking on his cigarette, as if it would help him clear his mind. While a slow waft of smoke emanated from his nose, he perused his thoughts and tried to put them into words.

'Marco is a good friend, over time I really started to like him. He works very hard to make the JV function and at the same time he's very dedicated to doing what his bosses tell him to do. The problem is he wants results too fast; he has no understanding of the local market requirements, or the expectations of us Chinese. He's been here for over three years and it seems as if he still doesn't want to recognise that you need patience to succeed in China.' Pointing to Adam: 'You, as a Chinese, understand the situation. It's very hard for me to explain to him that all his numbers won't add up without a human touch and an understanding of realities on the ground. We really treat him well, but he seems only to think in terms of quarterly reports and targets that the sales people need to reach. He would often get into a rage because this or that objective had not been reached while he was gone. But the staff needs time to make it work. Jieke, you barbarians often look for simple answers to complex problems. Everything always needs to have a clear-cut solution. But it really doesn't work like that. The situation is much more Byzantine than you'd like to admit and if you barbarians don't show enough flexibility, you die in China.

'The one thing that Marco does is offend our staff when he comes over. I often receive feedback from the employees that he is too pushy, loses his temper too easily, and is disrespectful towards China. Does he really think this attitude will win him any friends in the workplace? I'm not even sure if his own countrymen would accept such a work attitude.

'Italian workers would want to be treated with more respect when the boss asks them to implement his strategy. Why does he think all the problems with the JV are because the staff is incompetent or not really doing their work? This is not Europe, where you can make things happen by yelling orders into a phone.' This rhetoric was not unfamiliar territory. We had heard it all before.

Why is the partner not cooperating any longer? What has happened to all the well-intended pledges? Why, after such long negotiations, does everything have to end in confrontation? These questions could be asked of many a Chinese Mom-and-Pop joint venture.

But in the end it often boiled down to the parties' different interpretations of the paper they had fiercely negotiated and finally signed in good faith. For Marco it was a strict framework of how both parties would work together, trying to lay out all the what-ifs, if-thens, profit margins and reinvestments over the following five years. Any deviation from this piece of paper constituted a major no-no, and it was often used as a shield in case of changes in internal or external factors.

From the Chinese point of view it was merely . . . a piece of paper. A statement of good intentions regarding the potential develop-ment of the relationship into a real long-term partnership. In which, furthermore, the goal of making money is subjugated to the value of a long-term business relationship.

Probably adding to the confusion, Mr Lei's team and Marco often wrongly believed that they had understood each other's culture, but unfortunately a lack of cultural insight had led them to underestimate the differences. In the end, this created major misconceptions on a personal level, but also on the issues of how the factory should be run, or a market strategy implemented in China.

'Mr Lei, according to the Italian shareholders, the factory is underperforming because of a misappropriation of funds. Do you have any idea what they're referring to?'

This statement hit a nerve. His relaxed mood turned instantly to anger.

Talking to Adam while pointing at me, he said 'Who do these barbarians think they are? I don't need them to be able to run my other businesses. I'm very successful without this water plant and don't need their money. I did them a favour by building their factory on my existing premises. They always think that we're selling bottled water behind their backs, inflating the prices of raw materials or purposely turning accounts receivables into bad debt and splitting the profit with our customers. Who invented the Mafia? Not me! The books are open for anybody to look into! How do they dare tell this to outsiders. . . .'

Mr Lei stared furiously at me while a thrust of cigarette smoke gushed through his nose.

In a sense he was right. When we discussed it with Marco before flying over he didn't have solid proof that bottles were leaving the factory unaccounted for, or that raw materials were invoiced at an inflated rate.

The three of us sat there quietly for a while, breathing cigarette smoke and listening to the humming of the air conditioner. Finally I gathered the courage to ask if it would be okay with him if I stayed over for a while, so that we would be able to rebuff Marco's negative impressions of the place.

A grumble dislodged from his mouth that I took for a yes. Slowly our meeting returned from the sudden frostiness to a mildly warm discussion, which lasted for another two hours. Although we all knew that a one-time meeting couldn't magically turn the situation around, we listened to his grievances. We did what we could to mediate the situation while laying the path for the JV to get a new lease on life. In the end, Mr Lei decided we had more important issues to take care of: Enjoying a meal on the factory premises.

Above the worker's cafeteria was a restaurant area partitioned into eight different private dining rooms. A corridor in the middle divided the area in two, with four doors on either side. The place oozed opulence; each space lavishly decorated and immaculately clean, as if the restaurant had been transplanted from a five-star hotel. No expense had been spared; each room had its own gigantic TV and sophisticated *karaoke* machine, with a private bathroom. It was the perfect place to clinch a business deal, maintain relationships with the local authorities or pacify suppliers who were eager to collect their accounts receivables. Mr Lei definitely knew how to entertain his customers, and it was one of his secret weapons in resolving any kinks in a business relationship. As we walked through the hallway, the *karaoke* machines were chanting their tunes to the left and right. It was easy to deduce from the singer's pitch the amount of rocket fuel that was flowing through his veins.

Once we were seated around the table, the food started flooding in. The staff was scurrying around with drinks and cigarettes, doing their best to make sure nothing went wrong as long as Mr Lei was in the room. For my part I couldn't figure out if Mr Lei wanted to impress or annoy. The food consisted of braised frogs, but not of the normal kind. The Cuban frogs were a giant version, an XXL variety of the French type. Their meat was plentiful and tender. With bones the size of a young chicken it was not really a normal dining experience. *Ganbei*-ing our glasses for several toasts of XO Cognac, we continued into the next exotic dish. In came boiled goosefeet, from which one would nibble the sparse meat around the bones while holding it steady with a pair of chopsticks. Never having eaten it before, I welcomed the novelty. But while I 'indulged' in the treat, my brain suddenly made a completely different observation. Somewhere in the dark corridors of my unconsciousness my grey cells began to insist that the goosefeet were actually human hands. Looking at them, the feet certainly resembled sets of fingers. From that moment on, my stomach squeezed itself closed. My heart rate went up a few beats. While sweat dribbled from my forehead, a touch of panic settled in. Another bite and I would throw up. Looking away from my delicacy, I stared at Adam who was indulging in a second helping. I asked Mr Lei for another XO toast, while asking the waiter to take away my plate. We drank at least two glasses, and I kindly refused to have another 'human hand' tossed on my plate.

Mr Lei's enthusiasm grew more intense: 'Jieke, we Chinese are very poor and have to make sure we never get hungry again. The fishponds outside aren't merely for decoration but are also practical: They're used to grow a wide variety of living creatures: frogs, turtles, sweet water fish and eel. All very fresh!'

Then came the soft-shell turtle soup. I always loved the taste of turtle meat and welcomed it on my plate anytime. However this time I had been outwitted – as the guest of honour it was my privilege to chew on the soft carapace of the poor turtle. It didn't taste like anything in particular, and rather gave the impression that I was gnawing on a piece of rubber. In the meantime Mr Lei was effusively explaining to me all the advantages it would bring to my manhood.

While I waited for the elixir to take its effect, a new dish was plunked on the table. A succulent deep-fried fish, the head of which had remained intact during the cooking process. Still alive, the fish's eyes stared right at me while its mouth gasped for oxygen. Although it was definite proof that the fish was fresh, I couldn't bring my chopsticks to touch its body. As the evening wore on other blubbery goodies rolled by in revue: sea cucumber, deep-fried pork fat, and soup of goat penis, to name a few.

It definitely was not my best meal ever, but Adam seemed to love the notion that he had eaten half a zoo of exotic creatures. Probably he was craving more.

The next day Adam returned to the office in Beijing, while I stayed on. Although the factory hadn't produced or bottled water for several months, the office staff was still present every day of the week. Having nothing to do, most of them read newspapers, tended to their files, or answered the odd telephone call that filtered through.

Mr Lei himself introduced me to the staff, who were instructed to help me in any way possible. At the outset I spent time meeting the accountants, sales staff and engineers to get a feel for the company's history and past track record. My initial anxiety that they'd resist my presence proved well founded. To them I was just another barbarian walking into their territory. They had already seen so many people waltz through the place that another clown trying to steal the show was nothing but a turn-off. The only thing I could do was try to gain their confidence over time. Trying to understand what had gone wrong with the company, I hoped to convince the employees that I wasn't there to judge anyone. I welcomed their help in finding a way to get the whole JV machine back on track. This was certainly in their best interest, as their job security was probably on the line. All of them must have their grievances, their embitterment with the present situation and how it went wrong.

While I worked in a corner of the office, I often saw through the window frantic activity in Mr Lei's other factory opposite the water plant. Nobody really informed us what other businesses Mr Lei and his partners were involved in. The 'Aqua Minerale' trucks drove carton after carton of unknown contents out of the factory gates. It certainly couldn't be Aqua Minerale water, as the filling line hadn't run for months, ever since the relationship broke down. It might very well be the traditional copycat plant running the show at the expense of the JV. Those misgivings quickly dissipated.

The next time I sat down with Mr Lei, he informed me that that particular factory was involved in electronics. Although I found it a bit surprising, I took him at his word.

While one spot was churning out products, the other one was lying idle. This was particularly painful as Chinese New Year was around the corner, normally a peak period for the retail business. It was the one moment when prices for fast-moving consumer products were inflated, and the company's profit margins could make up for the weaker sales cycles of the year. Unfortunately for the joint venture, no gain could be had from this season's celebrations. It was even more distressing for the office staff, as incoming telephone calls from large supermarket chains and hotels had to be rebuffed with a litany of excuses, from: 'We've already sold out our inventory for the coming three months' to: 'We are willing to sell but unfortunately at a very high price', a favourite in getting rid of persistent purchasers on the other end of the line. In this depressing atmosphere, I was listening to anyone who was willing to speak their mind.

My chore was to dole out carton after carton of Panda cigarettes while holding informal discussions over extensive lunches, rocket-fuel ignited dinners and *karaoke* sessions spread over several weeks. As my waistline increased and I became acquainted with most of the girls in Mr Lei's favourite massage parlours and *karaoke* bars, the fog of mystery surrounding the JV slowly dissipated. Snippets of information were coming in.

The accountants explained how Marco resisted paying cash on delivery for ordered goods, apparently worried that large cash transactions would lead to funny business in the workplace. Initially, he decided that all payments should be made on extended credit terms. However, many of the suppliers were disinclined to deliver goods without a cash handover. Several quarrels and verbal attacks later, he agreed to operate with cheques. This practice, too, rebounded and antagonised many of the brokers, staff included. Banks and affiliates outside of Hainan Island would not accept cheques from a local bank in Hainan. This created so much tension and vitriolic argument that the accounting staff of Aqua Minerale refused to buy any more goods that didn't originate from within the factory's county.

If there was one thing to avoid at all costs, it was getting too cosy with the extended family/friend network that operated locally. Not only did the JV buy raw material at less competitive prices, it opened the door wide open for the funny business Marco had been afraid of in the first place. A striking example was the PVC caps. They were made of recycled plastic instead of virgin plastic, often resulting in leaky bottles. Ultimately, his lack of understanding of local business etiquette had an adverse effect on the products coming off the production line.

As for accounts receivable, most large supermarkets and distrib-utors worked on consignment and might only pay three to six months after the goods left their shelves. In some badly-run shops, goods disappeared on a regular basis due to a lack of internal control systems. To make matters worse, during transport some of the bottled water never reached its destination, ending up in a parallel circuit, and needed to be written off immediately. Although the in-house organising of transport decreased this 'evaporation' of goods, it was an undeniable fact that a loss of cargo was unavoidable and should have been taken into account early on. The fact that Marco was suspicious of all those peculiar transactions, and blamed the staff for the erosion of profit margins, didn't create the right environment for openly discussing those specific problems.

Sales people, as anywhere in the world, are normally a happy lot who have learned to take rejection with modesty. They generally know that with enough persistence they'll be able to sell. In the case of this JV, however, the whole sales team had left the company when they started getting a sense of how the wind was blowing. The secretary put me in contact with some of them.

Apparently, Marco's insistence that the buyer should accept a 35 percent price difference because the JV's products were superior to the competition's had killed many early opportunities. Not realis-ing the fierceness of competition with local producers, he had created an 'unanticipated' setback in the business plan by pricing

Aqua Minerale out of the game. The cost of positioning the product through advertisements, dedicated sales booths in shops and sales promotions was disproportionate to the small amount of sales that resulted. Initially, Marco blamed the sales people for the bad results and insisted that they write visiting reports. The problem was that the sales team had a hard time knowing what to write in those reports: What was he expecting to read? The reality on the ground, that the shop's purchasing department wanted a fee before the bottles could hit the racks? Good news or bad news? Didn't he know that water was simply a commodity to most Chinese?

In the end they settled on making no report.

Interpreting this as laziness, Marco went into a rage. This lost him the respect of his sales team and killed their enthusiasm for making Aqua Minerale a household brand name. When Marco was finally forced to dramatically lower price levels, he couldn't get his team to sell with the necessary dedication. Many of the staff left or were fired over time, which resulted in the joint venture losing the relationships necessary to collect accounts receivables, as well as relationships with the customers' purchasing department and the office staff. The crucial *guanxi* relationships on the ground were cut off one by one as the sales people were withdrawn from the field. Mr Mussolini was left alone to face the war.

Flicking through all the sales projections and marketing plans Marco had written, they looked neat and meticulously thought through. It was a textbook business plan that certainly could have worked out in the West without too much fine-tuning. It showed cash flow, business growth estimates with worst-case and best-case scenarios, estimated break-even point, expected return on investment, how profits were to be ploughed back into the expanding market, how the Aqua brand would be best positioned in China, what competitive advantages the jv would have over local competitors. All in all a beefy file that I'm sure Mr Lei never read and would not be interested in. His business instincts led him to profits. He didn't need all those graphs and figures to tell him when or how the money was flowing in.

Wanting to copy and paste a Western plan into a Chinese adventure was normal behaviour for our Italians.

Unfortunately for them, the Chinese market has many unquantifiable factors which influence a company's operations. For a start: business regulations, local and national level taxes and accounting rules often change before the ink dries on the paper on which they were written. Not seeing the vague and sometimes contradictory rules and regulations as a business opportunity, Marco often got entangled in a morass (as he saw it) of unexpected requests and arbitrary demands. What to do with the tax officers who knock at the door and ask for more dues because they either suspect double bookkeeping, or worse require more money to support megalomaniac building projects for the city government? Mr Lei's entertainment complex was one of the most efficient tools his business empire had for dealing with Chinese reality.

The engineers were the worst lot of all, and complained at length about their unjust treatment while the equipment was being installed. The Italian engineers had screamed their way through the equipment assembly and start-up phase. The local engineers, having been treated as idiots, didn't want to help any longer. When the Westerners left, so did the Chinese engineers' enthusiasm for running and maintaining the equipment according to HACCP standards – an international set of rules and regulations for the sanitary processing and packaging of food. The consequences of this appeared right away when an impromptu examination by local hygiene and sanitation inspectors discovered traces of microbiological contamination in the mineral water two months after operations began. This resulted in a two-week shutdown of the plant. Such events recurred at regular intervals, as the international standards didn't take into account the squalid living conditions of the workers, nor the need to train them in the plant's basic hygienic requirements. The unavailability of running water in their private homes was the source of many contaminants, and was only resolved by providing staff with showers in the dressing rooms and clean uniforms on a regular basis.

At the same time, the equipment was designed to run with raw materials that met specific standards. Unfortunately, most of the local chemicals didn't meet the high standards that the plant was designed for. Therefore additional filters, supplementary processing steps and maintenance procedures were required. The water analysis, mineral content, dry residue and pH never added up to what was listed on the bottles' labels. The Italian engineers, who were flown over more often than required, didn't quite see it that way, and thought that the equipment had been willfully sabotaged. They even succeeded in having Mr Dong, the head engineer, fired. Mr Dong was a school friend of Mr Lei and the latter certainly saw this as a personal insult.

Having made Mr Dong, and therefore Mr Lei, lose face, the Italians' relationship with their partners worsened considerably. Since the workers thought very highly of Engineer Dong both as a problem solver and a leader, the situation turned gloomy pretty fast. The eventual result was that the workers refused to work any longer for the JV partner. Mr Lei decided to keep quiet and stand with the workers.

From Adam I learned that the JV's agreements seemed mostly okay. There weren't too many discrepancies between the Chinese and English versions. As usual, the devil was in the details. What worried him was that access to the JV's leased land through Mr Lei's 'territory' wasn't explicitly specified. Or, to a lawyer's twisted brain: the JV by-laws did not clearly lay out the neighbouring rights of the land for the twenty-year lease period. Since the negotiations were conducted in an atmosphere of good faith and friendship, nobody was really bothered by the issue. However, as relations hit rock bottom, Adam's red flag resulted in another string of sleepless nights for the Italian investors.

Having spent several weeks at the JV, I didn't want to overextend my stay and decided that it was time to return to Beijing a couple of days before Chinese New Year. As if to test my resolve and patience, Mr Lei quietly instructed his secretary to inform me three hours before my departure that he and his wife would like me to stay over for the festivities. Most probably, the secretary was expecting a categorical no, and maybe a bit of haggling, before she gracefully accepted my refusal to adjourn my departure. Unfortunately for her, and maybe her boss, out came my response: 'Well, why not, I've nothing to do in Beijing during the holidays and over here the weather is much warmer!'

In the end it only cost me a ticket and a few hotel nights. But in return, I hoped to hear whatever nuggets of information Mr Lei might unintentionally let slip about his intentions regarding the joint venture.

On the evening of the New Year, a total of roughly twenty people shared two tables in an upscale Cantonese restaurant. Present were Mr Lei's wife, his sister and two brothers with their spouses, his son and parents, all celebrating the departure of the Tiger and the arrival of the Rabbit. The initial uneasiness over having a barbarian in their midst was quickly dissipated when Ms Lei got excited over my bits and pieces of Sichuan dialect. The fact that Chongqing was my favourite of all Chinese cities intrigued her. When I told Ms Lei that her city was the cradle of my life in China, it put her in the right party mood and set the evening going. She beamed at Mr Lei and threw in a barb of her own: 'You see, even foreigners love Chongqing.'

Her eyes were full of sparkle and Sichuan passion. From then on, I had a new drinking ally on my side of the table. It was the Chongqing clan against the others. Her capacity for rocket fuel was impressive and unquestionably showed her ability to handle any business situation, not to mention Mr Lei himself. At that moment I really pitied him, the untouchable, tackled head on by his wife. After draining I don't know how many bottles of rocket fuel, the end of the party was finally in sight. Two hours of feasting finished up with a fruit platter and the social gathering dissipated into smaller groups.

Mr Lei stealthily proposed a *karaoke* night together with some of his pals. My initial protests that he might want to spend the rest of the evening with the family were quickly silenced when Ms Lei ordered me to have a good time with her husband. We got on with a full massage at his favourite parlour, followed by a steam bath to evaporate the alcohol and then yet another full massage. As midnight was still far off, a *karaoke* session ensued with a messy yet entertaining extravaganza of topless women, XO and singing. Showing off the breasts of his current conquest, Mr Lei was a happy man. In Hainan, it's not every day you have someone of Mongolian pedigree sitting next to you. Between the flashing of mammary glands, the opening of yet another bottle of xo, and the howling of songs the night moved along effortlessly.

The next day, Mr Lei woke me up for brunch with his family at one of the five-star hotels in Haikou. Still beleaguered by a bouncy headache and uncontrollable *baijiu* burps, and mostly unable to stand, I sat under a hot shower for half an hour, hoping all the night's leftovers would swiftly evaporate in the water curtain. Walking out of the hotel I was picked up by the driver and shuttled to our destination.

At the table, a bright grinning Mr Lei looked at me as if to say 'we shared a great secret party yesterday.' It was probably nothing different from the other *karaoke* sessions I had had with him, but the fact that we were sitting there with wife and son made it, in his eyes, more exciting.

By the end of the lunch, my headache had slowly subsided and an irrepressible urge arose in me to ask about the venture: 'Mr Lei, why did you start this business with the Italians, if you really don't care about the water business anyway?' Pondering his answer, he slowly sipped his tea and took a deep drag on his omnipresent cigarette.

'Jieke, you're my friend. I can tell you a little secret. The factory next to the bottling plant is making cds. Millions of them every month, and I need an alibi for the movements of the trucks. Pressure from the us government on China has been mounting in recent years. They make pictures of my factory with spy satellites and show them during official meetings in Beijing. With the mineral water factory I can work under cover. For a while some "friends" would inform me when one of the satellites was passing over, but that became too risky for everyone involved. Now, with the new plant, everyone can better explain why there are so many trucks coming in and out. Everybody is happy.'

I had to take a good long look at him to see if he was joking. I've often experienced unlikely situations, but this one made the top of the list. 'Are you serious?' I asked, half-laughing, half-inquisitive.

'Sure. Makes good money. I had just hoped that the barbarians would take better care of the water business. . . . We were actually expecting Marco to act more rationally and not really depend on me. I thought that by not getting involved too much, the business might actually take off.'

This James Bond story seemed to be pretty close to the truth. A couple of months later I was invited to see the real venture. How wrong I was to think that the pirated CDs I had been stashing up over the years were printed in a scruffy garage in some back alley. In a clean building spread over three floors, row after row of copying equipment was churning out the latest movies on VCD, DVD, music CD and CD-ROM. Maybe Mr Lei hadn't invented the Mafia, but he seemed oblivious to the fact that his factory was a perfect example of Corleone ingenuity.

Everybody was certainly not happy with this story. Marco was pretty upset when he heard what Mr Lei had hidden up his sleeve. Like any good warm-blooded Southern European his immediate response was to sue them and expose this 'little secret'.

'You'd be losing focus on your prime reason for being in China: To make your business run. Preparing for legal recourse will waste additional investor resources and grind your operations to a total halt. Trying to win the moral high ground will get you nowhere. Mr Lei didn't do anything to undermine the JV. He even gave you carte blanche to run all operations. In a sense you should be happy you ended up with such a passive partner. It could have turned out much worse. You'd better try to save whatever can be saved of the JV.'

Lacking nerves of steel, Marco had a hard time weathering the unpredictable daily hurricanes buffeting his business. He'd probably lingered too long in the eye of the storm to realise what was heading his way. Having focused too much on trying to manage the people and operations from a strict Western perspective, he had lost control.

The unforeseen extended stays of overseas staff, loss of merchandise, faltering production equipment, and lack of sales devotion had all taken a serious toll on the expected margins, and the money would be hard to recuperate. Unless he accepted realities on the ground, the business would die a slow death.

Ultimately the Aqua Minerale JV closed down, as it became impossible to reconcile the two parties. Because the equipment was on Mr Lei's property, which also included other facilities, it was impossible to physically split up the land and sell the piece with the factory to the Italians. We initially tried to make Mr Lei pay in part for the equipment that remained behind, but he staunchly refused.

At this point, the Western investors decided that suing their (ex) partner was the best way to vindicate themselves. In early May we huddled up in our office discussing the best options for compensation. One sunny Sunday afternoon, while we were taking a break from one of these sessions, a crowd of young Chinese surrounded us on the street and asked if we were Americans. Having been asked this question a million times, I had my auto-response ready: 'No, we're lucky to be from Russia,' as from experience I knew this was an immediate turn off to young Chinese and no further questions would follow.

But one of the Chinese in the crowd started speaking Russian to us. They immediately realised we were a fraud, and the gathering suddenly got pretty nasty. People started pushing and shoving us around. This open aggression, coming from nowhere, was extremely intimidating and had me quite bewildered. These skirmishes were totally atypical of the Chinese I had come to know. Four versus twenty-something angry people certainly was unfavourable odds, and it didn't look good. We hurriedly explained that it was all a mistake, that we were from Europe. This seemed to appease them somewhat. Luckily, we escaped the volatile situation with only one Italian business suit and shirt damaged. White-faced, the adrenaline still pumping in our blood streams, we quickly returned to our office. Unsure what had just happened to us, we were in no state of mind to continue our discussions. Marco and Co. left for their hotel, while I went home. Initially it occurred to me that Mr Lei maybe wanted to intimidate us. But Beijing was not his home turf, and anyway he had had the upper hand in the whole JV affair, it was hard to imagine why he'd try to pull something like this.

When I watched the evening news, however, things snapped into perspective pretty quickly: apparently, US jet fighters had mistakenly bombed the Chinese Embassy in Belgrade, Yugoslavia, with precision-guided bombs, thinking it was a military target in the ongoing NATO air campaign in the Balkans. The volley killed four innocent Chinese staff. When this news hit the Chinese TV screens, protests immediately erupted in all four corners of the country.

In Beijing alone over a hundred thousand students invaded the Ritan embassy district, chanting anti-American slogans, throwing rocks and bottles at the US embassy. In Chengdu, the US Consulate was burned down during angry night riots.

Fairly quickly the American government offered its deepest regrets to the people of China, but insisted that the bombing was an honest mistake.

The US spy satellites that could detect the details of Mr Lei's illegal operations were unable to spot a well-known location: the PRC embassy in Belgrade that had been there for well over four years.

The protests lasted several days, with some barbarian-looking individuals roughed up pretty badly. For big noses like me it was certainly not the best of moments to take a stroll outside. The now-emboldened Chinese crowds were not willing to differentiate between a Belgian fry and a Freedom fry. My best survival strategy was to stay put at home for a week till the tempest passed by. The day after the incident on the street, the Italians flew back to Milan, as they thought Beijing was about to explode. This event also killed the investors' appetite for returning to China or pursuing the planned lawsuit. Mr Lei agreed to let some Italian engineers come over and dismantle the bottling line, which was shipped back to Italy.

Then the whole episode slowly disappeared from the radar screen.

Many of the joint ventures we visited, assisted in, or set up for our customers have not survived the clash of cultures. The hurdles for both parties to adapt to each other's business styles and methods seem too high. Too often we saw JVs created with the intention to profit from cheap labour, the gigantic local market, or a mixture of both, without any interest in what made the employee, local partner or local market tick in the first place.

Too bad about all the wasted money, sweat and damage to mental health. Still, many are hopelessly attracted by the mating call of the JV beast, and insist that it's within their power to tame it.

Postscript

• Herewith an overview of the typical stages of the birth and death of a classic Mom-and-Pop JV, unfolding in some far-flung corner of Chinese territory.

  Desperation: When will we see the end of the negotiation tunnel?

  Euphoria: The agreement is finally signed.

  Doubt: About the local implementation of the business plan. Let's fly over some managers to train the local staff.

  Excitement: first products rolling off the line.

  Worry: The quality is not up to standard; please send in more Western technicians. Did we really need to invest in an entertainment room?

  Jubilation: A major sales contract is signed and . . . electricity is available twenty-four hours a day.

  Anxiety: Account Receivables are seriously behind.

  Relief: Creditors start paying up, superior raw materials arrive on a more or less continuous basis. We are the kings: Our business will be profitable soon, all is running smoothly, the local partner knows because he just bought a Western luxury sedan.

  Uncertainty: The audited accounts don't look that good after all. Wow! Things seem to be done differently in China.

  Nervousness: Why doesn't the Chinese partner want to implement the second investment phase?

  Resilience: We'll make them go for the second phase. Replace this incompetent Western manager who's upsetting the local partner.

  Misery: The local staff wants a salary raise, they refuse to continue to work.

Shock: Production has stopped, we're not allowed to enter the premises.

Comprehension: HQ, we have a problem; China is not so ideal after all!

Arrogance: Let's buy out the Chinese partner.

Negotiations: Again?

Anguish: When will we finally see the end of negotiations to buy the rest of the JV shares?

Delight: We bought out our Chinese partner, good riddance.

Discomfort: Did we pay too much?

- Roughly 125,000 people died on the Chinese roads in 2005, most of them with their eyes wide open.

- It was 1998 when I crossed the streets of Beijing with my eyes closed. At that time traffic was miles away from what it is now. Please *don't* try this in today's Beijing traffic. You will most probably *not* succeed.

- Four million new cars were purchased nationwide in 2006. A massive 13.5 million cars were sold in 2012 and that was the year when for the first time more cars were registered in China than Europe. In 2013 more than 120 million passenger cars were plying Chinese roads.

- After being fired by the JV partner, Mr Dong, the head of engineering, immediately took up a job at Mr Lei's other factory. A lifetime friendship that endured the Cultural Revolution is not to be messed with.

- In early 2000, most of Mr Lei's copying equipment was moved to Taiwan, where activities resumed. As far as I know he's presently only taking care of distribution inside of China and into Russia. None of the products coming out of this new entity land in the Taiwanese market, as this would mean the immediate end of the Taiwanese operations.

- Western companies still make a killing selling sophisticated CD-DVD duplicating equipment into China.

- In times of misery and failure, I buoy myself with Mr Lei's favourite proverb: 'Failure lies not in falling down. Failure lies in not getting up.'

CHAPTER 6

Flashback: A lawyer's beginnings

After 1949, Chinese legal institutions were reformed to be in line with Marx, Lenin and Mao's view of the world. Overnight, China became a wasteland for commercial law. Communist doctrine was paramount.

The extensive reforms that followed the opening up of the country in 1979 required a solid base of new laws and rules to achieve the nation's common dream: becoming an economically advanced country on par with the West.

As such, my old friend and business partner was sent to law school in the early 1980s to study a mysterious new line of thought: international private law. Herewith a flashback to how my friend became what he is today: a successful lawyer running a major law firm in China.

Wuhan, Monday June 30th, 1987

It had been one of those sweltering days in Wuhan. Blistering hot with the mercury easily creeping past thirty-eight degrees, humidity levels turning a stroll through the Wuhan University alleys into a sweaty, clammy exercise. Although lush trees enveloped the alleyways, the shortest walk would inevitably result in a sticky shirt uncomfortably clamped to sweaty skin. On these days students tried to keep themselves busy reading in class, or just did nothing, lying in bed in the dormitory and waiting for the cooler evening to come.

But today was different; for once the walk from the dormitory to the Department of Law was not a bodily nuisance.

My friend Adam was part of a group of thirty-nine students who were to receive their bachelor degrees in International Law. Four years of study and absorption of the intricacies of international rules and regulations had borne fruit. This was only the second batch of students who would walk out of a Chinese university holding a degree of this kind.

Professor Liu had arranged a small congratulatory gathering in one of the classrooms. While a ceiling fan provided irregular wafts of hot air, the whole group sat in anticipation, waiting for 'the big moment'. Their degrees, documents bearing a cherry-red university seal and safely placed inside a small red plastic booklet, were handed out randomly, just as they'd been delivered to Professor Liu by the university administration. The brief speech he had prepared went along the following lines: 'We are expecting to make great strides in the future, and tomorrow life will be even brighter for all citizens, as long as everyone commits to the cause of a stronger and better China. Our country is now well on its way to becoming an industrial nation and you are key components in further developing it. But most importantly you should dedicate your lives to the greater good of the people and with boundless enthusiasm contribute to developing the motherland into a great nation. Each of you has already been appointed to your work unit. Some of you will work for the Ministry of Public Security, the Supreme Court, the Supreme Prosecutor's office, the State Planning Committee and other organisations. If you work hard, Spring will be yours.'

It all started in 1981, when the Chinese government realised that the country was ill-equipped to develop further and open up to the outside world. It would need lawyers, engineers, economists, and diplomats able to undertake whatever was required to make the country an international player. The slogan and goal at that time was the Four Modernisations: Industry, Agriculture, Defence and Science all had to be upgraded to international levels. Previously, China had had no international laws to speak of regarding investment and trade. It was a book in the process of being written. Two top universities were appointed to convey knowledge of International Law to a small group of school graduates who had shown potential.

Peking University had become the focal point for International Public Law. International treaties, including United Nations tracts on water bodies, land and aerospace, were to be the main subjects taught in its lecture halls. Future graduates would find their way into international bodies and government organisations.

Wuhan University, on the other hand, got to teach International Private Law. The main objective here was to develop understanding of corporate law, international investment vehicles and the governing laws of contracts between companies in different countries. Indeed China had great plans to become a major trading nation, and needed people who could scrutinise contracts and make sure Chinese businesses were not treated unfairly or suffered a loss at the hands of unscrupulous businessmen.

The problem for the fresh graduates in Adam's group was that they didn't feel their academic knowledge had anything to do with the real world. The heap of abstract subjects they'd absorbed over the past four years seemed to have no practical application. They knew of no company in China that had shareholders, charters, articles of association or even the necessary contracts with overseas entities. Intellectual property was considered some bizarre concept produced by the Western mind. These ideas went no further than abstract theory. China had closed its doors to the outside a long time ago, and in its insulated worldview everything belonged to the people, and was for the people. Lacking any idea of how, where or in what form their studies could be put into practice, many students felt they'd wasted their time.

And no wonder: In 1949 all factories were magically folded into state-owned enterprises (SOEs). New factories got the same treatment, becoming 100-percent owned by the Chinese state. All this restructuring and kneading of organisations into one and the same mould was done in name of the new workers' paradise. The directives of the proletariat ruled the Middle Kingdom. Whatever Chinese company law that existed at the time the country was liberated slowly faded into the history books, to lie dormant for decades to come. The target for Chinese enterprises was to meet quotas issued by the central government. The balanced scorecards of socialism dictated the production of so many tons of steel, so many shirts, so many tons of coal, so many silos of wheat, so many bottles of soybean oil, so many kegs of beer, so many pairs of shoes, so many litres of human blood, and on it went. A business plan was unnecessary, as the state would allot raw materials to the factory and the goods produced were shipped to different units scattered all over the country according to planned allocations. Profit was a bourgeois concept and not required in communism's seventh heaven. Quotas were all that mattered. The state owned all and everything in the factory and in the market, and regulated the economy as a grand master who knew what was best for the population. Since profit was unheard of, a shareholder was an even more alien notion.

Chairman Mao was certainly no fool, and had an in-depth knowledge of how, in the past, emperors were able to use the bureaucracy to control the vast resources of the country. The state, as the main stakeholder, put a system in place that mirrored very much the structures of past bureaucracies.

When factories were built to address a need in the planned economy, the government allocated money, land and people as it saw fit. It would appoint the head or No. 1 of the factory (the *changzhang*). The closest equivalent by Western standards would be CEO. The No. 1 would be in charge of administering the factory. His main task was to orchestrate his unit in such a way that the yearly quotas were met. As resources were pretty scarce, every *changzhang* in the country jockeyed for sufficient coal, electricity, production components and other raw materials. To reach the targets set by the government, the No. 1 of any work unit needed to rely heavily on his *guanxi*. His end-of-year bonus wasn't measured in terms of money, but in additional status, bigger banquets and more influential connections he could rely on when the next quota came in.

In the constellation of relationships that surrounded the No. 1, one other figure was and still is extremely powerful: the Party secretary of the factory. Appointed through the Communist Party and representing them in the factory, this prima donna could draw on a deep well of political capital. In the ballet of power he could always pirouette and leap with more skill and grace than anyone else in his work unit.

Those two company positions were key in making sure all directives, political as well as economic, were carried out along the guiding principles set by the central government. The No. 1 motivated workers by making them proud of reaching the targets and becoming a model unit others could learn from. The secretary roused spirits through political slogans to make people aware that they were working for the betterment of the country.

These two important titles still remain in each SOE: the No. 1 and the secretary. In case of conflict, the secretary will prevail. Always.

And so the populace dutifully worked towards the dream of collectivism, toiling away in endless pursuit of shadows. That's also how those students felt: struck by collective confusion, clueless as to what they were meant to do with their newly acquired wisdom. They were thinking, 'How can this knowledge be turned into a practical slogan that will give guidance and certainty?' 'Did the state realise that the curriculum had been useless?' Impossible! The state couldn't be wrong; it wouldn't waste the country's resources on something worthless.

The only explanation was that the bigger picture was eluding them. Hopefully, with more knowledge and experience, the fresh graduates would be able to understand the larger plan they were meant to be part of.

But still they looked forward to becoming a freshly-minted cog in the greater machinery of a strong and powerful China. Whatever the state required of them, they would comply.

The 'visible hand' provided every graduate with a train ticket home, and after leaving the university Adam was headed for a month of R&R in Zhengzhou.

A twelve-hour train ride later, he arrived in the capital of Henan Province. Zhengzhou's much milder climate, a pleasant twenty-five degrees Celsius and a slight breeze, was a welcome change from the oven of Wuhan.

Adam hadn't been back since Chinese New Year.

Home was one of the larger steel factories in China, with over fifteen thousand workers labouring away at all hours of the day. A typical left-over commune from a grand-scale experiment for the country's self-reliance during the fifties.

The distinctive smell of the fumes belching out of the many chimneys scattered through the factory grounds was the neighbourhood's welcoming sign.

Adam's mother, who had received permission from her superior to take a break from her work analysing samples from the smelters, had come out to meet her returning son. Although the factory's desolate surroundings were pretty depressing compared to Wuhan University's oasis of green, it always felt great to be back in familiar surroundings.

The factory itself looked more like a small town with department stores, hospitals, meat and vegetable markets, schools, sport centres, police stations, movie theatres and housing complexes. As the factory was pretty far from Zhengzhou, its commune was self-sustaining, and people lived there all year round. Most only left the compound for the outside world on Labour Day, May First, and National Day, on October First. The large community, disconnected from the outside world for long periods of time, had even developed its own dialect and accents.

Adam's father was head of the planning department for production and worked right under No. 1. Therefore the family's place was a bit cosier: they were allocated a three-bedroom, eighty-square-metre apartment consisting of a living room, bathroom and kitchen. Incredible as it might seem in today's China, their accommodations looked exactly the same as those in factories scattered across the entire nation, as if a single architect had imposed his design on the masses. Not only were the places similarly structured, built with the same material, painted the same colours, and laid out the same way – they even came with the same smell.

Only a few houses in the factory had their own private cooking space and it was considered a great honour to have one. This was a sign that the pure ideals of collectivism were still a work in progress.

Those who really lived the good life, Marxist-Leninist style, used the public kitchens open to all housewives of the work unit.

As always, the excitement of being back quickly died down and transformed into boredom. During the day the house was empty while Ma and Pa tended to their daily chores in the work unit. The small black-and-white TV only showed political speeches and news alternating with Chinese opera, old war movies, programmes on how to grow corn and educational courses on mathematics, physics, chemistry, English, calligraphy, Japanese ... basically anything people might be eager to learn as part of the country's drive to modernise.

It was an instant turn-off for any younger viewer; hardly worth contemplating for hours on end. The only way to escape the dullness of the day was to meet up with old school mates and friends who'd grown up in the same factory complex.

Xiao Wang had just finished his civil engineering degree in Tianjin. Adam once played with him so often that both families had become close and the children would walk into each other's houses without so much as knocking.

'How are you, what's going on? Where has the government decided to appoint you?' Adam asked while blowing the leaves in his piping hot cup of tea.

'I've been assigned to the Architecture Design Institute and will draw up plans for those fancy Western-style structures. There's going to be a huge demand for grand new contemporary buildings. The country needs a new modern look to face the future.'

'Down with the old, up with the new!' Xiao Lei, sitting next to Adam, laughed.

Xiao Lei had majored in Management from the Dalian Trade and Commerce University. Apparently he'd gotten a position at the People's Congress Committee of Liaoning Province. 'I have no idea what they want from me. I'll show up, have a look and if I don't like it, start my own business.'

Everyone was laughing at this point. Start your own business! That was a strange notion. Why would someone with a university degree risk his future for the unknown? The state would allocate a job for you, wasn't that good enough?

Xiao Chen had been quiet the whole time; he just graduated from a trade and commerce college in Shenyang.

'My father pulled some strings and I'm able to work here in the factory.'

In a sense they all envied him. He, at least could rely on his existing network of friends and acquaintances when walking into his job. For the others it was a bit of a gamble.

'What about you Adam? Aren't you going to continue your Masters in Law?'

'I don't feel like studying any longer, I'm hearing so many stories going around about becoming rich and successful. Right before graduation my university tutor was able to snatch me a job at an investment company I've never heard of.'

CITIC (China International Trust and Investment Corporation) was in need of fresh graduates with an International Law background.

That's how, in the last week of August, Adam came to take an early morning train to Beijing. His luggage consisted of a woven reed basket and the brown-strapped leather suitcase his father bought in 1958 when he was sent from his hometown in Dalian to the Zhengzhou factory. It was just large enough to hold some law books, clothes and other personal belongings. The total value probably didn't exceed two hundred RMB.

In the morning, hundreds of people stood with luggage in hand behind the metal crush gates, impatiently waiting for the train to pull into Zhengzhou station. All were pushing and shoving, trying to secure a better position for what was to come. When the train entered the station, the throng of people got more excited and pushed themselves closer towards the gate, squeezing everyone in the process. The more privileged passengers in the soft-sleeper and soft-seat sections were allowed on before the proletariat was un-leashed onto the train. In the meantime everyone behind the gates was getting more and more impatient to get on and some scuffles broke out, followed by more shouting and cursing. Adam, with two pieces of luggage clamped in his hands, knew that the hard-seat section would be overbooked as usual, and he would need to make a dash to secure a seat for the twelve-hour ride to the capital. When the gates finally opened the mass of people started to move forward like a huge wave, with the fastest getting hold of their precious prize: a seat for the ride. At the entrance of each of the carriages people were jostling and pushing to get on while they dragged their luggage through the mob. The slower ones had to make do with standing places in the corridors, while others already on were assisting their friends and family members through the windows. Adam passed the exercise unscathed, with a seat next to the window!

When the train jerked into movement the hard-seat section was completely full: three squeezed onto each firm seat bench, while others sat on their luggage along the gangways, bags jammed into every hole and corner of the carriage. Some passengers even found a place slouching under the seats. Probably the best spot of all to relax during the long ride.

As the breeze started flowing through the windows, in the carriage tempers quickly cooled off. The rush had taken a lot out of the crowd, and now everyone was back in a good mood. All were on the road to the capital!

At dusk the train finally shuffled into Beijing Station.

At the exit gates, a crowd thronged around the people leaving the train station, and a sign bearing the CITIC logo was brandished above the swarm of heads. A couple of fresh graduates had already congregated around the sign. The CITIC staff ticked off the names on a list of new employees, meaning they now belonged to an exclusive group, working for one of the first modern Chinese investment vehicles allowing foreigners to pour their money into the Mainland.

A short drive from the station brought Adam to a small hotel next to Tuanjiehu Park. The whole place had been rented by CITIC to house the one hundred and forty graduates they hired that year.

The company, established in 1979, was still in the early stages of development. It was headed by Mr Rong Yiren, known as the Red Capitalist, who had been personally chosen by Deng Xiaoping to supervise one of the first Chinese investment corporations to be run in a Western manner. While most wealthy industrialists had opted to flee to Hong Kong or Taiwan during the fifties, Mr Rong was one of a few patriotic industrialists who chose to remain in Mainland China. During that period he handed over most of his factories to the government, while relentlessly pushing for the modernisation of the country.

The company's headquarters were next to the Friendship Store: the then-famous CITIC building. The first Western-style office in Beijing, nicknamed 'The Chocolate Building' because of the colour of the tiles. It was a coveted work environment for many locals as the place was top notch, with air conditioning, and the offices emanated a serene atmosphere of success. The urge to visit the tower was so huge that an entrance pass had to be introduced to ward off the throng of locals wanting to pop into the place. The office building was definitely made for another era and a new world.

The first day on the job, however, didn't take the new employees through those heavenly gates. The hundred-and-forty-something graduates were whisked away on a training stint to the outskirts of Beijing.

The college of the Ministry of Foreign Trade and Economic Cooperation in Changping would be their home for the next three months. Here their grey matter was to be fed the sophisticated strategies of international investment, trade and negotiation. No more theories but the real thing in practice. Genuine banking instruments, factual investment agreements, purchasing contracts, and legal disputes would be de-boned and discussed six days a week, eight hours a day. Experienced staff came and exchanged their know-how; explaining in minute detail the aim of a particular job. But practical knowledge sometimes had its limits. As very little foreign investment had actually entered the country yet, the pool of expertise was pretty shallow and for many senior managers it was a new ball game that even they were learning on the fly, as JV after JV was signed up. In one of the courses on feasibility studies an expert got tripped up in a discussion on how to use registered capital and total investment in a financial analysis. Although it was a key concept in evaluating the amount of assets and/or cash flow required for keeping operations up and running, his confusion between theoretical discourse and practice was thoroughly exposed ... to the embarrassment of the expert.

At the same time those three months in Changping also provided a chance to literally get a taste of the world beyond China's borders. The experience of chocolate melting on the tongue or the first mouthful of a sparkling cola drink was certainly as memorable as anything else that was being taught. It marked a new era in those young people's lives.

On one of those cold and dull autumn weekends, Ms Xu, the sister of a roommate, came to visit her little brother. She was working at the Ministry of Foreign Affairs and during a recent trip to Hong Kong brought back a small container of instant coffee. This would be the event of the day! She shyly said 'I tasted coffee in Hong Kong and thought you should also try it. However I'm not sure how many spoons a cup needs to make it taste as authentic as possible.'

In the end they settled for four spoons each, roughly the same amount of tea leaves that would be used for a big cup of tea. The hot and bitter flavour of the coffee didn't result in love at first taste. The brew induced a not-of-this-world sensation on the taste buds with a persistently strong aftertaste. Although no one dared to be seen as unrefined, none could understand how anyone could enjoy this bitter liquid. And the experience didn't end there. As none of their bodies had ever encountered caffeine, their brains remained alight for the next twenty-four hours.

The courses kept everyone extremely busy throughout their stay in Changping, and the three months went by unbelievably fast. By the end of November the recruits were now craving their first hands-on business experience. A hungry and ambitious team was finally ready to leave the college for better pastures.

A welcome ceremony was held in the conference room on the third floor of the CITIC building. Walking into the space, the first-timers were overwhelmed by such luxurious surroundings. The room could easily hold two hundred people. A soft yellow glow of indirect light filled the place, thick beige carpet covered the floors from wall to wall, and row after row of black leather chairs were evenly spaced over the area. In front, an imposing stage overlooked the room, from which it seemed only vitally important discourses could be delivered.

Adam had been selected to make a speech to the senior management. It was nothing he was prepared for, and the place made the adrenaline flow through his veins. His well-revised speech probably contained too much hyperbole in the style of 'we are all happy to be here, proud to be part of this big family, we'll be working very hard to make a contribution to our company. . . .' but at the same time, how could they not mean it sincerely? Everything up to now was so excitingly new and challenging. A far cry from the wildest dreams of most young graduates entering the workforce.

The following days the new CITIC members were appointed to different departments of the company. There was the business department in charge of investment and trade, the banking department, the personnel department and finally the general office.

Adam's posting was at the planning section of the business department headed by Mr Wang J. Mr Wang's presence on the floor was always palpable. A tall, charming man and clever negotiator, he could always ensure that CITIC came out victorious, even in the nastiest of situations.

The initial monthly salary for all graduates was three hundred RMB, a huge amount compared to their peers in other companies. University professors earned only a third of that.

The planning section was in charge of the company's investment strategy, checking feasibility studies and scrutinising any of the legal issues passing through CITIC.

As a young company, it didn't have enough assets to cover all the investments and purchases that were handled by the different departments.

Therefore one important source for CITIC's initial cash flow was bonds issued on the Japanese market. Thanks to a powerful companion, the Chinese Ministry of Finance, collateral to guarantee the overseas loans was available. The company borrowed heavily in yen-dominated loans from Japan, which were invested into China. Through this mechanism CITIC was able to command huge amounts of foreign currency to purchase equipment, set up joint ventures and restructure promising Chinese companies.

As history would later reveal, laws were often written using a mix of blueprints from European and American legislation, with a touch of Chinese characteristics. Frequently the laws were only suitable for a single case, or a short period of time, and often contained loopholes, which were then eagerly exploited. As the economy grew at breakneck speed, regulations written to address specific problems and situations could have unexpected consequences elsewhere, leading to runaway problems which eventually affected many layers of society.

Following the financial success of CITIC in Beijing, several copy-cat CITICs mushroomed in most of the outlying provinces. As, yet again, money needed to be raised on the international markets to fund the clones, the provincial bureaux of finance backed their local 'CITICs' by scouring for bonds on international markets without formal approval from the Ministry of Finance.

This led the central government to quickly lose control of the country's financial situation, as these international debts pushed down the artificial exchange rate of the RMB. Devaluation became a real risk.

To prevent any deterioration of the country's balance of payments, new investment laws were enacted in the early nineties to stop the wild growth of those international loans. Direct involvement of government bodies in making financial guarantees was no longer allowed. In the meantime, CITIC had been raised into a stable orbit among investment highfliers, while copycats, many of whom had invested in economically suspect projects, came crashing down when the money tap was closed. The collapse of Guangdong's GITIC became a prime consequence of this new law.

Most of Adam's time was spent probing JV contracts and financial leasing agreements written in English and Chinese. Contracts were in English because for some odd reason the Japanese investors held anyone with even the slightest bit of English in high regard. Chinese colleagues who spoke fluent Japanese were not respected and quite often looked down upon, to their initial frustration. This attitude frequently created strange situations as the spoken English of the Japanese delegation members was barely comprehensible, thus keeping their Japanese-English translator busy. To make sure everyone followed the negotiations and kept their face intact, complex sentence structures had to be hashed down into simple legal phrases. With every final negotiation rush, the poor Japanese translators were nearly exhausted, and the CITIC staff took pleasure in keeping them as close to the edge of their seats as possible.

The war of words and psychological mind games never ceased.

The Japanese had this funny superiority complex, and often insinuated that China had not reached their level of sophistication. But the Japanese didn't seem to realise that by putting themselves in an inferior negotiating position, their plans often turned to *kamikaze* missions. Revenge for the World War II occupation had to be taken whenever the occasion presented itself. Being able to work in one's own mother tongue, and having staff members who understood every nuance of Japanese spoken at the table, conferred a huge advantage. Most often this resulted in contracts that were solidly to CITIC's advantage. For all the arrogance displayed by the Japanese it was clear that they considered China a backwater not worth taking seriously. As long as the JV purchased Japanese equipment and a Japanese company had a shareholder's stake, they seemed to be happy.

To Adam and his team none of this really mattered, they were working towards a greater goal: to make sure that the company could turn a healthy profit, and that the Chinese partners could learn fast and position themselves as serious industry contenders in the decade to come. As long as the Japanese brought in production and technology know-how, CITIC employees could live with Japanese prejudices.

Another eccentricity of each new Japanese delegation that entered the CITIC building was the small gifts, mostly electronic gadgets, offered before the initial meeting. At first, unwrapping the presents was an exciting moment. However, as a never-ending stream of Japanese delegations came through Adam's office, the novelty wore off. Involvement in more than one hundred JV projects left its detritus in many staffers' cabinets. The calculators, digital watches, pens and small radios simply collected dust.

Adam and his team's own eccentricity was to invite their corporate guests to the restaurant on the top floor of the CITIC building. At twenty-eight RMB per head the Window on the World served the best Cantonese food in town. Satisfying the stomachs of their honoured guests was a must. . . .

Over the years Adam's company firmly positioned itself as a key player in setting up joint ventures in China. The initial JV laws that were passed through the People's Congress in the early eighties even included a provision that mentioned: 'For any foreign investment in China you may approach CITIC as a partner.' This clause is still valid as of this writing.

In order to profit from the preferential treatment on company taxes, land use, and import-export quotas that was given to overseas investors, an offshore subsidiary became a common tool.

CITIC's investment strategy most often involved a Hong Kong subsidiary together with a local company representing the Chinese party. Sometimes the Japanese company insisted on having CITIC directly involved as well; probably in hopes that a CITIC link would help them cut through red tape.

CITIC's staff were certainly always keen for such arrangements as it encouraged the foreigners to put up hard cash for the honour of using CITIC's local prestige and relationships. As they were talking intangibles, CITIC's value was negotiated case by case. The more one sensed that the foreign partner was insecure in dealing with the Chinese surroundings, the higher the valuation would be. Adam and his colleagues did everything they could to inflate CITIC's value with every passing contract. Depending on the type of project they would sometimes take a minority stake, or for strategic projects like pharmaceuticals, the automotive industry, or aluminium and gold mining the government would make sure CITIC had a majority interest. Finally the local company, which was often starved of cash, invariably provided the land, property and manpower to develop the JV.

Adam continued working with his first employer for another four years, but got fed up with the many headaches the JVs brought him.

As many of the same mistakes and conflicts were repeating themselves again and again, he became disillusioned with the job. Working for and representing one of the shareholders as he did, he was in no position to suggest changes that were in the interest of all shareholders.

In addition, all his hard work never resulted in a salary increase. This got him thinking seriously whether this work environment was the right place to continue developing his professional career.

Luckily, salvation came when CITIC gave some of the legal staff the opportunity to enter a lawyers' exchange programme initiated by the Ministry of Justice and the Law Society in the UK. Without hesitation Adam went to the UK for a period of one year.

Upon his return to the motherland, the vice-chairman of CITIC offered him a job as secretary, but Adam was no longer interested. After five years in a position like that, he could have taken the position of general manager in one of CITIC's numerous subsidiaries, a dream for many CITIC staff.

Hearing he had rejected this opportunity, his colleagues thought he was totally mad.

In the UK, however, my good friend Adam had tasted something special. Something he had never had been able to embrace before: freedom.

'In a sense I was indeed a fool to take such a risk, because I had no guarantees: No house, no career, no salary,' he confided to me. But still the lure of freedom was too sweet to ignore.

Postscript

- China's constitution and the Ministry of Justice were established in 1979.
- Adam's parents are happily retired and still living in the large factory compound in Zhengzhou.
- Xiao Lei never tried his luck in business but is now head of the Liaoning Province fiscal planning committee monitoring the lawful and proper use of the provincial budget.
- Xiao Chen is now head of the purchasing department in the steel factory.
- Over the years Xiao Wang found his job boring and after hearing Adam's tales of Beijing he took a shot at getting a

law degree at Wuhan University. He got his Masters degree but unfortunately it was useless to him, as he didn't know how to apply his newly acquired knowledge. He's still working as an architect in the Liaoning Design Institute.

- Mr Rong Yiren passed away on October 26th, 2005, after a lifelong dedication to the development of the Chinese economy. He once stated: 'As a man who grew up in capitalism and followed socialism for forty years, I learned the truth from experience: Only socialism can save China and only through socialism can China develop.'

- Many of the JVs negotiated in the eighties dissolved as misunderstandings of local market conditions created friction between the different partners.

- In the eighties the Japanese Prime Minister Yasuhiro Nakasone and Prime Minister Noboru Takeshita visited China on several occasions, each time providing generous Japanese government loans to the country. Those soft loans, a kind of 'We're Sorry for What Happened During WWII' gesture, were used for powering many JVs.

- Japanese investors have come a long way. Over 30,000 Japanese companies presently have subsidiaries in China and many can now boast their success. Having been at the forefront of the opening up in China, they learned many costly but invaluable lessons.

- Over 500 weekly flights link China and Japan, and help deepen bilateral exchanges while alleviating mutual suspicion.

- In 2005 CITIC was restructured and many of Adam's old colleagues were fired: Their compensation for fifteen years of loyal service to the company was 100,000 RMB. The stigma of having worked for a state-owned company proved hard to
get rid of, and many haven't found a job after a year of unemployment.

- On the other end of the spectrum, another of Adam's ex-colleagues is now chairman of a merchant bank.

CHAPTER 7

Dotcom delusions

In the 17th century a Chinese official once disdainfully declared: 'Barbarians are a money grabbing lot interested only in buying and selling.'

In the 20th century, Alan Greenspan talked of American investors' 'irrational exuberance' during the dotcom era of the late 90s.

Add these two together, and the result is a rush of fast money entering China; pie-in-the-sky business models; exhilarated predictions that the Mainland would soon be Westernised; and the frantic determination to ride the next great wave.

In the end the message is clear to the average Chinese: The modern day barbarian remains a money-minded creature who takes unnecessary risks.

Beijing, May 19th, 1999

The Chinese capital had already been abuzz for several months with stories about the Internet, and how companies were receiving loads of money to develop their businesses on the web. The new economy was waltzing into China big time, but for me the whole idea was still an abstraction. My business experience was worlds away from those whiz kids who were able to make money with the click of the mouse. The Internet was there to send and receive e-mails, read the newspaper and track couriers. I hadn't seen beyond the obvious.

Adam, however, had already assisted a Chinese Internet company with legal advice on ownership. Governments all over the world have always enjoyed interfering in business, and this was also the case in China. Because the Internet was categorised as belonging to the Ministry of Information, no barbarian was able to directly purchase into Chinese Internet companies. But by setting up offshore structures, combined with exclusivity agreements, Westerners would more or less have a legal cover to protect investments, which ultimately flowed into China.

Apparently this company did pretty well and a couple of months later they were basking in the glory of a multi-million dollar investment. This 'hit the jackpot' incident provided added incentive to look into the matter more closely, and that's how we ended up being part of the dotcom mania.

The largest Chinese cities were alight with website advertisements. Where before washing powder, soft drinks, instant noodles and cosmetics once called for attention on buses and billboards, now those traditional products were crowded out by the latest fad: websites. They screamed from every corner of the street, were plastered over every public vehicle and had even crept into prime-time TV ads. Most carried no message of need or desire. Name recognition was the only goal.

Often the measure of success was simply how many eyeballs were glued to the website, where the mouse was clicked, how long one's brain trotted around on a webpage. How revenues were to be created were worries for later.

Hong Kong, the traditional stepping-stone into China, was already far ahead in cyberspace, thanks to its sophisticated telecommunication infrastructure and reliable financial and legal environment. The obvious next step was to explore its neighbour with a billion-plus inhabitants. Critical mass would be easier to achieve in China than any other country on earth. All the investors and website owners were daydreaming: 'If all those people started clicking away en masse on my website, surely there would be some way to make loads of money.'

This was a new world where bricks and mortar businesses would have to adapt to the new economy or be flushed away along with Keynes's theories. Name branding and availability of fresh, ever-expanding content was key to getting people to visit a site. The only way to sustain this business model was to have an army of creative staff generating content, and to continuously spend money on splashing cities full of advertisements. Investors hoped this would create a loyal user base willing to click on ads or spend money at a later stage.

Most members of China's web generation were enthusiastic young people with overseas university degrees. Bright and full of ideas, having witnessed first-hand in the States how the Internet had developed from a simple tool into a sophisticated device, they were eager to dip into this multi-billion dollar business.

Initially we started attending seminars and discussion groups on the subject. It wasn't difficult, as each week brought a host of such meetings held in five-star hotels. Taking part was utterly confusing, to say the least. It was like learning a whole new language: B2B, thumbnail, B2C, 600-pound gorilla, NDA, pay-per-click, C2C, virtual sales networks, 3G, angel investors, 2.5G, VC, hosts, PPP, spam, URL, Y2K, Web ratings, XML, ASP, virtual CEO, USP. . . . It was a never-ending torrent of Internet vernacular we were totally unfamiliar with. The in-crowd at those seminars spoke in the same cryptic codes. They would nod at each other and reply in this strange lingua franca of the Internet. Having no idea what those guys were up to or talking about, we felt a bit like Dumb and Dumber, completely lost in this brave new world. But that didn't prevent me from opening an Internet stock trading account, hoping to make a killing on the NASDAQ.

Meanwhile, the letters V and C formed the expression that was most electrifying of all. Young entrepreneurs would often beat their chests and claim 'I'm in discussion with several VCs for my business plan, and hope to finalise an agreement with them soon.' Others were gazing into a crystal ball: 'I'll only disclose the plan for my website after I've met a VC worth my time and he's signed an NDA.'

I came away with the impression that this 'VC' had to be something really special, but I hadn't figured out what it actually was. Man or Machine?

In my mind the 'VC' were proud Vietnamese farmers, the Vietcong who emerged victorious from the war against the US. We'd never heard of any other type of VC. . . .

So, during one seminar, it was with a certain chagrin that I had to ask a twenty-something sitting next to me, 'What's a vc...?' After staring at me with a shrewd smile that said 'I know it all, you little lamebrain', he leaned over and whispered in my ear. 'Those are the guys with lots of cash! They put millions in a company and can make you rich very quick.'

'Oh Venture Capitalists, that's what "vc" is all about.' It took a few more uncomfortable question-and-answer sessions to get used to speaking in contractions instead of full words. All those acronyms certainly made everything sound cooler, less like stuffy boardroom talk. Once we were more fluent with the letter-codes, the time had come to peer over the horizon, trying to imagine how we could make a buck out of this. With no Internet experience and no idea how to program a computer, we couldn't dream up any of those bright ideas that could create magic and money. We knew nothing but boring old economy stuff. But at least the acronyms were mastered! At the very least we could pretend to be knowledgeable Internet addicts.

As we met more Internet devotees, our radar scanned deeper into the Internet environment. They seemed to be constantly searching for vc. It felt a bit like Forrest Gump always hunting for Charlie in the Vietnam jungle. We came to the conclusion that vc sessions were the shortcut to getting our share of the dough, and so began our hunt for a vc of our own. These guys were not the stuffy archetype of bankers in their black tailored suits. Thirty-something, hip, casually dressed, some even with long hair, for heaven's sake.... All enthusiastically speaking the same vernacular and yammering on about young Internet entrepreneurs they had already turned into multi-millionaires. Who didn't want to hear that kind of sweet story? And it could happen to any of us. If that wasn't enough incentive, the lavish parties that were held afterwards certainly ensured we'd remember the event. Never have I drunk so much champagne or eaten so much goose liver paté as during those sessions. Personally I certainly had something to celebrate, as my stock portfolio on the NASDAQ had increased over 40 percent in three months' time.

By the middle of '99 several Chinese Internet companies had made it to the overseas stock markets, and additional VCs were pouring into China by the dozen every week, providing more speeches and extravagant parties. VCs gazed from podiums or stood surrounded by eager people hanging on their every word. VCs were treated like rock stars and could always be sure of a dedicated following of hundreds of Internet entrepreneurs wherever they went. 'I'm a VC' became the easiest pick up line in China, and some could boast of having groupies.

Most of the discussions centred around business plans, which initially sounded weird. Why would a VC fly thousands of kilometres to talk about the basics of business? Then it quickly occurred to us that many fresh graduates had bright ideas but often no clue what business was all about. VCs needed some 'hard' facts or at least something to evaluate where revenue would eventually come from, how Internet traffic would be generated and where the investments would be utilised.

So it became clear that presenting ourselves as business-plan writers could ensure us a piece of the pie.

To avoid entanglement in Big Brother's web of ever changing rules and regulations, rather unorthodox company structures had to be set up. So we correctly assumed that VCs, sitting down with those dotcom owners, wanted to be sure that their investment in China had legal protection. Here, also, a piece of the action was up for grabs.

As was the case in the States, most of the Internet companies drew their vitality from the unbridled imagination and brainpower of university students. Thinking that our pool of customers would also be found sitting behind study desks, we plastered Tsinghua, Beida and Normal University with leaflets explaining our services. One week later nobody had picked up the phone and called for help, except for a couple of foreign students looking for a job. This channel was a dead end, as most Chinese students were too focused on their year-end exams. So our quest brought us back to the fertile hunting fields of the VCs. During discussion breaks we touted our new business and to our initial surprise a throng of people surrounded us. . . . For a brief moment I thought they had confused us for VCs. Luckily Adam presented himself as a lawyer and pretty quickly emotions cooled down to less tropical levels. Nonetheless a torrent of questions was unleashed from all directions: 'Do you know VC...? What are your references? How much do you charge for your services? When can you visit our offices? Would you be interested in our B2B platform that organises the sales of raw material?' And so on.

It was simply impossible to answer any of the questions without being interrupted by another eager would-be millionaire. Even the VC organiser came to see what all the commotion was about. Never having seen so much enthusiasm for our services, we thought we had already landed in the new economy. Customers falling from the heavens like fruit ripe for the picking. This was the bounty of the new and exponentially growing economy.

Eventually we traded name cards with all the Internet aficionados present.

The same frenzied scene unfolded during VC seminars in the following days and weeks. Each time we got in touch with people we thought were promising and invited them to our office to explain what their Internet business was all about.

Unfortunately, grasping their brainchild wasn't always that simple. Some were so fixated on technical descriptions we couldn't follow their ideas, and others had very flimsy concepts of how revenue would be generated. Writing a business plan for something we didn't understand was impossible. For the others, we could assist them with legal issues and write a plan that VCs might fall in love with. The topic of compensation soon became the next burning issue, as most of those dotcommers had no money to spend on us. Everything had been dropped on servers and salaries for the worker-bees ticking away at keyboards all day long. It became obvious that the only way we could be part of the new economy was by becoming shareholders in their company, crossing our fingers that a VC would be interested, and cashing out later. So only the start-ups which already had a legal structure or who were willing to pay for our legal services to set up a company were appealing targets. Not being compensated for organising the company and attracting a VC created a thorny issue, as now we had to be extra careful not to bet on the wrong horse. Instead of just making business plans, our time was spent looking more closely into the business, and also who the people really were. Did they have the talent to run a company? Were they gifted enough to deliver on their technical promises?

As time crawled by, we were sucked deeper and deeper into the www maelstrom. Our company became more entrenched than we'd intended. We clung to the hope of getting something out of it – it was close to playing Russian roulette. But it was a time of lunacy, and all bets were off. It was now or never.

From what was happening in the US we learned that only the ideas which materialised first would become winners. There was no second or third place. The winner would take all. Those who copied what had already been successful in the Chinese market were rejected right away.

Meanwhile my trading account continued its relentless growth as I slept. I really thought I had already become a NASDAQ trading expert. Each time I logged onto my account, I found my portfolio had grown. Therefore I poured more dollars in at every session, hoping to drive things up to supersonic speed.

By day, understanding our potential customers came close to a full-time operation. Checking up on their backgrounds and identifying the potential value of their business models absorbed much of my energy. Eventually the whole operation started to seriously affect other business activities. So we decided to stop wasting time, and bet on a couple of dotties we thought would be able to provide a return on time invested.

The next hurdle was negotiating a share in each of those companies, as every entrepreneur already thought he/she was a budding multi-millionaire. This turned out to be a major stumbling block: No one was willing to part with a substantial amount of shares from their micro empire in return for our services. Taking into account that these organisations were in the initial stages of development, we knew we were taking an enormous risk. Tomorrow could always bring total failure. Therefore we stubbornly held to our minimum target of 25 percent of the company, and wouldn't lift a finger for less.

Many heated debates were required to finally build up a collection of Chinese entrepreneurs who were willing to accept these conditions.

Our so-called portfolio consisted of one platform that would unite all the Chinese measurement and automation equipment makers, another for building a genealogy database so that a family tree could be generated for one's Chinese ancestors, another that focused on young, urban women's issues, and lastly one for creating software applications for mobile phones that could up- and download data via the Internet.

Luckily each of those companies already had their own staff, often operating out of someone's apartment.

Making the business plan was the easy part. More challenging was being a gun for hire trying to manage 'investments' in this myriad of companies. Many of the co-owners had huge egos and often our work consisted of dousing fires caused by personality clashes. Part-time psychiatrists, part-time business partners, we kept our distance from the creative end. But we felt that adding a bit of business order to the organisation was our best bet for attracting the attention of VC. The accounting was one area that, to an outsider, looked like a total mess. It was a mix of company assets, family loans, privately owned computers, purchases without VAT, tables and chairs borrowed from friends, an uncle's office space. . . . Although we owned a share in the company, in reality it was not always clear what was an asset, what was a liability and what was just on temporary free lease. The server could have disappeared the next day because someone else needed it. But I didn't worry too much: This was the dawn of the new economy and once VC dollars began flowing in, we'd be able to start with a clean slate.

While we nursed our babies, China became awash with capital. The reverberations of Chinese dotcom companies hitting the stock market had spread all over the world. No self-respecting VC could pretend to be uninterested in China.

Every time a Chinese company had an overseas IPO, more money came pouring in. Ultimately it became a tsunami of dollars chasing fewer and fewer opportunities. At a certain point in time one had only to utter the word 'dotcom' and a throng of VCs encircled their prey. At this stage most of the Chinese dotcoms still up for grabs were knee-deep in the pre-revenue stage, or had very flimsy business plans. None of the businesses we were assisting made any substantial revenue except for some ads that appeared on their websites. One crucial step remained beyond our reach: generating enough cash to make each of the companies self-sustainable. All were bleeding their meagre reserves of RMB with no way to stanch the flow. To our surprise, the VCs weren't bothered by this little detail. 'New economy. All rules of common sense are off.' I heard this half in disbelief, half in faith in all things new. Each night my trading account was reaching a new crest, and here cash wasn't an issue at all. In five months that account had made more money than I could earn in three years.

Some VCs hadn't even been worth the label a few months earlier, but they thought it would be a smart idea to jump on the Internet gravy train too. Thus high-risk funds were created with generous donations from private investors who were willing to gamble with their money. To us, the most interesting VCs were those without offices in China. Those were the ones with zero understanding of what China was about. They flew over determined to spend money before reboarding the plane. They had no idea about local Internet conditions, Chinese customer behaviour, or the average Internet user's profile, and didn't realise that credit card penetration was close to zero. Walking off the plane and into a limo waiting at the Beijing airport, they'd end up in a five-star hotel suite and spend their time in the conference rooms, eat in the Western hotel restaurants, watch CNN and go to sleep with the thought that China was not that much different from the West. Being completely insulated from the real China, those VCs equated China's Internet awareness with that in their own country. We considered them to be the easiest prey, most willing to part with their money. One only had to look in the trade magazines to learn when another busload of those 'would-be China VCs' would be touring through Beijing, and put our strategy into action. Our date with the devil was set.

In the meantime we crafted a plan to revamp the companies under our wing with a sexier look. The operation was nicknamed 'Moneytron' after an illustrious sponsor of the now defunct Onyx

Formula 1 team. Offshore structures were established and interdependency contracts were inked with our Chinese Internet companies so the VCs could invest with peace of mind. To stand out from the crowd, basic guerrilla marketing techniques were taken out of storage.

Three weeks before the arrival of our potential targets, we sent them lofty e-mails about our stable of dotcommers – their domain names and business models – and asked if they'd be interested in meeting the team during their whirlwind tour. Within twenty-four hours nine VCs had responded requesting more specifics about those companies. We sent them the sexiest business plans, with bloated revenue streams, exponential customer growth and frugal plans for spending money on staff, equipment and advertisement. All in all a cost-conscious and result-oriented plan. The women's website and the measurement and automation platform seemed to generate the most interest. Why those two, we never really knew. Soon our agenda was chock full of meetings at which we'd impress our unwitting hosts during the conference.

With so much at stake with this fund-raising game, all our partners' contacts were drawn into the mix. Our aim was to show some of our stallions' names in the newspapers and maybe on the sides of buses. Lack of funds meant we had to generate maximum exposure to impress VCs with a minimum amount of money burned.

Getting positive coverage about our dotcommers in the news was the easy bit. As journalists are plentiful in China, it wasn't particularly difficult to hook up with one. As is customary, we asked a friendly journalist at a main local magazine to write about us for a fee. A red envelope was exchanged after a dinner party and in return a lofty story hit the newsstands on the date of our choosing. Just to make sure we didn't end up in the wrong section of the magazine, most of the content was written by our side.

Buckets of RMB would be necessary to buy bus billboards for any period of time. None of the companies had that much cash, let alone the desire to spend it on this kind of advertising. Anyway, space was already blocked solid for months to come on all the buses that puffed around Beijing. There was no way we could have arranged for ads during the meetings with the VC. It was the insider spirit that would curry us favour, China style.

The young and elegant Ms Lin, the main partner for the women's website, knew an employee of the city public transport, and this person in turn was acquainted with some of the staff who dealt with advertising. Countless discussions, meetings, dinners, telephone calls and one *karaoke* session later, we had a verbal promise that something would happen. Knowing at which hotel the VC convention was to be taking place, we could easily identify which bus lines passed in front of the hotel, and thus which buses to target for advertisements.

The printing of the ad on a special plastic sheet had to be paid for at cost. Within one week our giant sticker bearing the women's issues website was ready to be flashed. A helping hand got the ad stuck on a spare bus that would be taken out for a spin past the hotel . . . again on a date of our choosing.

Emboldened by our recently acquired marketing artillery, we felt even more could be added to our arsenal of image 'beautification'.

The missing piece wasn't that hard to spot.

Opposite the hotel were a couple of bus shelters that could be put to good use for advertising our dotcom sites. Through our advertisement contacts, we probed the next revolutionary opportunities available to advance our campaign. But the feedback was negative: 'Too risky! There are other dotcom people who keep track of their ads all the time. It would be impossible to replace those just before the conference.'

The alternative was to foot the bill for a minimum of thirty locations scattered all over the city for weeks on end. We came to the conclusion that purchasing space on small billboards was out of the question, unless . . . there was an opportunity to go through the back door. There was – with another red envelope – and we got our flashy billboard exclusively on a bus shelter right next to our office. Although the location was not close to the conference, it wouldn't be too hard to lure the VCs out of their posh environment, or so we hoped. Bringing them out into the open might impress them after all.

In the meantime, at night, I was huddled in front of the money shrine, staring in amazement as my trading account grew by the day. I felt like a genius, having bought into those Internet companies and making money in my sleep. Figuring that I could outsmart the markets I went for margin trading, using my broker's money for a little fee to make more money! 'Guerrilla tactics on the NASDAQ' I smirked.

On a dreary rain-and-fog-filled Wednesday morning, the VC circus went into full swing. The hotel was bustling with activity. One area of the building was dedicated to an exhibition where glossy website brochures were distributed by the kilo. For the sake of impressing VCs, whole forests were laid to rest. By the end of the day the paper collectors on their tricycles were feasting on the piles of gloss. At least our guerrilla strategy was a little more ecologically friendly.

In the convention hall e-HR managers were promoting the benefits of share options as a sure way to keep the best programmers plugging away at their keyboards eighteen hours a day. The e-finance managers talked about their surefire business plan to convince VCs to leave their dollars on the table.

In the meantime our public transport bus and its advertisement was plying the road in front of the conference. Unfortunately, it wasn't really a public transport bus any longer. The vehicle turned out to be one of those retired buses still in use by the transportation company to pick up customers who were stranded when one of their regular people-haulers broke down. The thing made a hell of a noise and at a maximum speed of forty kilometres per hour left behind a trail of grey-blue-black smoke. The lone customer sitting in the bus was one of our guys, to instruct the bus driver when it was the right time to pass in front of the hotel. Or to give his position in case we wanted to walk out of the hotel with some VC. But it didn't look authentic enough with no one sitting on the bus. So for good measure we quickly decided to pay some grannies and retired city seniors to sit in the bus from 8 AM to 5 PM, providing snacks, hot food and drinks at regular intervals. They loved it!

A world away, the speeches of VCs had advanced to cloud nine. They spoke in superlatives: 'China is the final frontier for the world wide web'; 'With its immense human resources, this country has a huge potential to leapfrog into the new economy'; 'As China gets wired to the world, the world gathers here to connect into China'; 'Imagine what 1.3 billion customers could mean for the Internet community'.

In a country where slogans are a staple part of life, it didn't have much effect. The masses wanted to hear success stories and how to emulate them.

They weren't disappointed. During panel discussions VCs brought out the co-owners of the companies they invested in, showing them off as their most prized possessions. The 'wannabe millionaire' crowd was staring at them in awe, hanging on their every word, hoping they'd reveal the secret to getting a VC to pay for a 'get rich quick' scheme.

Afterwards, both VCs and the successful dotcommers were mobbed like rock stars. Everybody wanted to rub shoulders with them in the hope that some of this success potion would drip their way.

When a judgmental journalist asked a superstar VC if this entire obsession with the Internet wasn't just a bubble ready to burst, the crowd laughed the poor guy away as 'old economy'. The PR-hungry VC gave it an academic twist but the end result was the same: Anyone who didn't jump on the China bandwagon now would be a loser of catastrophic proportions.

Operation 'Moneytron' was jump-started that very day at 2 PM. Our first VC caught in the net of deception was Jonathan, a smart, socially-engaged British lad in his early thirties who had a particular interest in this women's website. He thought it was a revolutionary idea to launch such a portal in China. Once he'd read the business plan we chit-chatted on the sidelines of the conference, and after a while he agreed to spend some more time with us to better understand the business and meet the team. Our plan to get him to visit our offices was effectively quashed when time constraints kept him inside. Competing dotcommers were vying for his attention.

So we settled for one of the rooms that had been made available to discuss business. The meeting didn't turn out as we had anticipated either – the VC was brainier than we thought. His specific technical questions on how to run the operations using server capacity, cables, software, bandwidth and god knows what else caught us completely off guard. Our technical wizards could explain, but that couldn't be translated into a specific business strategy, or revenue. Even Ms Lin's sexy presence couldn't turn the tide. We were damaged goods before we could explain ourselves. Our lesson learned, we moved on to the next VC chapter.

This was a Singaporean VC representing a government fund. Mr Kwok was an atypical VC in our experience. In his late forties, balding, wearing thick glasses and a pinstriped Wall Street business uniform, he wasn't what I thought of as part of the Internet 'in' crowd. During presentations for both our Internet sites, we very quickly noticed that he was new to the game. Internet business was a novel thing, and his superiors had asked him to investigate. The Internet vernacular we were used to was still alien to him. But he had taken the time to dissect both our business plans and come up with some stuffy questions about tax issues. . . . He wanted to know about this because US Internet businesses didn't have to collect VAT on their delivered e-services. What was the position of the tax authorities in China? As the Chinese government itself was still grappling with the situation, much of Internet business was in a grey zone. How to explain to an orderly Singaporean that his question was irrelevant at this moment in time, and that we'd know as soon as everyone else did when the ever-changing rules would be promulgated? The question was skirted with the explanation that our business plan was in line with present accounting rules.

As the discussions returned to more familiar business territory, it seemed this VC was showing more and more interest in the automation business. Mr Zhang, a sturdy forty-something engineer who had come up with the idea for the website, got really excited when he realised he might be on track to win. Mr Zhang enthusiastically explained the benefits of his website to the Singaporean.

'Our web might finally ensnare one VC' I quietly exulted. Moneytron was working.

Ms Lin meanwhile received an alarming telephone call from the bus. She gave me a discreet signal to leave the room and presented me with a troubling situation. 'Apparently the police noticed the vehicle roaming around with all those seniors on board and ordered it to stop. What should we do?' she whispered to me. Her words were barely out of her mouth when another call came in. 'Could someone quickly come over and explain the situation? The bus driver might be arrested. . . .'

'This one could quickly spin out of control and get us all in trouble. Can you do something?' Ms Lin was implying that I should solve the problem. 'A *laowai* might have a soothing effect on the situation.' As she spoke she gave me a puppy-look of despair.

Dealing with the police was not part of my plans for that day. But options were limited. 'Risk major problems later and continue to court the vcs,' or 'lose out on this once-in-a-lifetime meeting while addressing the police issue.' As we were pondering our choices we knew that ignoring the problem would simply produce a time bomb that would explode in the future. So the barbarian broke down and went out to douse this most pressing fire.

Approaching by taxi I could see the bus from a distance, blocked by a police van with flashing blue and red lights. The bus driver was in fierce discussion with two policemen, while another checked the IDs of the bus passengers. The whole event was attended by hundreds of onlookers giving their usual comments and interpretations.

Breaking through the crowd, Ms Lin's employee spotted me right away and gave me a quick update of the situation. 'This is a public bus without a proper route number. Because it never halted at any bus stop and kept driving along the same road it drew the suspicion of the officers.' Seconds later I was surrounded by the men in blue asking me why a barbarian was standing there amid all the commotion.

'Are you one of those journalists? Do you have a licence?' they aggressively inquired. A barbarian had entered the scene: the crowd was pleased with this unexpected turn of events and became visibly more agitated. The whispers turned into louder voices. While onlookers shouted 'helpful' remarks to the police, another police van with blaring sirens arrived on the scene, slowly driving through the crowd in order to disperse them. Within minutes a police cordon was established. In the bus the grannies stared at me while munching on some oranges. The bus driver had no clue who I was but was clearly relieved that I was acting like a lightning rod to draw the policemen's attention. I trembled as I wondered what was to come next. Three policemen took me aside and pressed for information.

'Actually I asked this bus driver to drive around for us. This is a publicity stunt for the Internet exhibition at the hotel a bit further down the road,' I stammered. 'The people on the bus are paid to sit there. They're part of this advertisement campaign.'

After listening to my story a couple of times and ascertaining that I wasn't a journalist, they loosened up. I wasn't that evil after all. The grannies were ordered to get off and go about their business. The bus driver's details were written down and I was taken into the police van.

Ms Lin's employee quietly disappeared. From the van I could see the driver arguing again, pointing at me and pleading with the police. Half an hour later he disappeared with his smoky bus into the Beijing rush hour. Hopefully he was off the hook.

My ordeal was still ahead of me. Sitting in the van, I was pondering whether the money fever was really worth all the hassle. When my turn came, I was again asked a multitude of questions as if I'd built up defences they needed to break through. Another hour of discussions was necessary before the three officers confronting me seemed satisfied with my arguments. I was finally asked to write a self-criticism and promise never again to assemble any group of people without formal approval. Then came another round of discussions as I could only write it in English. My handwritten Chinese looked like that of a seven-year-old, not to mention that I tended to make many *biwu* or 'spelling' mistakes when I wrote Chinese characters. On this one I wasn't willing to lose face.

In the end we compromised: a friend would translate my text into Chinese and I would hand-copy the Chinese text. The following day, my nicely written self-denunciation in hand, I arrived at the station in charge of my case. One of the policemen who had been on site the day earlier got all excited and introduced me to his fellow colleagues. Apparently the bus story had made the rounds, and all smiled and shook hands before continuing with a serious reprimand for my misconduct. Handing over the papers, I was once again warned not to encourage disorderly behaviour in public places.

Finally off the hook, I asked Ms Lin to tell her contacts at the bus company to keep the vehicle inside. The guerrilla team had lost one of its weapons but the war was far from over. Moneytron would limp to victory, one way or the other.

The second day of the conference was already well underway, and our VC meetings had already kicked off by the time I joined them in one of the meeting rooms.

The VC was from Silicon Valley. What I didn't know when I sat down at the table: While I was being cross-examined by the officers the day before, Mr Zhang and Ms Lin had gotten into an argument after Mr Zhang sneered at the women's website in the presence of the Singaporean VC. Our friends had apparently become foes, and the dust hadn't settled yet.

As Mr Zhang and team weren't fluent in English, he was being sidelined by the Lin camp who spoke English to perfection.

Minutes after joining in I could see the tension buzzing through the conversation. When the VC asked Mr Zhang a question, Ms Lin's staff would reply for him without bothering to translate. And if Mr Zhang said something they'd translate it poorly, making sure he came out looking bad. I innocently intervened to explain to the VC what had actually been said, which touched the spark to the powder keg. Mr Zhang, realising he was being misrepresented, insulted Ms Lin's staff. In no time both parties were openly rebuking each other. The VC, flabbergasted by the sudden squall of high-pitched Chinese voices, stared in disbelief at the theatrical squabble unfolding in front of him. Beijing opera it was not. There was little more that could be said, literally or figuratively. Once past the initial surprise, he shook hands with me and walked out with a smile, leaving Ms Li and Mr Zhang to continue screaming at the top of their lungs.

Another day, another disaster at the office.

In hindsight it hadn't been the smartest choice to have people with competing and diverse interests negotiating together in one room. Bad blood was bound to arise. Future VC meetings would be held with the cats and dogs separated to avoid cross-fertilisation of the worst kind.

While we were trying to put our house in order, the place was buzzing with stories of VCs making deals with other dotcommers. Corrective action was required ASAP or we'd leave empty handed and would have to wait for the next circus to come to town.

That afternoon was spent browsing through a whole collection of American VCs. Some of them had clearly been hit by culture shock; others were convinced that their short stay in the Middle Kingdom had turned them into China specialists. With each 'ni hao' that came from their mouth, Mr Zhang and Ms Lin smothered them with praise. As long as they were willing to part with their cash, we'd be willing to praise them to the imperial heavens.

One of the next VCs to sit at the table seemed to have walked straight off the set of *Baywatch*. Mike was a tall athletic guy in his early thirties, with curly blond hair, a suntan and beaming smile. One might easily wonder if he'd attended the wrong conference. Hearing Mr Zhang's exposition, he started to warm up. The numbers seemed to fit; he was convinced that the business model might actually work. Mr Zhang walked out of the meeting room convinced he had nailed the deal. Next up was Ms Lin who, with her charming looks and well-oiled presentation, raised his interest one notch higher. His wide range of questions were all answered to his satisfaction. At the very end, Mike insisted on a one-on-one talk with me. It suddenly dawned on me that at long last we might have a case. 'Having met all these companies in the last couple of days, I'm starting to get a pretty good picture of the situation here in China. My problem with these two presentations is that they either lack business experience or have no commercial sense of how to turn their plan into reality. In addition, our company normally doesn't do first-round investments. If you stay on, we might have an interest.'

Fed up with working for bollocks, I said, 'Only if I'm getting paid decently. Without that I've no interest.'

'OK. That's understood,' came the cold reply. Mike stood up, gave me a pat on the back and walked out.

What the hell did this mean? Was this a yes, a no or a maybe?

The rest of the evening was spent pondering his words. Had I interpreted him correctly? Was he willing to invest? Had I made a mistake by not offering to work for free?

That night it was time to kowtow in front of the money shrine. On the screen flashed a dollar number not far from the million mark. I couldn't really believe this was my account. Logging out, I logged back in straight away. The amount was still the same. . . . So this was my account after all. Over the last week it had received an overdose of testosterone. 'Yabba-dabba-doo!' was an understatement.

Around 11 PM a call came in on my cell phone. It was Mike, with an urgent question on his mind. My heart ticked a couple of beats faster in my throat. Was this the moment of truth?

'Hi Jack, would you have any idea where I can buy some cocaine? I've been to some of the discos but there's nothing I can find.'

'Shit,' I thought to myself. 'How the heck can I please him with this kind of Wall Street craving?'

'I'll come over. Where are you?'

In one of the mega-discos of Beijing I found our VC Mike at the bar surrounded by a number of long-legged glamour girls sipping cocktails. Beijing by night is never dull, with the disco beat pounding until the wee hours. Above the pulsating bass rhythm I shouted in his ear that I only knew of hash, but that it might be hard to get so late at night. 'Okay sounds great to me! Let's go. . . .' This was followed by a broad smile.

The open-air charcoal grilling stations run by Uighurs were known for hashish. But at this time of the evening I wasn't sure they'd still be open and loaded.

Mike, myself, and one extremely sexy glamour girl were on the road in search of something to open the guarded gates of the endless mind. With *Wish You Were Here* playing in the background, the car carried us through the desolate streets of Beijing. Some red and green neon lights to the left and right still advertised their wares well past bedtime. We passed some places where charcoal grills would be operating; most were gone but in a stroke of luck, I saw one guy still spinning lamb skewers under a dim naked light bulb.

A couple of minutes later, Mike was busy rolling a joint and sharing it with his glamour girl while I munched on a lamb skewer.

The car slowly filled with the sweet aroma of burning oils and resins. Pink Floyd was our guiding light. We were sailing through a storm of neon warps. Number 9 was at my right.

The next morning – the last day of the conference – our 'news' article came out. It covered a good part of a quarter page in the economics section and rambled on about the stallions in our stable that were ready to enter the home stretch, forever changing the Chinese Internet playing field.

Was this the attention-grabber we were desperately looking for?

When I walked into the main conference area, I was immediately grabbed by one of the VCs we'd met a day earlier. 'Would it be possible to have a meeting now?' he asked.

As we stood there I spotted Ms Lin out of the corner of my eye, surrounded by three other VCs. Mr Zhang tapped my shoulder, asking me to join him in a brief discussion with yet another VC. Help! VCs were encircling us. At long last we had caught their attention. The power of the written word had made the difference.

Spaced-out Mike was nowhere to be seen. Probably still hitch-hiking through la-la-land.

How, in such a short time span, could we channel so much VC power to our advantage?

We decided that the best course of action was to hold 'intimate' discussions in our office so as to create a bit of a distance from the competing conference participants.

This was good thinking indeed because all the interest had pushed Mr Zhang and Ms Lin's discord to a peak. Once real money opportunities seemed to be surfacing, jealousy, intrigue and deceit bubbled up close behind. Not wanting the earlier scene to be re-enacted, we set up a schedule with six VCs willing to stray from the familiar confines of the hotel.

While we were on the way out I saw Mike with a droopy face walking straight towards us.

'Jack we've decided to invest in the women's website. We need to sit down to discuss the details!'

'Hi Mike, this is Ground Control, have you commenced your descent?' I joked, but he seemed cold sober already. Despite that he couldn't refrain from whispering *'Cannabis Libertad!'* in my ear. A real pro.

And thus our fairytale began.

In an office far, far away, VCs came and went. They haggled, bickered and squabbled. Contracts were scrutinised, drafts rephrased, translated and approved. Holding structures in exotic locales were portioned out and cut in pieces like birthday cakes. Eventually hands were shaken and . . . hugs exchanged. The IPOs were set for within two years.

I remained on board for our share and a salary was allotted. We now were one big family.

For the record, nobody seemed to have noticed our ad on the billboard in front of our office.

Finally we'd made off with some crumbs of the VCs' cash reserves. The valuations they came up with were more than we could ever have imagined. Surprisingly enough, the VCs were convinced as easy as ABC, with the least expenditure of effort. Nobody looked any deeper than the people and papers they were presented with. Our unique selling proposition was all that counted. Who cared how the business worked and if our strategy was the right one? Money for nothing seemed to be a shatterproof part of the new economy.

In the end both companies made off with over seven hundred thousand dollars each, which, if everything worked as planned, would be boosted with another cash injection at an even higher valuation eight months down the road. Our 'angel' investors were actually thinking about a return on investment in the range of eight to ten times their initial deposit.

My trading account, continuously fed with the new vein of cash combined with margin trades, swooshed past the one million mark.

Over the following couple of months our dotcoms grew dramatically in size: the latest fads in servers and software, designer chairs and cool office tables were acquired. Employees were hired by the dozen, and left at the slightest hint that a competing dotcommer would provide a better incentive. We were all running our lives at full speed, working seventy-plus hour weeks and partying like animals. The allocated money arrived in the company accounts at regular intervals as milestones were reached. We knew we were going places!

During that time everything seemed to go our way, except for some minor hiccups:

The office building where Mr Zhang was based experienced occasional loss of Internet access. Fibre-optic cables would mysteriously disappear. The problem was only solved when a clearly visible note was placed on them: *This cable contains no copper: Please don't steal!*

In the meantime, outside our office walls, Beijing was preparing to impress the International Olympic Committee with some guerrilla marketing techniques of its own. The city grass, turned yellow in the winter cold, was spray-painted green along major roads. Colourful plastic flowers decorated the cold streets. Building walls that would come in view of the committee members received a fresh lick of dark-grey paint. Driving along the 'official route' in the opposite direction, one could see dreary dull walls alternate with painted ones.

A couple of months later our initial VC guys introduced new VC candidates who were gearing up for the second round. We were going to see the end of the dark snaky tunnel I had plunged into. The dividend was in sight; the exit strategy was finally around the corner. We would at last be able to cash in our shares and put ourselves out of our misery.

Then one day, logging onto my trading account, I noticed something odd. The value hadn't grown. Some of the companies in my trading basket were heading downhill. But others had kept up – all in all only a 5 percent loss. I wasn't too worried, as everybody knew that stocks may go up as well as down. But I had obviously forgotten the rest of that tune: 'Past performance is no guarantee of future results.'

Three days later a margin call from my broker came in. I urgently needed to sell some stocks to bring my account back to a minimum maintenance level.

So I duly chose a couple of stocks to sell into cyberspace. My computer sent my passwords over the 33.6 kb/s modem, and waited for the trade to go ahead. Usually it would take roughly one minute to get into the system, as the encryption used for security crunched numbers through a pretty complex algorithm. But this time it seemed as if every buyer and seller on the NASDAQ had had the same idea. The servers in the States seemed overwhelmed. That night I didn't receive the handshake of bits and bytes that would allow my trade. I didn't worry too much as I'd be able to get online once New York was sound asleep the following morning.

The next day, logging onto my account, I got an enormous shock looking at my basket of shares. The broker had sold my workhorses like Amazon and Yahoo, leaving me the message: 'As no heed was given to our warning to maintain a minimum level, we were forced to sell on your behalf, blah blah blah. . . .'

I was left with the likes of Webvan, eToys and Excite.

Again I didn't worry too much and would make up for my loss with future trades. We were part of the brave new world. Weren't we?

We continued working the long hours, preparing ourselves for the second round of investment. The trips the VCs were planning to China had already been postponed twice, but that wasn't too worrying. Those guys certainly had a hectic schedule and would make some time to fly over soon. Everybody seemed too busy to realise that in Beijing, VC forums had already disappeared from the landscape and the expensive champagne parties were only a distant memory. What was happening on the stock market at the other side of the Pacific seemed completely detached from our own activities. But at a certain moment things came to a head.

Ms Lin and Mr Zhang became nervous as cash was running out rapidly and they might have to lay off people. On top of that they'd made promissory notes to family members for shares in return for their cash.

That day, after trying to reach our angel VC, I knew something was wrong. Normally they were always available, but now my calls were deflected at all times of the day.

At long last I had to admit that there was an embargo against our calls. The VC didn't seem interested any longer in our labours.

Our fairytale quickly spun out of control and headed straight into a nightmare.

In the weeks that followed our people were laid off one after the other. Then bills could no longer be paid: this was the end. All our sweat and efforts had been in vain. Our offshore shares could finally be put to good use: as wallpaper to decorate our rooms. Apparently . . . the bricks and mortar economy was back.

Somewhere else in cyberspace I was fighting my own financial loss. A couple of margin calls later, my basket of shares read like a casualty list of the dotcom companies. Basically all value had evaporated.

It was a time when everyone had thought they were on the way to retirement at age thirty-five. The whole experience was one of joy and playfulness, as long as the champagne kept on bubbling. The feeling certainly was incredible with plenty of advisors and boiler rooms spreading the gospel of get-rich-quick.

In the end I was just another victim of the financial vanity act that had rippled through the world.

Postscript

- The person who helped us with the bus received a bonus from his company, because he'd been able to sell ads even on that particular worn-out vehicle.
- When the next bubble hits the markets, some fools will still believe that 'this time will be different. . . .'
- VCs are back in China in droves. This time they're investing mostly in Chinese bricks and mortar companies.
- In 2006, over one billion euros in venture capital was invested in China. 2012 saw hungry VC invest 3.7 billion USD. That was down from 2011 when more than $6 billion poured in. Internet censorship might have a hand in the declining investments.
- In July 2001, Beijing was awarded the 2008 Olympic games.
- On 8/8/08 at 8:08:08 PM the Olympic games in Beijing officially began.

- The NASDAQ composite index first closed over the 1,000 mark in July 1995. The peak was reached in March, 2000, with a value of 5,132. From there it declined and hit rock bottom at 1,108 in October, 2002.
- Ms Lin is now living in LA with her American husband, a VC by profession.
- Mr Zhang is working for a large European conglomerate managing a 60 million euros account in automation equipment.
- VC Mike vanished from the radar screen. We never heard from him again.
- As for the dotcommer creating software applications for mobile phones, the one none of the VCs was interested in; he reinvented himself in the past few years and now runs his own 7,000-plus-employee software outsourcing company.

CHAPTER 8

In exile to Taiwan

Taiwan is often depicted by China's Ministry of Propaganda as the disobedient son who refuses to return into the embracing arms of the motherland.

A wonderland of Confucian values, centuries old. . . .

This world of traditional Chinese customs was a fascinating new playground to discover and enjoy. Some of my hard-won China know-how came in handy, but still. . . .

Taiwan seemed descended from a Chinese DNA strain that had branched off centuries ago, whose traits popped up in the most unusual of places: thoroughbred Taiwanese businessmen getting caught up in a net of deception by their Mainland Chinese counterparts.

A new business opportunity was around the corner!

Taipei, April 1st, 2001 (or April 1st, 90, by Taiwan's Republican Calendar)

As an economic refugee from the battlefields of high finance, I ended up taking a job in a Taipei-based trading company, and with no further ado found myself exiled to Taiwan. Apparently the barbarian who hired me thought I would be able to transfer my Mainland business experience into a Taiwanese setting. This certainly was a remarkable philosophical approach, and worth further scrutiny. But as is usually the case with theories formulated behind a pile of beer glasses, it didn't hold up for a day. The rules and dogma I had soaked up over the past twelve years were completely incompatible with my new Taiwanese biotope.

For one thing: when we landed at night at Taipei's Taoyuan Airport, a huge, brightly-lit banner greeted us with a sincere FALUN GONG WELCOMES YOU! There was definitely something unusual in the air here.

Seeing the banner, a passenger sitting across the aisle mumbled in a heavy barbarian accent, 'At least there are no scary *apparatchik*s here trying to control the free world.' Those words struck me as overly cynical, as on that very same day a US military surveillance plane on the verge of entering China's airspace south of Hainan Island bumped into and brought down a Chinese fighter jet. This resulted in the death of the Chinese pilot, while the US plane had to make an emergency landing in China. Since Bush's appearance on the world scene he had already injected a venomous level of mistrust into Sino-US relations. One of his first actions after becoming president was to agree on a multi-billion-dollar weapons sale to Taiwan. Overnight, the strategic partnership between both countries turned into strategic competition. After this particular air incident tensions were cranked up another notch or two. When in recent years the US government called on China to become a responsible country, one had to wonder if it wasn't a bit of tactical sarcasm.

But all this seemed far away now, as my new home was giving me a kaleidoscope of fresh sensations.

For over fifty years the island had been run as a dictatorial franchise. The end of the eighties, however, heralded a new chapter, this one in favour of the people. Expressing political, religious and personal ideas became a way of life. The wide range of political parties, the cacophony of TV channels, the rainbow of websites and jungle of magazines competing for attention reflected the general mood of Taiwan. Even Mainland Chinese TV channels were piped in, uncensored. A pinch of anti-communism and a touch of extreme democracy demanded that every type of public debate could and must be conducted on the island. A shiver of excitement went through my body. This island had a trace of something exceptional I hadn't experienced for a while.

The beginning of the nineties had already brought me a couple of times to Taiwanese shores, but at that time the place was rather dull. In those days Taipei was a polluted, dusty, worn-out city with crumbling buildings, unbridled traffic and a thriving prostitution industry. It looked like a dump from which everyone, including some of the Taiwanese, were hoping to escape sooner rather than later.

But this time, my motivation for labouring away on this island had more to do with China's persistent and tenacious obsession with trying to get this rebellious place back into its ranks.

Indeed, Taiwan started blinking on the Chinese radar screen every time a politician across the strait made the slightest noise about self-rule or independence. For the Mainland, Taiwan is a province; for many Taiwanese, there is China and there is us.

In 1992 government officials from the Mainland and Taiwan huddled together in some hotel in Hong Kong where they came to the following agreement: 'There's only one China, but each side of the Taiwan Strait can have its own interpretation of the meaning of "One China".'

The Kuomintang, the Taiwanese nationalist party in power at that time, came out of those consensus meetings saying: 'One China, different interpretations.' For the PRC, however, the outcome of the meeting was simply 'One China.'

This certainly sounded reasonable, but didn't take into account that the Kuomintang's version was 'Republic of China', while Beijing officials were adamant that one China meant 'The People's Republic of China'.

The fog of confusion grew thicker when the passports carried by Taiwanese citizens travelling abroad were altered slightly. When the original Republic of China passports had the word 'Taiwan' added, it drew the ire of the Chinese government.

Apparently 'Republic of China' had become relatively acceptable.

Just to make it more confusing for this freshly arrived barbarian, the licence plate of his car read: PROVINCE OF TAIWAN.

Even the wording of 'peaceful solution' versus 'peaceful resolution' was reason for a good bout of bickering.

Depending which side of the strait one was standing on, Chen Shui-bian was either 'the president of Taiwan' or 'the leader of the Taiwan authorities'. His actions certainly didn't help to smooth out

China-Taiwan relations. Whenever he found a microphone pushed under his nose there was a good chance he'd mention 'Taiwan' and 'country' in the same breath. This would, without exception, result in a tongue-lashing from China and sometimes also from the US, depending on the size of the commercial interests being negotiated with the Mainland at that moment.

The US would in return also get a bashing from China when weapons deals with Taiwan came to light. Invariably the panda huggers and dragon slayers in the States got in a fight whenever the equilibrium shifted too much one way or the other.

Without a doubt I'd never seen so many American weapons dealers in my life. They crawled over the island, fervently promoting the 'benefits' of their vast array of weaponry: anti-tank rockets, submarines, jets, anti-submarine warfare, Patriot anti-missile batteries. . . .

This soup of emotional ferment seemed interesting enough to pass over other job offers in Shanghai and Hong Kong, and make a detour to Taiwan.

Once in Taiwan, the subtle tensions and differences didn't take much time to float to the surface.

In the office, some employees' grandparents had been among the one-and-a-half-million Chinese refugees who fled to Taiwan after Mao's victory over Chiang Kai-shek's army.

These people definitely had strong inclinations towards Mainland China and were called 'Chinese from the outside provinces'. Most were preoccupied with retrieving their family's Mainland China property, which had been seized after 1949. Most had never visited the PRC, but proudly stated 'I'm from Shanghai', 'My roots are in Wuhan' or 'My grandparents still have a house in Nanjing'. Asked if they'd like to visit their ancestral homes, the common response was: 'It's too dangerous at the moment!' Apparently, the Qiandao Lake incident in 1994, when robbers murdered over twenty Taiwanese tourists on a boat, was still reverberating.

Others in the office were descendants of Mainlanders who had arrived two or three hundred years ago in search of a better life. They invariably had no sense of belonging to the Mainland, spoke fluent Taiwanese dialect, and considered themselves born-and-bred Taiwanese.

But all Taiwanese passport holders had one thing in common: A strong sense of Confucianism, respect for ancestral Chinese culture, and superstitious beliefs ranging from fortune telling to feudal rituals.

My job was to replace a bright and humorous department manager, Mr Tsai, who was – according to the European boss – past his use-by date. His staff and customers revered him just as much as the barbarian general manager loathed him and his business ethics. Mr Tsai was the child of a Shanghai businessman and an Italian mother. His father had run a China-trading business from Europe from the mid-thirties until the closing stages of World War Two. When the family business in China was annexed by the new government during the turbulent late forties, they ended up in Taipei. Their thought at that time was: 'Very soon we'll be able to return to our family home in Shanghai.' That day never came, and against all odds Mr Tsai grew up in Taiwan.

Possessing a positive outlook, fluent in several languages, and able to connect with people easily, he came to know the ins and outs of Taipei's elite.

During the seventies and eighties the Taiwanese economy rushed into overdrive. Being at the right place at the right time, he was able to handsomely capitalise his expansive *guanxi* network among government agencies and the private sector. Having hauled in billions of euros for his present employer over a thirty-year career, he had been once the star of the company. The guy could certainly look back on a successful trading career. But now the Taiwanese economy had entered a mature phase, while at the same time members of his *guanxi* network were all reaching retirement age. His flamboyant style of entertaining customers was now viewed with displeasure, in light of the company's bottom line. His department had bled money for the past two years, and top-level patience was running out waiting for the new orders to come in.

'He seems out of place in the company,' thought the barbarian boss. 'Change is what we need in his department. Fresh blood will make the difference!' He had run the show for the past five years, but never appreciated or trusted Mr Tsai's business approach.

Mr Tsai was able to pull in several million euros in commission for the company by successfully taking part in large government tenders. The boss, still a Cartesian at heart, wanted straight answers, while Mr Tsai could only come up with tangled, contorted explanations of how things got done, and called for more patience. Historically, Taiwanese political parties were deeply involved in running large business consortia and the government had monopolies on a wide range of industries. This meant that big egos had to be stroked to capture the orders. Therefore, there simply were no easy linear answers. Only trustworthy people with Mr Tsai's track record would be able to penetrate the closely-guarded circles of power.

Sacking Mr Tsai meant blowing most of the bridges between the company and government-linked enterprises. But the boss remained adamant that our company no longer needed this monkey business. Luckily, some other seasoned managers in the company were able to pick up the slack when Mr Tsai's legacy was transformed.

It was my task to revitalise the department and add something novel to the basket of products the company represented. The staff inherited from Mr Tsai were clearly antagonistic to my presence, and they couldn't be blamed. This barbarian was the evil embodiment of those who had forced their beloved manager into early retirement.

Anyway, there I sat interviewing a legion of new staff for the department. Many well-educated people passed the review, most of them male and having spent as much as eighteen months in the military. Intrigued by this draft thing, I questioned one guy who had been posted on a destroyer during his service. 'Have you ever seen Mainland Chinese military vessels?'

'Sure we've seen them. We approach within a few miles of each other.'

'So what happens when the ships come so close?'

'We go into high alert and the whole ship is put into fighting mode. Airplanes from Taiwan are scrambled and at the same time Chinese jets go into the air.'

I asked, 'How often have you experienced such an event?' expecting him to answer: 'A couple of times over the course of my military service.'

'Oh this happens all the time. We never had a full night's sleep. That sort of thing happens night and day on the high seas along the demarcation line.' He reported this dryly, as a matter of fact.

'But that means there's a good chance that something might go wrong,' I said, surprised.

'Not to worry. Both sides have highly professional militaries. They've been constantly testing each other and looking for weaknesses in each others' defence strategies for the past few decades.'

Another one of my interviewees had once operated one of the early warning radar systems that were in place all over the island.

Eager for another juicy story, I quickly steered the discussion with a question: 'What goes on in the skies over the Taiwan Strait?'

'Chinese jets fly in configuration towards the demarcation line, only to break formation a few hundred feet before crossing the artificial line, and then return to base. Or even more irritating: a rival jet flies along the delineation, flying into and out of our territory every few minutes, creating visual and audible alarm signals that have to be cleared with other stations. Jets are scrambled to the point of intrusion and this unfortunately is followed by written reports. Really very boring!' he laughed.

'I assume this teasing is reciprocated?'

Annoyed by the question he only said: 'Maybe. I don't know. . . .'

So most probably, at this very moment, somewhere along the 160-kilometre-wide Taiwan Strait, submarines, fighter jets and naval vessels are playing a high-tech version of Battleship.

As the Taiwan economy becomes more and more interconnected with the Mainland, this line of demarcation has become an important discussion point among local politicians and company owners. Opening direct transport links with the Mainland, signing a peace accord, and increasing cross-strait exchanges require tackling some thorny issues for the Taiwanese. Often those discussions result in pretty tough fist fights in parliament, which are beamed all over the world to serve as the lighter part of primetime evening news.

As debates opened, editorials in local newspapers vigorously discussed the pros and cons of direct links. It would certainly benefit the island's economy, but in the eyes of others it could create a security risk.

The debates often centred around procedures for civilian aeroplanes approaching from China, and having to zigzag before entering Taiwanese airspace to demonstrate that they had no evil purpose. But what about military jets that might be hiding under the body of a jumbo jet? Should every civilian plane be escorted into Taiwan?

If freighters sailed from a Chinese harbour into Taiwan, should each and every container be checked for hidden soldiers? The debate raged on.

Even today, train spotters and other thrill seekers still gather in Taiwan for the yearly full-scale military drill.

Sirens all over the city blare for an imminent attack. Drivers are requested to pull over and pedestrians to halt on the spot till the drill is finished. To make it even more exhilarating, for the military brass anyway, fighter jets are expected to land on highways and take off again. Attack helicopters fly low over the highways making swooping manoeuvres, looking for an imaginary enemy. Beach landing invasions, Normandy style, are executed and repulsed.

For a spectacle out of the ordinary these are great times to visit Taiwan.

Extensive meetings and discussions followed my taking over from Mr Tsai, in which I explained what changes were to be implemented and why. Everyone agreed in theory, but in practice dark forces continued to play conniving games. Mr Tsai's ghost hovered everywhere; loyalty was to him, certainly not to a barbarian fresh from the bush. As the new sales team was being put together, and new products entered the business, the existing department members did their best to torpedo the changes. Under these conditions we were taking three steps backward for every one forward.

Although unconditional free rein was given to carry out reorganisation, any decision to fire the most die-hard anti-reformists met with the boss' adamant resistance. The wrong pretexts were given for keeping the recalcitrants on board: that this person had worked loyally for the company for ten years, or that person had kids to take care of, or this man possibly had the right contacts. All very noble thoughts, but not commensurate with the short-term demand to generate cash. It also didn't take long for the old-school staff to smell hesitation and weakness in the decision making of the barbarian boss.

One day, while we were negotiating our way out of this political cesspool, the whole office suddenly began to bend and wave. As if we'd become part of an Escher drawing, pillars and walls adopted all angles but the right ones. Bent shelves dropped books; twisted tables spilled tealeaves, and painting frames swayed into new axial dimensions. Before our minds could adapt to the new environment, everything went back to normal. Total silence. . . . Our senses had barely even registered the rattling noise that had surrounded us. Each pair of eyes searched for another pair, looking for mute confirmation: 'Did you just feel that?' The whispers built into a ruckus. A pretty heavy earthquake had struck, which was followed by some severe aftershocks. This time only a couple of souls lost their lives in Taipei. A buckled crane that came crashing down from the 101 Tower had caught some people by surprise.

There was no better way to escape from this ambiguous office disaster area than to hit the Taiwanese markets. With a couple of fresh team members, the hunt for orders was on.

The economy, heavily dependent on the electronics and biotech industries, included a whole chain of sub-suppliers, from specialty plastics, novelty steels, and high-precision mould manufacturers to high-tech equipment designers, all densely littered along the Western strip of the island. In the last ten years 'just in time' delivery around the world had made the place a marvel of logistic competence.

Our visits took us to the most decrepit of places, where complex robots were developed and assembled on badly-lit factory floors, under broken windows, and then exported to the Fortune 500 companies of the world. At the other end of the spectrum were giant plants, protected like fortresses, which churned out the latest in electronic gadgets, TFT screens or bio-engineered products.

Two different worlds met on a cloud of knowledge and entrepreneurship.

Expecting a good session of *karaoke* and a couple of large dinners to seal a deal, I was totally mystified when the first negotiated contract was settled with three meetings in the customer's office. And during business hours, for heavens sake! It was an unsettling experience. Could business really be so easy? Where was the joy of buddying up as a deluge of rocket fuel, songs and food boosted us into an orbit of trust? Nobody seemed to care; they didn't have the time or the need to waste resources. Efficiency and quality permeated the customer's requirements.

I was starting to lose confidence in the ability of Taiwanese businessmen to wind down until. . . .

Karaoke was still alive and well in Taipei. But it was a watered-down version of the fiery brand on the Mainland. Everyone sat graciously on sofas, forming small islands of people sharing a large common area. Properly clad ladies walked from group to group, filling empty glasses and exchanging civilised chitchat. While sipping whisky we politely applauded any outstanding performance.

The raunchy part had apparently been shifted out of these cultural palaces to somewhere else. This was the direct result of Chen Shui-bian's cleanup of Taipei city when he was still mayor, and dreaming of greater and higher things.

But evidently, 'somewhere else' was not too far away.

After the conclusion of our daily business meetings outside Taipei, where we'd kept the bottom line firmly in mind, we slept in small motels that during daylight hours acted as love hotels. As those places only allowed their all-night guests in after 7 PM, we had to wait in front of the gates for the seven strikes of the evening. This meant enjoying the spectacle of couples sneaking out of the hotel into the open. The businessmen behind the steering wheel had just enjoyed a dalliance with their secretary, escort lady, mistress or girlfriend.

To minimise interaction with outsiders, or to avoid peeping eyes discovering the misadventures of their spouse, the rooms often had their own closed garage. Driving in and jumping straight into bed was as easy as one, two, three.

The rooms were often decorated with the most bizarre of paraphernalia: from a gynaecological table, mirrors on the ceiling, or a low-hanging swing, to special ornaments in the bathroom. Menus listing costumes for rent were available so guests would be able to impersonate a policeman, nurse, vixen or student. At least here a businessman would be able to escape the daily routine and indulge in some quality time between four walls. Not to be forgotten were the deluge of sex channels focusing on copulation between all races of the world. Japanese babes, Western chicks, graceful Africans, they all made an appearance. Sometimes there was also the odd animal channel but it definitely wasn't Animal Planet.

In addition to their escapades those businessmen also had companies to run. Most of the ones we visited were in search of better margins, as purchasers around the world squeezed them for their last cent. This often meant that production was shifted to China, while R&D and the latest know-how were kept safely locked within their Taiwanese fortresses.

Some of the most adventurous of Taiwanese companies took their investment to the furthest borders and deepest areas of the Middle Kingdom. Their Chinese heritage enabled them to easily navigate local government waters, past loudmouth officials, and embrace local business ethics wherever they ventured. Unfortunately this wasn't always enough to lead to a match made in heaven. We crossed paths with disillusioned businessmen more than once.

Having kept in touch with a couple of lawyer friends on the Mainland, I realised this was a goldmine yearning to be worked. Delving a bit deeper into the business community, it wasn't too difficult to pick up news of JVs gone awry. Putting small ads in Taiwanese newspapers and aiming our services at distressed companies, we saw some handy pickings coming our way.

The resulting data was dutifully funnelled back to Beijing for analysis, to single out the juiciest of the bunch.

This also meant acclimating to a double life. I was tending to the needs of the company on one end, while during the weekends taking care of 'personal' matters. The window of opportunity for the latter was from Friday night till Monday morning.

One of our embittered businessmen was Mr Hsiao.

He was a thoroughbred Taiwanese with a balding head, the legacy of his recent Mainland troubles. Extremely superstitious, he refused to take any taxi that had an 'unlucky' number in the car's licence plate and spent thousands of dollars to get the 'right' mobile phone number, hoping it would bring him wealth. He even confided to me that he had seriously been thinking of changing his name so that Yin and Yang would have a positive effect on his life. Before moving into his Taipei office a *feng shui* master was requested to ensure the position of the furniture, colours of the walls and the right number of tropical fish in the aquarium would bring him luck. To prevent any bad omens from befalling his business, he'd have special red-labelled inscriptions placed under desks, chairs, flowerpots and behind picture frames. Just to make sure all his bases were covered, he went so far as to build a small temple in the neighbourhood to get in the good graces of his ancestors.

At a certain point in time however, all those efforts seemed to have been in vain.

His particular story went along the following lines:

In 1994, Mr Hsiao set up his real estate development company in the Chinese hinterland, with the idea of developing a residential complex of 230 apartments plus a large luxury shopping centre.

In agreement with the local authorities a plot of land was purchased, on which over one thousand families were then living. A provision in the agreement stated that he would pay roughly 2,800 RMB per square metre, or a total of more than 95 million RMB, to the dispossessed families whose houses were to be flattened.

After surmounting a mountain of tribulations and losing a good deal of hair, he put the shopping mall into operation in 1998. At the same time, the first batch of owners took possession of their apartments. Just as his cash flow was turning positive again, Mr Hsiao had the misfortune of finding himself smack in the eye of the Asian financial crisis. Subsequently, much of his operating funds were entirely depleted, and to continue the second phase of apartment-building a cash injection of eighty million RMB was borrowed from a local bank. This was provided to his company against the shopping complex he still owned. At that time the bank estimated this property to be worth 520 million RMB.

During one of Mr Hsiao's overseas trips, some of his most trusted employees had the great idea of using the company chops for their own benefit. After pulling some strings, another bank subsidiary was persuaded to provide a small local company with an additional loan of 46 million RMB, also using Ms Hsiao's shopping complex as collateral!

For this second loan, however, the mall was only appraised at 155 million RMB, far below the appraisal made for the official loan. The wives of Mr Hsiao's employees owned the small company, and had entered the scene like soldiers in a Trojan horse. Upon receiving the second loan, the money was put to good use on the Shanghai and Shenzhen stock markets. As the local markets went into an upswing the small company dutifully paid its part of the bogus mortgage.

Then one day in 2001 the payments stopped. Apparently some bad investments, combined with a betting spree in Macau to make up for those losses, led to the evaporation of most of the second loan. After that the nest egg leftovers, together with the loyal employees and their wives, disappeared overseas, never to be heard from again.

For Mr Hsiao, the nightmare had just gotten out of the starting blocks. He was suddenly slammed with an additional loan payment he considered illegitimate. Obviously he was in no mood to pay to cover up the scam. But from a legal point of view Mr Hsiao had no strong footing, as his company's stamps were littered all over the official documents and banking papers used to obtain the loan. The trick for him would be to bring his employees to court and convince a judge that he was the victim of a swindle.

In the meantime the small bank branch, faced with non-performing loan number two, got a court injunction to sell the shopping centre to repay the loan. To Mr Hsiao's dismay, the place was auctioned for much less than the official initial appraisal. Pulling in just 175 million RMB, the sale earned the bank its loan, interest and legal expenses back again. Now that the collateral for the genuine loan was gone, however, the other bank also weighed in to recoup its loan, which was being used to build the second phase of apartments. Ultimately Mr Hsiao was faced with an additional avalanche of accounts payable from construction companies, architects and tax authorities whose bills were left unpaid. To top it all off the embittered apartment owners, left with nothing but a concrete ghost, also got organised. Mr Hsiao, fearing that he would end up locked in a hotel room by his suitors, took the only option left and fled his erstwhile paradise. Considering all his tribulations, maybe – just maybe – he should seriously have considered adopting a more auspicious name before beginning the whole adventure.

Thus I came to know the embittered Mr Hsiao, constructing his case in a Taipei office. Having already spent a fortune on trying to retrieve his assets, he didn't mind wasting a bit more time talking to a barbarian and his lawyer friends.

Meanwhile, during the days, circus politics were spinning along. Mr Tsai's secretary, whom I had inherited, released small doses of toxin wherever possible to kill off newcomers' enthusiasm and send them running for the nearest exit. Orders from customers were purposefully misplaced or shipments sent to the wrong address. Putting out the fires she set in the four corners of the island became a daily routine. Successions of sleepless nights intensified my daily misery. Cutting the secretary off developed into an urgent priority. But the boss continued to stall on implementing steps to create a healthier business environment. He continued holding on to her like a lifebuoy. On the one hand she was his direct link to the long-term outstanding government contracts that were due for payment, and on the other hand she turned out to be the only one who understood the 'complex' agreements inside out. Having already fired her once, the boss pulled her back three days later. Feeling that her power over the boss, and therefore over me, had grown stronger, she flaunted it on every possible occasion. When I couldn't resist trying a second time to put the house in order, I got an earful. Fed up with the wall of indecisiveness, I stood my ground. Although this meant that the barbarian boss lost face, at least she was finally gone . . . and others started taking notice. Mr Tsai's moral legacy had weakened considerably. Liberated from the dead weight, the department went into overdrive. Sales moved again in the right direction. We were making a foray into the Taiwanese companies. Orders grew from a trickle into a steady stream.

Anticipating satisfaction from the boss about where things were heading, I instead got a strong dose of negative emotion. Apparently the boss had totally miscalculated the timing of Mr Tsai's physical departure. Although he'd told everyone that Mr Tsai was a short-term loss for the company, the 'cosmetic' changes were costing the company dearly in revenue. The anticipated income streams from the last outstanding contracts were stalled. No one in the company had the magic touch inside large government organisations to make things happen. In the end that money never arrived in the company's bank accounts.

The boss's wounded pride had not yet fully recovered. A depressed captain, unable to direct the crew, was the last thing the company needed.

Having to face internal sloppiness and at the same time hunt for staff, chase orders and re-organise the department, the demands were slowly sapping my vigour to perform.

Then like a thunderbolt in clear daylight, we received an e-mail from Singapore HQ that our barbarian boss had been fired.

An hour later I had Mr Tsai on the phone, listening to him bask in the realisation of his predictions of a year earlier.

'I told you so. You didn't want to believe me, but now the results are out! Tonight I'm having a celebratory dinner with my ex-staff. Do you care to join?' Having been fond of the charming guy since I'd first met him, I couldn't refuse the offer. The event was held at a top-class Italian restaurant. At first, my presence at the table wasn't taken well by the others. Seated near a few of the people I had fired, a bit of tension was unavoidable. Mr Tsai's charisma, however, worked wonders in smoothing out some of the outstanding grudges, and he declared; 'We're all here tonight to commemorate the good times we've had together. I'd like to thank each one of you for the friendship and dedication you've given. We all know that the barbarian seated at the table over there came to replace me. However you should not blame him for the wrongdoings since my departure. He's not as bad as you think. It's the boss who never realised what a tightly knit family we are.'

Mr Tsai's hidden message said it all: 'The old experienced leader, having won the hearts and minds of his staff, was irreplaceable. Nobody ever questioned his authority and business experience. By letting Mr Tsai go, the boss had created the mechanism of his own downfall.'

Thereafter we all enjoyed a great night out.

At the conclusion of the dinner Mr Tsai, indulging in the moment, was serenely blowing smoke rings with his cigar. He had finally been vindicated of all imputations. Bending forward he revealed what I suspected all along: 'You know I've been in contact with several of my old customers and they all assured me that any future payment would be blocked. In the meantime, I've heard through the grapevine that you're involved with some business in China. What's that all about?' However carefully one tried to hide one's private business, nothing was safe from the all-perceiving eye of the well-connected *guanxi* network.

Revitalised by the sudden change, the department got a shot in the arm and grew by leaps and bounds. Another barbarian who was already running the show in Shanghai was temporarily put in charge of dealing with the Taiwan office as well. The guy hated being responsible for the Taiwan business. Clearly prejudiced about the island's potential, he quietly hoped the Taipei office would meet a slow demise.

In his mind Mainland China was the only place worth his while for doing business. 'Managing' us through a dribble of e-mails from the Shanghai office, he declared a freeze on the headcount, which brought my department's growth to a halt.

The human resources manager was let go. Business operations were put in line with those on the Mainland: Travel to visit customers had to be requested in advance and . . . approved. Our sales people were demoted to a tribe of pen pushers; sales margins were dictated from Shanghai.

To his dismay however, he discovered that the talents of the local Taiwanese managers ran deeper than he could imagine. After one week his rules were subtly bent to get back to business. Nobody was going to order Taiwanese businessmen from across the strait. As a statement of protest sales figures from all departments went one level higher. This forced him to acknowledge results, and spend at least two days per month in Taipei. Narrow-minded about cross-strait relationships, he never missed an opportunity to flaunt his opinions. Staff shrugged it off by chalking it up to a possible brainwashing he had experienced over the past years.

When the two of us shared quality time in the meeting room nothing but barbarian grunts were exchanged. It was clear from the very beginning that there was mutual contempt.

The lure of Mainland-related business became more appealing over time. 'Burning the midnight oil' took on an entirely new connotation. Evenings were now dedicated to the emerging China business, which seemed to be my lifeline out of the darkness. Encounters with embittered investors became more frequent during the week.

We were mainly on the lookout for cases that hadn't matured for too long, that had occurred in locations not too far from civilisation, and that involved amounts above 500,000 euros. Where a good chance existed to recover some of the lost spoils, we dug a bit deeper in the hope of finding the right ingredients to recoup our time and money.

But nothing could compare to the experience of jumping into the bush. As direct flights between Taipei and the Chinese capital didn't exist, flying into Beijing over the weekend was too much of a hassle. I travelled to Hong Kong, where meetings were set up in Shenzhen just across the border.

On one of those trips in wintertime, I found the hotels less crowded than usual. Mr Xiao, a local lawyer with whom we were discussing Mr Hsiao's financial entanglement, mentioned stories making the rounds of a mysterious disease that had already killed over one hundred people in Guangdong Province.

Rumours had it that the most effective preventative measures were to smoke, eat loads of garlic and inhale vinegar vapours on a regular basis. Sure enough, looking through local shops, the shelves where vinegar once stood were empty. On the street people were still puffing the same amount of cigarettes, but the roads seemed a bit less crowded than usual. The saturated garlic breath in taxicabs remained a constant – nothing had changed in that department.

Then one month later Hong Kong newspapers reported that a doctor from Guangzhou had been admitted to hospital with a respiratory disease. Two weeks after healthcare staff had treated him, they also fell ill. Slowly a picture emerged of clusters of sick people all over the world, all of whom had had contact with virus carriers weeks earlier. The name of the illness was SARS (severe acute respiratory syndrome). Apparently the source of the disease was Mainland China, more precisely Guangdong Province. Here vinegar manufacturers had discerned the mysterious infection months earlier, and were already devoting marketing campaigns to promote their fluid as a cure-all. Factories couldn't churn out enough of their magic potion. Meanwhile the World Health Organisation took notice and sent staff to China and Hong Kong. The organisation recommended postponing all essential travel in Hong Kong and the south of China.

Local governments, hoping that the disease would magically vanish from their provinces, initially put some WHO workers under house arrest. Then, when the cover-up was no longer possible, the full controlling powers of the Chinese government went into action. Draconian measures were taken to control the spread of SARS. Schools, restaurants, *karaoke* bars, exhibition centres, offices were all closed down. No one was allowed to travel in and out of cities. Whole areas were hermetically sealed off.

In the meantime, in Taiwan, preventive measures were also taken. Everyone travelling from Hong Kong or China had to go into quarantine for a period of ten days, either at home or in dedicated hospitals.

In our office building everyone's body temperature was measured with an infrared thermometer. Even entering a parking lot meant stopping for an officer to take a measurement. 'You're thirty-three degrees Celsius. You haven't got a fever!' the guy told me before entering a restaurant. Before I could figure out if he was being serious, a small smiley sticker was slapped on my shirt stating, 'You're cool!'

Every evening on the news, Taiwan authorities beat their chests, proudly stating that there were no SARS patients on the island. Taiwanese politicians declared that the SARS epidemic in China was slowly undermining the Chinese government. They predicted that internal unrest would soon follow, as the economy had ground to a halt. Overseas tourists, business people and investors were terrified of the disease and fled in droves. It was a doomsday scenario; dissidents and dragon slayers alike sucked blood for days on end.

Meanwhile I kept in contact with my partners on the Mainland, trying to move forward with some of the cases our Taiwanese customers had entrusted to us.

Although I still needed to be able to visit China over the weekends, a dilemma arose. I could not afford a ten-day quarantine. The Internet was the great saviour of those faced with the same dilemma. Checking into Taiwanese discussion forums it quickly emerged that the solution was fairly simple. Flying through either Tokyo or Kuala Lumpur on the way to and from China would preclude the nasty ten-day lock-up upon returning to Taiwan.

As local travel restrictions in China were pretty harsh, the only way to meet face to face with my contacts was to fly into Beijing myself.

On the Tokyo-Beijing leg of the flight everyone was wearing a surgical mask, as if we'd all been invited to a masked party at ten thousand metres.

Once in Beijing I could see how drastic the measures had been. The whole place was in hibernation. Only those who thought they could take a measured risk wandered into the open. Restaurants were closed. Offices were closed. Shops were closed. Exhibitions were cancelled. Buses drove around with very few riders, all wearing white masks on their faces. Some taxi drivers still scoured the road in hopes of catching some brave soul who'd dared to venture out. One of the taxis I took drove with the windows open, just in case I might hit him with the virus. Another taxi driver took even more drastic measures: he kept his head out of the window during the whole trip. The money I handed over was sprinkled with some kind of alcohol and left to dry on the dashboard. The hotel where I stayed smelled of chlorine from the constant floor cleaning. Elevator buttons were wiped virus-free every half an hour. Guests walking into the lobby were scanned for their body temperature. All this undertaken by a hotel whose occupancy rate had sunk to 6 percent. Needless to say the trip became a total waste of time. The people I had spoken to before flying over were either not allowed by their families to leave the apartment or were stopped by road blocks on the outskirts of Beijing.

Flying back to Taiwan via Japan, the plane was fully booked with Taiwanese returning home. Upon arrival at Taipei Airport the heat detecting sensors, which scanned passengers' body temperature after disembarking, were switched off. This equipment was only to be used for planes originating from areas were SARS had been detected. . . .

As the SARS tribulations continued all around the world, Taiwan seemed to have been spared. But one evening watching the local news, the first potential Taiwanese SARS case was being reported. The authorities emphasised that this was an isolated case. There was no reason to panic. A couple of days later more patients came in. Hospitals went into quarantine. When it appeared that one virus carrier had travelled by bus from Taipei to Kaohsiung, all commuters who had taken that bus were requested to come forward. More dreadful information came out. Passengers who had flown from China through Tokyo to Taiwan were contacted one by one. The virus had hopped onto the plane and more people got into hospital beds. Although I had entered Taiwan fifteen days earlier, definitely past the incubation period, a call came in to see if any fever had developed. Suddenly scores of people were infected everywhere on the island. All hell broke loose.

The Taipei office put preventive measures in place, lest one person got the disease and the whole company had to be quarantined: half of the office went to work on even days, the other half on odd days. Some key people from the accounting department were consigned to work from home. Our Shanghai-based barbarian boss took three months' leave and remained in Europe. We all received a box containing masks to cover up our nose and mouth while we sat at our desks. . . . Every few hours, hands and phones were cleaned with an alcohol gel. The same aseptic smell I had experienced in China was now also tingling our nostrils here.

Sales calls to customers were no longer possible, because only essential staff were allowed to enter factories, companies and purchasing departments. Sometimes downtown felt as if a neutron bomb had just exploded: empty restaurants, a few cars, shopping malls where nobody was shopping. Only a couple of water trucks spraying disinfectant along the streets disturbed the monotony of the landscape. In the subways people were looking for any suspicious hands moving to mouth or nose. An innocent cough sent everyone scurrying for the exits at the next stop.

Sales figures collapsed like a badly baked soufflé.

The new boss got his wish. Departments were streamlined and unnecessary fat trimmed.

I was set free again, finally liberated from conformist business visions.

Postscript

- A 2006 PRC national defence white paper states that the struggle to oppose and contain separatist forces for 'Taiwan independence' remains an important but difficult task.

- China has always vowed to reunify with Taiwan, by force if necessary. Mainland China considers the secessionist forces in Taiwan the greatest threat to peace and stability across the Taiwan Straits. The Chinese government has reiterated on several occasions that Taiwan is an inseparable part of China's territory.

- In 2007, Chen Shui-bian's wife was investigated for allegedly accepting department-store vouchers for lobbying services offered. For a president who was elected in 2000 on a platform of eradicating graft and corruption, it didn't bode well. Chen Shui-Bian and his wife, Wu Shu-jen were incarcerated for more than seventeen years on bribery and corruption charges. They should be free in 2028, but taking Taiwan's dynamic political landscape into account, Chen Shui-Bian was released from jail on humanitarian grounds in January 2015 and now lives in Kaohsiung. Chen's son-in-law was jailed for six years for insider trading.

- As requested by the US government, the US surveillance plane that landed in Hainan was dutifully returned, but only after Chinese engineers had dismantled, inspected and boxed it into wooden crates.
- In 2007, at sixty-five, Mr Tsai was still pulling in the dough, but for his own account. He retired in 2010 to take care of his grandchildren.
- A devastating earthquake with a magnitude of 7.6 on September 21st, 1999, killed more than 2,000 and injured over 10,000 citizens across Taiwan.
- Mr Hsiao earned an acknowledgement that his staff had wronged him. However any cash reimbursement will have to wait until those people can be found and brought to justice.
- Corruption scandals continue to plague some Chinese banks, with officials either jailed or dismissed when anomalies come to light.
- From November 2002 to July 2003, more than 8,100 probable SARS cases and more than 770 deaths were recorded worldwide.
- At the peak of the SARS epidemic over 12,000 people were quarantined in Taiwan.
- 'Thanks' to SARS, in larger Chinese cities spitting has mostly been consigned to a thing of the past.
- The National Palace Museum in Taipei contains the very best of the Chinese emperors' art collection. During the thirties, afraid that Japanese forces might damage it, the Nationalists shipped the invaluable treasures, legacy of Chinese culture and history, out of the Forbidden City.

- Chen Shui-bian's push to hold a referendum in 2008 to join the United Nations was seen as ill considered by both Beijing and the international community.
- 'A scum of the nation who attempts to split the country won't escape the punishment of history,' quoth the spokesman of the Taiwan Affairs office in Beijing.
- 'Mr Chen's referendum plan is a needless provocation. We don't recognise Taiwan as an independent state and we don't accept the argument that provocative assertions of Taiwan independence are in any way conducive to maintenance of the status quo or peace and stability across the Taiwan Strait,' quoth the US deputy assistant secretary of state for East Asian and Pacific affairs.
- 'War is the highest form of struggle for resolving contradictions, when they have developed to a certain stage, between classes, nations, states, or political groups, and it has existed ever since the emergence of private property and of classes.' [Mao Zedong]
- Direct flights between China and Taiwan are now a non-event.
- In November 2013, Taiwan President Ma Ying-jeou said that the country was not ready yet to have a political dialogue or a peace agreement with China. Meanwhile PRC President Xi Jinping said that political talks could not be delayed indefinitely.

CHAPTER 9

A dislocated joint

When investors believe they have every parameter in their Chinese business model under control, they're in fact sailing dangerously close to terra incognita.

On the ground, far away from the barbarian boardroom, the absurdity of reality can often surpass the imagination. But with a touch of cultural intelligence and a modicum of appreciation for social differences, one has a good chance of blending into the local scene.

This may assist in steering one's investment into less turbulent waters.

Understanding heaven and reaching for earth are not for the faint of heart.

Beijing, Monday August 16th, 2004

'I'm fed up with working for those barbarians. They're the worst customers I've ever faced. I really want to leave this place and go back to Beijing,' Xiao Gao said between a sob and a tear.

Trying to calm her over the phone, I was eager to know what had upset her so badly.

'Cool down. Tell me what happened. Enlighten me.'

Xiao Gao was one of a group of top-notch translators who freelanced for us when one of our customers required translation and didn't want one of the expensive busybodies from our company.

In this particular instance Mark, the new production manager of Pressure Tubing NV (PT NV), had arrived in China along with two engineers to visit the company's JV and had requested an independent translator to assist him with technical discussions.

While weeping softly she explained, 'These barbarians expect me to pay my share of the meals. I don't mind paying for my meals. It's not much money but I find it so strange. But worse, yesterday they slept until noon while I had been waiting downstairs since 8:30 in the morning. They told me they would work on Sunday morning. Why can't they be more professional? Now they are complaining that the daily translation fee is too expensive. Yesterday evening one asked me to reduce my fee from seven hundred RMB per day to five hundred because they'll be staying longer than expected. I'm really sad and disappointed you know. This is the first time something like this has happened to me.'

'Crikey!' I thought to myself. 'Why are they playing hardball with this girl? The one person they need to rely on in the middle of the bush, and they're giving her a bashing.'

I tried to douse the flames: 'Xiao Gao, probably Mark and his team are under stress. I don't think they mean it. I'll give them a call in the evening when all of you return to the factory guesthouse.'

Having followed their company's tribulations in China over the past couple of years, I knew the Chinese JV partners pretty well. They definitely weren't the type that could be handled without first donning a tough pair of work gloves. Staunch SOE employees, they were masters in playing all registers of the negotiation process. Those unversed in Chinese bargaining antics could find themselves climbing the walls in no time. I could imagine how a stressed out, jetlagged barbarian might erroneously take his frustration out on Xiao Gao.

PT NV specialised in the manufacture of the high-pressure pipes used in gas distribution and in power and petrochemical plants. Those industries were experiencing double-digit growth in China, and projections for such plants were mind-boggling.

After a new Electric Power Law came into force in 1996, the business of generation, distribution and consumption of electric power was turned upside down. In the past, provincial- and municipal-level electric power bureaux managed power supply. The new law stipulated that power generation and distribution would be administered by separate companies, which would introduce competition into the cosy business environment and hopefully improve efficiency. Previously, electricity rationing was a common occurrence in all major cities in the deepest parts of the country. One or two days of blackouts a week were meted out to every city district on a regular basis. Since working by candlelight wasn't particularly propitious to the construction of a world-class economy, the power grid was wrested from the bureaucrats' sticky hands. It was expected that the reforms in power generation and distribution would lead to the creation of many new power plants, and get Chinese industries working at a steady hum.

In the nineties many Western power plant equipment suppliers and engineering companies operating in China imported these PT pipes for their Chinese installations.

Because of the expected surge in oil and gas transportation and power generating installations, the Chinese government wanted to cut costs and absorb some advanced know-how. Therefore the multinational power plant designers, and their suppliers, were asked to localise as much as possible – either to provide technology transfers or lose out on this lucrative market. In turn, PT NV was forced by their Western clients to follow them into China or fail to secure future contracts with them. For the majority of medium-sized suppliers in the industry this was a once-in-a-lifetime opportunity, and many of them were eager to jump into the China fray. As usual, both China and the multinationals got their wish.

Due to national regulations, which required safety approvals for manufacturing high-pressure vessels and the like, a JV was highly recommended. After long, drawn-out discussions, PT NV signed a JV agreement with a local partner in 1998, manufacturing high-pressure pipes. Located roughly seven hundred kilometres from the Chinese capital, they partnered up with the ramshackle old state-owned pipe manufacturer Guandao Ltd.

Strategically it was not a bad move, as the power industry was projected to grow from around 220GW of installed power generating capacity in the mid-nineties to 350GW by the end of 2004. That meant at least one hundred new power plants, which translated into many kilometres of pressure pipes. 'Bingo!' the investors would shout as they watched the value of their company's shares balloon.

'*Chenggong le!* Success!' was probably the cry of relief on the Chinese side when the last remaining booby trap in the JV agreement was disarmed: The retired staff living on the factory's premises would be allowed to keep their housing, while their pensions would be the responsibility of the Chinese partner.

The communists were acquiring their first taste of capitalism, as the capitalists took a step towards communism.

As the factory got a second lease on life, the employees were invigorated by the new opportunities the JV would give them. Luckily, the venture agreement clearly stated that all existing SOE staff were to stay on board in the new company. The former general manager of the state-owned enterprise remained in charge of production and kept his title. PT's permanent staff in the JV consisted of a vice-general manager, an engineer and sales manager.

Immediately following the JV's birth, a whole team of barbarian technicians was brought over to recalibrate existing machinery, train staff in the technical visions of PT, and upgrade certain sections with state-of-the-art equipment. Despite or perhaps due to the fact that these stints were short term, their arrogance often soured the Chinese employees' respect for their counterparts.

Therefore, the vice-general manager's main duties over the short term read as follows: diplomat, technician, fire fighter, cultural attaché, people's manager, teacher, trouble shooter, finance manager, psychologist, problem solver, trusted counsellor and human-resource manager. Basically the kind of multitasking usually only a woman would be able to pull off.

Luckily, real supermen do exist in the world. The one PT appointed was named Dirk, and he somehow had a good practical grasp of the daily mix of yin and yang, with a blend of extensive management experience.

Able to adapt himself extremely well to his new Chinese ecosystem, his qualities gained the trust and respect of the partner. He was an asset every aspiring China investor would love to have on his/her side.

The other key position of extreme importance to PT's Asia strategy was the sales manager. He acted as conduit to Western and Chinese power-plant equipment suppliers, tracked bids, identified possible projects in Asia and at the same time built up a capable sales team.

The ink on the agreement was not yet dry when the first problem hit the barbarian investors smack in their innocent faces. The JV's sales manager, full of enthusiasm, had initiated a marketing campaign informing PT's major Chinese customers and research and design institutes about the JV's new manufacturing facilities in China. 'PT, in its relentless drive to serve its customers with the best possible service, has set up a JV with the famous Guandao Ltd. From now on piping will be made at Chinese prices but with PT's high quality standards.' The Western customers operating in China also raved about the new JV which had joined their ranks.

In their Cartesian minds nothing could go wrong; this strategic move was a sure bet to unlock China's riches! PT's HQ was already dreaming up rosy pictures of extravagant sales revenues, new products and plans for expansion. Their aim was to become the market leader in China six years down the road.

To the barbarians' initial surprise, local orders dried up soon after the promotion campaign went into full swing.

Chinese customers insisted that if PT's pipes were not manufactured in Europe they'd buy from the local competition. Which they'd probably end up doing anyway, because of the aggressive pricing and import restrictions the Chinese government had imposed on this specific product line. But nobody could understand the logic behind the refusal to buy from the JV. Months went by without any sales to Chinese end-users. The Chinese partner played innocent, and blamed the barbarian sales manager for stirring up bad feelings among their customer base.

Meanwhile the poor sales manager, unable to escape from his Cartesian box, was carried off the sales battlefield, bruised and shaken by the behaviour of the enigmatic Chinese customer. I was told his last words were 'Never will I put a foot on Chinese soil again. China is just a trap to suck in Western money! This country is going down the drain! Those Chinese will never understand what they're missing.' Then he was safely strapped into his airplane seat and shipped back to familiar surroundings.

That's how I got sucked into PT's story line. Through a friend of a friend of the JV's superman Vice-General Manager Dirk, I was retained to find a Chinese sales manager, and discreetly asked to find out why customers had turned their back on them. The search for a sales manager was relatively easy compared to the second task.

The road to twisted insights led me to many places, from Mr Yan, the chairman of the JV, to old sages working in industry-related institutes scattered all over the country.

Through the haze of discussions, research, incense burnt and offerings made, a faint oracular truth emerged about PT's choice of partner.

No Chinese company was willing to place orders with PT's JV. No major institute was prepared to back the JV's products. The news that the famous PT NV had put together a JV with Guandao Ltd had been met with total bewilderment and scepticism in the Chinese research centres, engineering companies, chemical and power-plant manufacturers. In the tightly-knit industrial community the gossip was buzzing: 'Why would a well-established barbarian company want to link up with Guandao Ltd?'

This company had never been considered a major player in the business. It was third-rate in all respects and had never built a reputation of reliability. There were so many other more qualified high-pressure piping manufacturers along the east coast with whom PT could have aligned themselves, but no ... for some incomprehensible reason Guandao was chosen. 'These barbarians will never understand China,' was the oft-heard comment.

So PT's reputation took a major blow even before the first pipes rolled off the production line.

Due to a lethal mixture of opaque market information about the Chinese players and shareholders' eagerness for a cheap deal, PT had walked into this adventure more or less blind. Having found Guandao Ltd, they latched on to it without looking any farther than the company's gates.

Eventually foreign equipment suppliers in China became their main buyers, and because of the lack of further demand the Chinese pipes also ended up on the European market.

Although the JV had additional teething problems, involving employee conflicts and expensive equipment collecting dust, light was clearly visible at the end of the tunnel.

But when the superman vice-general manager retired a couple of years later, the synergy went out like a candle.

What followed was a travesty of professional management. Believing that superman's performance had 'effortlessly' brought the JV up to speed, PT's HQ assumed that any manager, adventurous, thoroughbred or otherwise, could be transplanted into the Chinese scene and set to work. They expected superman's replacement to keep the enterprise purring on autopilot and get the anticipated full return on investment a couple of years down the road.

That was a big mistake. It was something they wouldn't have considered doing in a million years if the JV had been located in another European country. But HQ had thrown common sense out the window the moment China inched onto the radar screen. Having put blind faith in the new manager, the China investment drifted away out of the spotlight as more pressing issues closer to home caught the investors' attention. It no longer seemed to matter so much what happened on the other side of the world.

This may sound like a bad management decision, but surprisingly enough it's part of a well-rehearsed script used by many JVs (or wholly-foreign-owned enterprises for that matter) and many an enterprise is thus wrecked midway through the long dark tunnel to profitability.

The hungered-for synergy never materialised at the PT JV.

Even now the relationship was rather wobbly. Earlier a call had come in from Europe that some of their key staff in the JV had gone over to the dark side. . . . In the understanding of the Europe-based general manager, Patrick, his Chinese staff had defected and were now defending the interests of the local partner.

And now back to our crying Xiao Gao, who was quickly developing a hatred for the barbarian mindset.

Around 9:30 PM Mark finally answered the phone. 'How are the technical discussions going?' I asked. 'Not too many problems, I assume.' I got the same old story replayed in a slightly different version.

'Are you mocking me? You know we're having problems with our partner. Every step we want to take to improve the JV is scuttled. Although the factory is producing at near full capacity, we seem unable to generate a profit. The quality of the product isn't always to our satisfaction. Since we have this stupid buy-back clause in our agreement we need to be sure the final product is up to our specified standards. Too many of the pipes can't be used and are written off. All this because the material and finishing don't meet the specifications set forward in the purchasing agreements. At the moment the JV is costing us more money than if we'd produced in Europe. China should be cheap, not expensive.'

'Yes, I know, I know. In the past we've already had many of those discussions with Patrick. Is he actually coming over any time soon?'

'No, he has no time to spend in this remote area. This is really the end of the world.'

Then, completely out of the blue, he switched to an entirely different subject. 'Speaking of Patrick, he negotiated this deal and I can't understand why those provisions about the workers' union were included in the agreement.'

'Oh, you're also taking time out to renegotiate the JV? Normally this scheme belongs exclusively to the Chinese party.' I was pulling his leg.

'No, it's just that since I was coming to work here in China I read about this agreement on the plane flying over,' was his stoic reply.

The JV's most pressing problems were still unsolved, but he was already tackling the next imaginary thorn in the JV's side. . . . Having felt the sting of worker unions in Europe, he had gotten pretty worried about what could happen if this power was unleashed on the JV work force.

'Mark . . . at PT NV nobody seemed terribly bothered by spending the investors' hard currency for a piece of land, outdated buildings and equipment, and the possible pension liabilities of retired Chinese staff. Now, for once, you're worrying about something you shouldn't be. Setting up a trade union is an obligatory JV clause. You'll have to live with it. And as far as I know it hasn't produced any problems, right?

'No. . . .' was his sheepish admission.

'Don't worry too much. In this worker's paradise the unions are usually reduced to organising entertainment for the workers, things like *karaoke*, tourist outings, training courses and birthday parties. And if you really fear the worst, the present Chinese constitution has no provisions that allow for a strike.

'Actually I called you because I heard that Xiao Gao is not so happy with you guys. What's going on there? She's a bright lady and never failed any of our customers. Please have a bit more compassion for her. She's on your side you know.'

This comment seemed to catch Mark by surprise, and he replied with a pinch of sarcasm in his voice, 'What happened? I don't know anything. We've been treating her fairly.'

When I explained the situation he snapped back at me: 'You're in no position to tell me how I should handle the situation here. I've been told you always have to argue about price and never give in, otherwise the Chinese will take advantage of you. We'll be on the losing end every time unless we play hard ball.'

'Who told you that?' I asked, a bit irritated.

He explained with an air of confidence: 'At HQ we received a one-day training course on cultural awareness regarding China. The trainer discussed this with us.'

'Come on Mark, please! Stop this rubbish. You don't have to generalise. You're not buying shirts and pants in a market. Xiao Gao is on your side. Why can't you treat her like a colleague? Do you want her to defend your interests or do you want her to scuttle your efforts?'

'Mmm. I'm sorry, I really don't like her attitude. Why didn't she talk to me directly about those problems? We could have solved this easily.'

'Mark, you're starting to get on my nerves big time. First you go on about the union system, now you're full of little bits and pieces of China wisdom. When you go back home ask your trainer why the translator talked to me and not to you. Don't you have any common sense?'

'Maybe she'd better go back to where she belongs.' Those were Mark's last words before hanging up on me.

Rather than assuming the worst, I needed to sound out Xiao Gao and hear her part of the story.

'How are things? Did you have dinner with the barbarians?' I feigned ignorance.

'We were invited by Mr Chen, the general manager of the company, for a nice meal.'

'And . . . how was the mood?' An anxious me was keen to know.

'Not too bad. You really want to know?' Excited to gossip, she eagerly went on: 'The barbarians drank too much rice wine and made complete fools of themselves. One of the engineers even wanted to impress Mr Chen by knocking back two glasses for every glass of rice wine he drank. The man definitely went past his comfort zone. He insisted on hugging Mr Chen and gave him a kiss. When he went to the bathroom he tripped, and then fell asleep in his own vomit. It was a real mess.' The phone went quiet for a fraction of a second.

'Oh! I almost forgot: This guy ate some *jiaozi* with his hands. That really bemused Mr Chen. None of the barbarians even tried to stop him. Now I hope you realise what kind of long noses you saddled me with.' She had nothing but scorn for the job at hand.

'Wow, now that's what I call my type of party. We barbarians love to go all the way. "No limits" is our motto. We always celebrate as if there's no tomorrow. Next time we'll have a barbarian drinking session to get you up to speed,' I teased her.

Afterwards I didn't want to talk about my conversation with Mark, because I was hoping that rocket fuel had marred his thoughts while he spoke to me. With a bit of luck, he might regret his harsh comments the following day.

Indeed, when I called Mark the next morning and mentioned last night's conversation, he quickly professed there had been a misunderstanding. 'Of course we need Xiao Gao here. Who else can help us but her? You can rest assured that we'll take care of her.'

Four days later they were back in Beijing. Apparently the technical discussions hadn't gone as smoothly as the binge drinking in the evenings. An additional crack had appeared in the Sino-PT relationship. Most probably, more cultural training was urgently required at HQ to plaster over the crumbling business alliance. Meanwhile, on the morning of their departure from the city, Xiao Gao dutifully went to the hotel lobby, expecting to meet up with them one last time to receive her hard-earned translation fee. After fifteen minutes of waiting in the lobby, she called Mark's room.

No answer.

She quickly glanced in the breakfast area. The place was full of barbarian faces, but none were familiar. They had apparently sneaked out an hour earlier, leaving our Xiao Gao once again empty-handed and in tears. 'These days appearances are deceiving, even when dealing with barbarians.' Xiao Gao sent me a text message an hour later.

Wanting to keep the image of the barbarian pure and clean, I wired the money to her account. How those guys could walk onto that plane with their dignity intact, I will never understand.

That afternoon I couldn't resist calling the general manager in Europe. There was still anger in my voice when I got him on the line. 'Patrick, the attitude of your new production manager is really pitiful. Taking revenge on Xiao Gao for his failed attempts at the JV was pathetic. This shows how carelessly you're handling your Chinese investment. If you continue sending uninterested or insensitive people the situation will only deteriorate, probably to the point of no return. The JV agreement you signed six years ago was the beginning of a relationship. Why can't you nurture this business bond a bit better? It really reminds me of "out of sight out of mind". Listening to all the recent stories coming out of this JV, I've got a horrible feeling that this is an accident waiting to happen.'

A hesitant Patrick replied, 'You certainly know our history. I don't want to sound like a broken record, but. . . .' And here we went again with the JV gripes.

'Personally I'm fed up with the mental energy this company is sapping out of me and my staff. Since our first Vice-General Manager Dirk left the Chinese factory and retired in 2002, we haven't found anyone who could replace him. After all the past troubles I thought that Mark would be able to handle this more diplomatically.' And so the story was repeated for the nth time:

... about the experienced manager sent over from Europe to replace Dirk: The harsh living conditions and the missed family resulted in his stay being cut short after only eight months of 'forced' labour in China.

... about the fact that the JV factory seemed to be running smoothly and that the Chinese staff over time seemed to be thinking in a more Western way.

... about another young upcoming manager sent over for miracle healing. 'He definitely wanted to prove his credentials in the company and was a good match, or so we thought. In the end we really didn't know any more what it meant to be a qualified replacement for our Chinese JV. As long as the person could manage the factory with his technical expertise we felt OK.'

Stopping the story in mid-repeat I said 'Yes, we all know the effect of that guy's presence on the mood of the employees. Not to mention the never-ending production problems. Although I wasn't present when Mark knocked on the JV's door, I've kind of got a feeling that he also had a talent for blowing up bridges.'

An annoyed grumble was clearly audible on the other end. 'Really? I understand you're upset because we didn't involve you this time, but that's the way Mark wanted it. He promised that on his return the JV would be spinning as smoothly as the company he managed in Africa before joining us.'

'Well how you manage the place is your choice. But do you really think we appreciate the way our past efforts are methodically ruined by the sloppiness of your staff? This also affects our reputation with the JV partner. You're stubborn as a mule, and only call for our services when you're running out of options.' On this the conversation swiftly ended.

A month or so later I got our PT family on the line once again.

'One of our bids came out for an important customer and we need to make sure that this time our deliveries go without a hitch. Would you be so kind to assist us with the discussions?'

This request surprised me a bit. 'What about your permanent staff in the factory? What about Luk the engineer you've got working there? They're all at the front line. I'm not an expert in pipe production. Can't Mark rely on them to work out the issues at hand?'

In a most coaxing voice he replied 'Well . . . he will, but we think there might be more going on than meets the eye. I know from the past that your relationship with the Chinese partner isn't too bad. Maybe you could mend some fences.'

Teasing him a little by picking up where our last conversation broke off, I said, 'So you do admit that you only need us when you're running out of options?'

'Jack, please don't stir that up again. I'm really calling you in good faith.'

'Mmm, I've got to think about it. In the meantime could you be more specific about the quality problems; and how will Mark will be entertaining us this time round?'

'From our lab tests we discovered that the steel being used is often of inferior quality, which influences the structure under stress. Also the accuracy of certain batches is way off scale. They're certainly not manufactured according to PT blueprint specifications, which leads to connection problems. Another unexpected problem is the way the pipes are being shipped out of our factory. The transport handlers treat the pipes so badly that they never survive shipping unscathed. If you agree we'll e-mail you a copy of all the different reports and pictures.'

Always in the mood for a piece of China action, I was eager to go through some of the evidence. 'Well, just send them over as we speak!' While the bits and bytes trotted through the gazillions of servers in the world, I couldn't wait to open the files on my computer.

Taking a quick look through the pictures I was mildly disappointed that the problems didn't seem that severe. 'What's Patrick complaining about?' I thought to myself.

'But these are issues that could easily be resolved locally,' I protested.

'Actually our expat engineer Luk and the others are completely worn out. Every time they come over the staff is retrained and shown how to manufacture the parts according to specifications. Once they turn their back the problems reappear: The wrong material is ordered, machines are not maintained or calibrated correctly. . . .' Pausing briefly, he took a deep breath and kicked in again:

'But you also have to realise that the relationship has become very bad. At present it's hard for us to talk business with our Chinese counterparts. Since Dirk's retirement they've considered us out-siders, none of his replacements were ever able to build up a relation of trust. We're no longer considered the major shareholders in the company. Even as a customer we're not treated correctly. We really have a serious situation that needs to be solved urgently. My shareholders here in Europe are very worried with the performance of the JV. We don't meet the financial targets we set forward, we're losing important customers, and on top of that we're facing a hostile partner. It's not a situation I was expecting and really hope we can do something to save the JV before it's too late. Gossip about our failed China operations has been making the rounds in Europe, and the board of directors has put a lot of pressure on me recently. I hope you understand the dilemma I'm in.'

'The good news is that you're not the first JV desperately looking for profit. I'm glad you've finally realised that working in China is a little bit different from what you're used to. Chinese labour may be cheap, but the operational cost of "unforeseen" circumstances can quickly spin out of control. During our last meeting in Europe, roughly a year ago, I mentioned that the core problem remains with the qualification and motivation of the PT management you bring in. You're kind of running this place as an unhealthy appendix. A willingness to understand and learn the Chinese way is really necessary for it to have a shot at profitability. There's not much that can be done if you're demoralised by all the setbacks, and let the problems fester for extended periods of time. As long as you bring in inexperienced or unmotivated people you'll continue reaping what you sow.'

'So what do you suggest?' he snapped in response to my dull, worn-out sermon.

'I've kept in contact with Mr Yan, the chairman of the JV. This is maybe a good angle of attack? What do you think if we try to get his point of view?'

A couple of days later, an appointment was set up with Chairman Yan in one of the poshest restaurants in town. Appointed by the Chinese shareholder, a state-owned investment company, he almost never set foot in the factory. A lean, sturdy ex-army officer, he was taller than the average Chinese. He was in his mid-fifties, with greying hair dyed black, and he radiated an aura that demanded respect. Typically chain-smoking expensive cigarettes and dressed in the latest brand names from Beijing's upscale shopping malls, he was accustomed to a life worthy of a chairman. Seeing me walk into the private room, a huge smile was followed by an extroverted, loudly echoing 'Jieke, old friend, how are you? Glad to see you're back from Taiwan. Have you been able to liberate the place? If not I'll do it!' His voice bounced through the dining area.

Since he'd been diagnosed with high blood sugar, rich food was off the menu for him. But face demanded that he only patronise restaurants that were all glitter and dazzle. His hunger was satisfied these days by spoiling the twenty-something-year-old beauties by his side. The *er nai* – second wife – was his way of decorating the dining table. This time a well-manicured woman dressed in a gown worthy of the Oscars adorned his side. The big-breasted, fine-legged lady looked like the kind of model you only see in fashion magazines. When she shook hands, the braless Xiao Mei showed off her curves in the best light, and the sparkling diamond on her necklace was nicely tucked between her female assets. Trying to concentrate in this type of setting wasn't easy, at least not for me. For a man of Chairman Yan's age to be able to gather, maintain and handle this much beauty took real artistry. It had to have been an expensive undertaking, but one that displayed his capacity to spend money as he deemed fit. Allowing her to mingle with me, a mere mortal, was a way of displaying his status to me, and doubtless also to everyone else in the vicinity. Actually 'second wife' was an understatement, as he made a point of bringing along a different sexy lady to each of our meetings. Probably he had a whole stable of racy girls, spoiling them with brand clothing and cars, even apartments for the more loyal ones.

Any one of them could have been mistaken for his daughter or, with a bit of luck, his granddaughter.

While expensive Cantonese seafood arrived on the table, small talk about Taiwan ('the province of', to be more accurate) filled the private room, followed by the amazing fact that Xiao Mei could afford not to work, pollution in the capital, and how Beijing had won the honour of hosting the Olympic Games. As our fascinating discussion shuffled along at a pleasant pace, Chairman Yan insisted on serving Xiao Mei and me with deep-fried oysters, steamed crab, stir-fried shrimps, ginger lobster and the like. Whilst he was satisfied with a nibble here and there, I tucked into the delicacies with unbridled enthusiasm.

As if his body had to be oiled like a car engine every so many kilometres, the most expensive rocket fuel was ordered and poured into our glasses 'to dilute the blood', in the words of Chairman Yan's doctor. Both of us drank only a tiny glass from the 130-euro bottle.

I took a fleeting glance at our lady, who was being quietly beautiful, and noticed she had only played with the food on her plate. At most half a shrimp and an oyster had landed in her stomach. It didn't bother me too much as my eyes were comforted by the diamond still safely tucked away in her cleavage. The tablecloth on my side of the table, however, was full of cracked crab shell, streaks of yellow ginger sauce, lobster carapaces, spilled soy sauce and stains of jasmine tea.

'The barbarian at his best,' I observed wryly. Not that anyone noticed the carnage: the messier the table the better the food. Halfway through dinner I got into the meat of the conversation about the JV.

Initially he feigned disbelief that the barbarian JV partner was still unhappy. 'What more do they want? The factory is running at full capacity! I knew that bringing those barbarians into this deal meant trouble! Barbarians can't be trusted. Now we give them our land and labour. Still they're not satisfied. We need to remember how they treated us a hundred years ago. They destroyed the Summer Palace and handled our people like dogs! Never again! China is strong now and will never be bullied again!' The soldier in him vented his frustration.

'Don't worry Jieke, I don't mean you. You're my friend, but some other barbarians can be so inconsiderate.' This while toasting me with a cup of jasmine tea.

'Let me talk to General Manager Chen of the JV and see what the situation is. If there's anything we can do to improve the business we'll do it.' Then he waved his finger in the air with a determined look. 'But the efforts must be mutual. Don't expect us to give in without them making any efforts to smooth the situation! Come let's have a last drink for our friendship.'

Mr Yan was there to make sure the government didn't lose control of the strategic state-owned property that was part of the JV. From behind his desk in Beijing he had more influence than Patrick ever could imagine. The thought that as a majority share-holder PT was in a position of power and decision-making was simply a mirage. In the end many a foreign investor had to realise that once they'd coughed up the money, they could easily find themselves knee deep in the shit.

The government's idea of reform was to let foreign investment flood through the once-closed gates to assist with the modernisa-tion of the country. When in 1979 China opened again to the outside world, the first joint venture law was published. It allowed foreign investors to pour their money into several sectors, not including telecoms, insurance, distribution or power generation. The law was fairly simple, but left many issues open for interpreta-tion. Unfortunately not many small foreign investors actually bothered reading the few pages of the law, or going through the hassle of consulting with a lawyer familiar with Chinese rules and regulations. The JV articles clearly stated that certain decisions taken by the board, such as any change in the articles of association of the company, suspension or liquidation of the company, increase or decrease of the registered capital or mergers and acquisitions, would have to be unanimously approved. So even with a 99 percent majority vote the JV would still be unable to change course. On top of that the chairman of the board would 'preferably' be a Chinese national. While in the West this is an honorific title, whose only real value is breaking a tie during board votes or maybe promoting corporate responsibility in the company, in China the chairmanship remains of major importance. If the company's by-laws don't state otherwise, the chairman is the legal representative of the company and quite often holds the company seals used to sign off on all legal documents. Along with this power came responsibility, however: the chairman is legally responsible for the wheeling and dealing of the company. In case of bankruptcy he might be sued as the physical person responsible for the loss. Creditors would always have someone to run after, if not to retrieve their accounts receivables, at least to have the pleasure of putting someone behind bars. However, Chairman Yan and most other such chairmen thought little of the possible legal ramifications their position entailed. As long as the *er nai* stayed pretty and did as the chairman pleased, life was beautiful.

I picked up the bill, which clocked in at close to 500 euros. My sigh of relief was clearly audible above the sound of flicking banknotes – it was pretty cheap by the chairman's standards. Shaking hands on our rediscovered friendship, we promised to meet again in the not too distant future. The deeply buried diamond disappeared elegantly into Chairman Yan's car, never to be seen again.

The chairman's visions of cooperation were seen in too broad a historical context, covering more than a century of Chinese suffering, and I hoped that the discussions with Mr Chen, the general manager of the JV, might be a bit more fruitful for the short-term progress of the PT JV.

Meeting the man in question meant a five-hour train ride through the arid landscape outside of Beijing, followed by a three-hour trip in a minivan into the mountainous hinterland.

Farmers were busy harvesting corncobs and spreading them in a yellow carpet along the roads to dry. The first signs of autumn were already visible: Although the trees were still a busy green and the sunlight was strong, autumn's fruit had appeared in the stalls along the narrow winding roads to the JV. The stacks of orange persimmons and small burgundy-coloured apples screamed for attention. Often these were the only colours visible against the brown, overworked earth, clay houses and white-grey mountain stone. Kids dressed in bright red also helped to break the monotonous landscape. Rush hour here meant swarms of noisily bleating goats following their master back to the farm. Most probably they would be the only major traffic jams along the road for decades to come. We crossed bridges spanning dry riverbeds, the empty waterway snaking alongside the van for a while before disappearing into the backdrop. I couldn't help but think how in those remote areas people's lives had changed so little over the last centuries, even while we were so close to the capital. During the winter this area had to be completely desolate. When freezing temperatures settled in for what must feel like an eternity to the inhabitants, they were totally cut off from the outside world. In those isolated places life would go into hibernation until the first rays of sunshine melted the snow and the farmer was able to tend his land with love again.

After many more dry rivers, harvested fields and villages scattered along our narrow road, we suddenly arrived at a straight, three-kilometre stretch of widened, brightly-lit blacktop four-lane motorway heading directly to the gates of the JV. Adorning a roundabout roughly fifty metres before the gates was an abstract stainless-steel sculpture with pointed ends and copper-plated balls reaching for the heavens. It was hard to describe in artistic terms, unless measured on a scale of ugliness, but it symbolised modernity in this godforsaken part of China. Surrounded by the Chinese, European and PT NV company flags, it stood there proudly, welcoming all guests visiting the factory.

The general manager, Mr Chen, was close to retirement age, and stood about 1.65 m tall with locks of long hair tenderly combed over his balding head. He wore high-heeled shoes and thick solid spectacles with the brand label still stuck to one of the lenses, emanating the dignity of a veteran state-owned company GM. As I was perceived as a good friend of Chairman Yan, I was met with open arms. Having lived for months on end in what could best be described as a backwater he was definitely happy to see a new face. Trying to make me feel comfortable, Mr Chen suggested I take a good rest at the factory's guesthouse, have a dinner with the remaining PT engineer Luk, and meet again in the morning. But I was in no mood to put off the anticipated discussions. Accustomed to city life, I couldn't see myself wasting too many nights in this desolate spot. The factory's odd location originated in the sixties when Mao ordered whole industries to move into remote areas so that in case of war with Russia or the US they couldn't be easily destroyed. Indeed, those pressure pipes became an extremely valuable commodity when seen as part of a tank or cannon.

But why someone, in times of peace, would want to invest hard currency in this place was beyond me. The Chinese shareholders must definitely have been good negotiators to get the PT party to shell out money for the privilege of making glorious pipes in the bush.

'Let's have dinner together. We can meet Luk tomorrow.'

During that evening we exchanged pleasantries while Mr Chen avoided my questions with the adroitness of a skilled politician. At a certain point he must have realised that I was not there to admire his factory, and he tried to seduce me with a local brand of rocket fuel. Knowing the deadly effects of a Chinese binge-drinking session on the brain, I took a polite rain check for a better occasion. The meeting in the morning would still stand as scheduled: 7:30 AM.

The following day, in the early morning chill, Mr Chen had already inspected production at the manufacturing halls before sitting down with me. Joining Mr Chen were the production manager Mr Cai and Ms Luan, who occupied the all-in-one post of HR-accountant-import-export manager. While I explained that Patrick was worried about the direction the JV was going, everyone dutifully took notes on flimsy rice paper with a red embossed company letterhead. They only interrupted my talk when they thought they might have misunderstood something I said.

Once my points were on the table Mr Chen appointed Mr Cai to address the quality issues. 'Jieke, have you visited our factory? You should see our equipment, it's maybe a bit old, but top of the line. It's really quality machinery imported from Russia over forty years ago. Any of the problems it gives us, we can easily solve. We even manufacture our own spare parts! But now with these barbarians, it's different. The precision on the PT drawings is much too strict. How can we manufacture pipes with such accuracy? They need to understand the performance of the equipment. How can somebody in Europe decide what accuracy we should be working with here in China? It's as if they want to show they're still superior to our country. We've discussed this issue many times with Mr Mark, but he only told us that we needed to work more meticulously, that we should be studying the technical drawings more carefully and listening to the advice of the PT engineers. I tell you, they have no idea what they're talking about.'

'Mr Cai, you surprise me. They've invested a lot of money in new equipment. The Chinese investor in the JV even required a certain level of technology transfer. Why are you still insisting on using old Russian-made stuff?'

As if to make his point clear, his voice got louder and more strident.

'You should see the maintenance bills for this equipment. Each time someone from PT NV flies over they rant about our workers mishandling the machines. Their equipment is first class, no doubt about it. But it's not really made to operate in China. The cost of the consumables and spare parts is too high. Everything that breaks down on those machines needs to be imported. It takes weeks to get them here. Almost nothing can be copied. We've blocked the purchase of those parts, because it's ridiculous. A pure waste of money! If we had known all the maintenance these machines require we'd never have allowed them in.'

'But with well-maintained machines you could do a better job and sell more. You can't deny this fact.'

Mr Chen scraped his throat for a good spit through the window and went on. 'The workers. They don't understand how to maintain such complex machinery. Therefore the old way is still the best.'

'What about the material quality?' I asked Mr Cai. 'Is it true that the quality is not up to the drawings' requirements?'

'You know Jieke, the European standards for brass and steel are different from our national standards. Where can we find such steel in China? Do you expect us to ask Capital Steel to make a batch according to DIN norms? It's just a joke. The demands of the PT partners are way too absurd. They need to work according to the quality standards of our country. All this nagging about the inferiority of our material is pretty annoying. What is available in China is top quality, but they're always talking from their own experience, this or that standard. We're not idiots. We've done this business for over fifty years. We know what we're doing. Those guys in Europe don't seem to realise this.'

In a corner of my mind I was thinking that these claims didn't match the profile of the Chinese companies I was accustomed to. It seemed strange that there was no real hunger to learn from PT's technical proficiency, or make use of the top-of-the-line imported equipment. Normally, Chinese engineers would jump at such an opportunity to learn more.

This negative thought swiftly evaporated as Ms Luan's high-pitched voice grabbed my attention. 'It's impossible to work with those PT people. If they really want to work with us, then they should accept our standards. What's that saying about the Romans again?'

'When in Rome, do as the Romans do,' I interjected.

'Yes, yes that's it. Mr Luk imposed penalties on people who don't work according to the production schedule he set forward. He shamelessly took away part of their salary! This is illegal exploitation of the workers. This is a decadent bourgeois capitalist game! Our country was liberated from this and now you barbarians want to impose it again. Our country's leaders will never accept this!'

'Aha, there's the party member in the organization.' I mentally ticked that off on my list of to-dos.

'We already informed the local labour bureau and we were told that if the workers' rights are trampled on once more, we're allowed to rally for a strike. Mr Luk says the orders from PT NV are to be respected to the letter, because customers at the other end of the world are waiting for delivery. But he's always saying the workers are lazy and mishandling the equipment. In Europe it wouldn't be a problem, and this and that. Well if it wouldn't be such a problem, why do they come to manufacture in China? Because we can do it better than they do, that's why! We've been manufacturing pipes for many years, we've received many "model worker" and "model work unit" awards, and no Chinese customer ever complained about quality or delivery. Why suddenly all those complaints?'

Everyone seemed to agree with this statement, and they nodded in unison while slurping at hot cups of tea. Mr Chen, full of appreciation, thanked her for her convincing words.

Ms Luan enthusiastically continued: 'Where transport is concerned, it's their own problem. We told them from the beginning that we don't have thirteen-metre three-axle trailers to move the pipes out of the factory. The length of the pipes is too long for transportation along our narrow roads. The PT NV design department is not qualified to draw pipes for our factory. We should be in charge. Now we need to use our smaller Liberation trucks to ship them out of the factory. A good part of the cargo swings out in the open air. In some of the villages we even had to ask that some vegetable stalls be torn down so our transport could pass along the turns. This has meant a lot of work with the local party officials to get things done. On top of that we need to respect the delivery schedule. Well, we can only do this by overloading our trucks and making our drivers go too fast. Due to the bad road conditions and the weight of the pipes, the tail end starts swaying, which ruins the original shape of the payload.'

'Luckily we've got a 100 percent buy-back clause with them for overseas sales,' Mr Cai chuckled, 'so we get paid anyway.'

Since, in the past, this type of industry was an integral part of the planned economy, the managers were accustomed to offloading their goods without having to listen to their customers. Everyone at the table still seemed ignorant of the demands of a free-market economy. No one grasped the concepts of marketing, supply-chain management, quality control, or least of all competition. Apparently, news about the major changes the country was going through had not yet trickled into this outback. For Mr Chen and his team the buy-back agreement looked like a win-win proposition. A win for the Chinese investors who sent hard currency flowing into the company's bank account, and a win for the factory's people who remained employed. The foreign party didn't appear in the equation, and was merely an annoyance they had to live with.

The PT NV investors, who assumed that business was business, certainly got a wake-up call once reality hit home.

In the afternoon, the nastier issue of profitability was put on the table.

Smooth talker Mr Chen took the lead. 'What about my salary? Have you heard how much the PT NV managers are making? It's shameful. They order us around and how much do we make? Not one penny more than before we sold out to the barbarians. Why should we make all the effort while they're the ones making the money? It's unfair. They take away the iron rice bowl, we need to work harder but at the same time we still get the same salary as before. But we do it, because we're proud of our factory and our workers.' By now Mr Chen was almost in tears. If it was an act, then it was the act of a movie star.

Ms Luan, already a bit nervous about this subject, gesticulated angrily while delivering her point of view: 'The barbarians meet among themselves and make decisions without ever consulting with us. They even eat separately. How can you expect us to respect them and understand what they want?

'The barbarians are always asking us to lower our prices, but in the buy-back clause it's clearly written that the prices can only increase by a maximum of 3 percent annually. A decrease can only be expected when steel prices fluctuate out of a certain range. I'm sure they're cheating us and making a lot of money behind our backs.'

'Could it be that cost of materials has increased over the past year in this part of China?'

Ms Luan went on the defensive, and scornfully lectured me. 'You know that demand for steel and brass is high. Prices have gone up dramatically, we need to get our hands on raw materials. This costs money. As you can see the factory is running at full capacity. I don't understand why the barbarians are complaining – they get their pipes. Do we get to see any of the profit they make overseas with our sweat? Why are they so annoyed with the profit margins in China? The money they lose here can be compensated by all their capitalist habits of making money outside of China. I really can't understand them. When I think of it, those barbarians only want to exploit us workers, there's nothing else on their mind. Why should we be nice to them? Actually we should retaliate and tell the workers to stop all activities.'

By now her hands were shaking with emotion and her eyes burned with disdain.

The topic of profitability seemed to have fanned the flames and stirred up unexpected emotions. This hadn't been my intention, as I had actually hoped to mend fences instead. The virulence of the conversation and the lack of enthusiasm for profiting from PT's technological know-how also tweaked my sixth sense for a swindle. Their act on both these subjects hadn't been rehearsed well, and got me thinking.

On my return to Beijing, with an accountant on hand, we scrutinised the financial activities of the last year in more detail.

Interestingly enough, we discovered that the Chinese JV shareholder, a state-owned investment company, had demanded from the board that the JV pay a salary comparable to international standards for the more important positions. Mr Yan's official salary was in the range of US$12,000 per month, but he could spend almost none of that on life's pleasures. Mr Chen got a feisty US$8,500 per month. But both these salaries were symbolic – sucked out of the JV and ending up in the accounts of the Investment Company – Chairman Yan and General Manager Chen continued to receive their regular income of a couple thousand RMB per month. Talk about motivation!

Had we not dug deeper than the numbers in the official accounting sheets, nobody at PT NV would have realised that this was happening.

This situation obviously opened the door wide to fraudulent activity. Knowing exactly what they were supposed to earn, they actually went home every month with a fraction of that figure.

I knew that Mr Yan, Mr Chen, Mr Cai and Ms Luan were in positions of power, and could at any moment make money at the expense of the shareholders. Having worked in familiar surroundings for many years, they had created a massive network of business partners and political contacts. Without any real leadership from the PT NV partner, the opportunities were too tantalising to ignore.

We dug up a side business not soon afterwards. Most of the raw material and fuel wasn't procured directly from the source, but went through an elaborate set of middlemen and front companies whose names were very similar to the factories producing the material. Along each step of the way a little money would remain behind, adding up to a nice nest egg.

Inferior raw materials were purchased at the price of the superior materials, with 'updated' invoices to match, and the difference was pocketed along the way. Some of the raw materials were resold for scrap even before they were processed.

Also the quantities and types of commissary goods going through the books were bizarre to say the least: Large amounts of cigarettes, rice wine and beer were purchased, along with an excessive volume of meat and vegetables that never ended up in the workers' stomachs.

Much of the frivolous purchases were part of a scam to stock family-owned shops in the different neighbouring towns and villages.

The so-called wasted food was resold to outside catering facilities below cost.

For a fee, the factory trucks dealt with the transport logistics for neighbouring factories.

Electricity hadn't escaped the resourceful eyes of the factory's managers either; the power was tapped off the main and resold.

After literally digging a bit further in the factory's area, a T-joint on the main gas pipe was unearthed. The drawn-off gas ended up two kilometres down the road, feeding the boilers of a small chemical factory.

All these transactions appeared only on the cost side of the factory's books. It involved no expense for the people implicated and was pure profit in their pockets.

Most probably everyone in the swindle kept an eye on each other to make sure that the loot was fairly divided. We never were really able to find out if this only began after the JV agreement, or if it was already a well-established practice before the long noses' arrival.

Actually a small part of me couldn't blame them. The fact that they weren't compensated fairly had created resentment from the day the factory operated as a JV.

But my mixed feelings of 'forgiveness' were partly due to China's long history of turmoil. The pain and sorrow of an entire population were engraved in their spirits, reminding them that tragedy could strike at any time. Most of those managers had vivid memories of the tumultuous Cultural Revolution. Everyone during that period had to fight for him or herself, deceive, blame and sometimes betray family and honour to survive. Nobody came out of that episode unscathed. These were lifelong scars, and the survival instinct still kicked in whenever the slightest opportunity arose.

As the safety net was slowly dragged away, potentially undermining one's social status and livelihood, personal interest prevailed. It was of the utmost importance to protect oneself and one's family against a rainy day. One had to make sure that 'opportunities to prosper' could be turned into valuable personal assets (money, relationships, goods) for when the good times inevitably turned sour.

Two days after reading our findings, Patrick and Mark flew to China. They were on the path to war with the local factory management and the Chinese JV partner.

In the months that followed, a whole team of skilful PT managers remained full time in the JV. As the barbarian executives started to tighten their grip on the JV, less-obvious scams began to come to light. Within two months of his presence in the JV, PT's chief accountant discovered company stamps on a wide range of inappropriate invoices, all of which led cash astray. When adequate checks and balances of all the company's internal purchasing and sales procedures were implemented, many of the local management team appeared to have been involved in financial irregularities of one kind or another. Even the names of mid-level government officials, the selfless servants of the people, bleeped on the radar screen as having received 'gifts'.

As was expected, the request to oust Mr Chen turned into a first-class brawl pitting the outside and inside shareholders squarely against each other. Workers went on strike for extended periods of time. Mr Yan, the chairman, played an extremely active role in fomenting resistance against the barbarians. Having survived many class struggles in the past, he knew how and when to play his cards. In the end politics won out over all manoeuvres to get rid of them. The Chinese investment company insisted that both gentlemen, although stripped of power, remain on the payroll of the JV until their retirement. Ms Luan was transferred to another state-owned company. Others got the boot.

The new CEO of the JV, an experienced China hand, had leverage and moral authority to implement changes. After that, pipes were manufactured more closely to equipment and material specifications.

Mark, with his phenomenal library of Asia 'wisdom', was right for once when he cited a Japanese proverb: 'Vision without action is a daydream. Action without vision is a nightmare.'

The bright side of the story?

China's infamous 'manager's pension syndrome' – in which a manager aged fifty-nine, a year from retirement, would make arrangements to siphon money out of the company's bank accounts and disappear into thin air – was *not* part of PT's joint adventures.

Postscript

- Patrick has had difficulty accepting the compromises, and has worked very hard to buy out the Chinese partners. He's now recovering from a heart attack.
- Mark married a Chinese lady he met in the JV. They divorced roughly one and a half years later.
- Mr Cai was politely asked to leave the company when he continued to refuse to operate the digital production equipment.

- Over the years, prosecution of graft has become more effective while newspapers and TV programmes are encouraged to dig up dirt.

- After the dust settled, I never had the pleasure of Chairman Yan or his *er nai*'s company again.

- Although PT NV initially sent inexperienced staff to run their Chinese subsidiaries, we've noticed on several occasions that foreign companies send over managers who are useless in HQ, whom top management wanted to root out of their own corridors of power.

- The installed power-generating capacity in China exceeded 700GW in 2010 and will reach around 1,800GW by 2020. The Three Gorges Dam, which included twenty-six separate 700MW generators when completed in 2009, produces a total of 18.2GW.

- In 2006, on average one new coal-fired power plant was linked to the electric grid somewhere in China every eight or nine days. That year beat all previous records: 100GW of new capacity was made available. This trend will continue unabated for the next ten years. Global warming doesn't seem to be a concern.

- This is in comparison with wind power which in 2007 received an additional 2GW of capacity. In 2013 more than 15GW of windpower was installed. China expects to have more than 200GW of wind-power on the grid by 2020.

- Even when communicating across cultures in English, the message often comes across differently than the messenger intended. This was proven during a conversation with a Chinese friend of mine: 'Melting of the poles? What? You barbarians use any excuse to deny us our prosperity. The inhabitants of Poland are not affected by our power plants.'

- Having seen too many cases of abuse of Chinese workers in the form of low or delayed payments, physical maltreatment, non-signing of employment contracts, and unhealthy working conditions, the All-China Federation of Trade Unions has received the go ahead to grow some

teeth and protect workers' rights in the last couple of
years. Since then, multinationals seem to be complaining
the most about their perceived right to treat workers as
they saw fit. Not any longer. Joint ventures, wholly-
foreign-owned enterprises and other investment vehicles,
you have been warned.

CHAPTER 10

Chaos in the boardroom

In the 19th century the foreign devils flooded the Chinese market with opium under the protection of the superior military technology of the British, French and Americans.

The tide only turned when an advisor to the Imperial Court stated: 'Learn the techniques of the barbarians in order to control them.'

To the present day the strength of this advice is still alive and well in the Chinese business mind.

Add a snippet of Mao's strategy and the road is wide open to conquer the world.

'We stand for self-reliance. We hope for foreign aid but can't be dependent on it; we depend on our own efforts, on the creative power of the whole army and the entire people.'

August 5th, 2006, Düsseldorf, Germany

Flamboyant Mr Zhang had finally been able to purchase a most coveted asset from a main European competitor, a producer of let's say 'widget equipment'. Basking in the glory of now owning the brand name of this century-old family company for a rather small fee, we were to celebrate on the Reeperbahn in Hamburg. But for me it also meant the agony of having to sit in the passenger seat on the autobahn while Mr Zhang pushed the rental v8 engine to his driving limits.

Hearing him shriek, 'I'm short-sighted like a seal,' while sliding into the air stream of another car refusing to get out of his way, certainly got the adrenaline flowing. Or was it listening to the

Beijing opera songs blaring out of the CD player while the landscape flashed by that gave me the usual anguish? I'm not quite sure any more.

However all this sorrow was quickly forgotten when we plunked into one of the theatre seats to watch a porn show consisting of short sketches rotating around hard-core sex performed by actors dressed up as Superman, Zorro, King Kong, Snow White, Dracula or other fairy-tale creatures.

In the eyes of Mr Zhang, the most entertaining part was during the intermission when friskily dressed ladies walked around the audience with a carrot, a vibrator and a cucumber, with the understanding that any of the objects were allowed to be used on those performers who'd fake a quick orgasm and move on. This and other memorable shows had been part of Mr Zhang's pilgrimage whenever he flew into Europe. During many dinners thereafter the Bahn's experience remained the subject of discussion whenever there was a dip in the conversation around the table . . . only to be spiced up when he'd mention the classy Costa Rican escort girl I ordered for his forty-third birthday.

As tough as he could be at the negotiation table, he would agreeably part with cash to have a good time out with his friends. Mr Zhang lived by the slogan 'work hard, play harder'. But this certainly had not been the case when roughly fifteen years earlier he had been forced to jump into self-employment with a fistful of dollars. . . .

Working as an engineer for a state-owned enterprise specialising in 'widget equipment', Mr Zhang was part of an assembly and testing team. His task: to make sure that all the screws and bolts on the equipment would be tightened strongly enough. The design and technology used on those Chinese widgets was from the fifties and hadn't seen a major upgrade since, which in a sense was normal as there was no real need. Everyone was manufacturing from the same blueprints which came from a research institute that had copied it from an imported West German machine in 1957. Competition was nonexistent. Making sure the yearly production quota was reached was more than enough. Always being able to deliver, the factory was one of the bright stars in the widget industry.

By the beginning of the nineties, however, foreign widget equipment makers slowly but surely discovered the Chinese market. Selling at prices roughly thirty times higher than the local equipment, the managers in Zhang's factory couldn't envision too many customers eager to shell out such an amount of money. But as the economy became more and more open things changed drastically. To the surprise and despair of many SOEs, the Western widget machines took the place by storm. In quick succession many of the old mammoth companies lost market share. Unsold equipment clogged inventory and in desperation for cash, the machines were sold below cost.

During that period the central government also pushed many of its SOEs to reform and adapt to the new realities on the ground. No longer fully supported by loans, panic-stricken, the factory began delivering equipment that wasn't assembled properly and performed poorly. This was the straw that broke the camel's back. Unsatisfied customers turned away in droves. Consequently his employer, unable to compete any more against the sophisticated foreign onslaught, went bankrupt in 1992. Overnight Mr Zhang was made redundant. Having only known the world of widget equipment and end-users, he took the brave decision to become self-employed, taking with him whatever drawings, know-how and customer lists he could carry under his arm during his last days in the office.

With a capital investment equivalent to three hundred euros, borrowed from family and friends, a company for the maintenance and repair of widget machines was established. His office space consisted of the twenty-five square metres flat on the old factory premises where he had been living since marrying his wife several years earlier. Initially servicing for a small fee the machines sold by his ex-employer, the business got moving. Grabbing business wherever he could, the message of his magic touch spread in the widget community. By word of mouth he quickly became known as the man to contact when the widget machinery was failing once again.

With a disarming laugh he often told how he'd drawn his first spare parts with pencil and paper, knocking on doors of old schoolmates to have them manufactured in their work units during spare time. Without initially realising, he grasped the key to his present success: designing and manufacturing parts. As his experience grew with each machine repaired, his self-confidence got stronger. His first staff member, Mr Wang, an experienced machine tool operator, sometimes went without salary for several months, as money was invested in the spare parts delivered to clients who'd pay only months later.

Two years after having left his iron rice bowl he came to realise that his know-how was more than enough to actually also design the whole widget machine by himself. His first system was sold when still on the drawing board. Although it was nothing more than a slightly improved copy of the Chinese model, he found a niche market of customers who trusted his abilities.

While American and European widget salesmen swarmed the Chinese coastline, lots of potential Chinese customers were faced with a myriad of technologies they weren't familiar with. Some of the equipment initially purchased was so sophisticated it demanded too much maintenance or required special products to remain operational. It quickly dawned to government importers that they needed to organise themselves better to be able to identify which overseas system might best suit their customers' needs. Those buyers, in search of an expert, hired Mr Zhang as a technical consultant to assist them with technical specifications during tendering, advising on equipment set up and add-ons.

This is turn gave him the opportunity to directly ask Western makers very specific questions, who innocently or out of pride gave him the technical answers he needed to develop his own widget machinery. On top of that Mr Zhang was always present during fine-tuning and acceptance tests, observing the very best in the field. With copies of maintenance manuals in his possession, he slowly but surely got familiar with the ins and outs of Western widgetry equipment. With a staff now of ten his after-sales business further expanded by taking on the maintenance of overseas brands. And in no time, he was designing and manufacturing spare parts and consumables for Chinese customers at one tenth the cost of what was coming out of the West. Adored by clients who saw their maintenance bills shrink in size, demand for his services grew. When he got the bright idea to insert 'Made in Germany' on the packaging, who could resist such an offer? Sales went through the roof.

Other Chinese entrepreneurs who saw the success of Mr Zhang started to emulate his business. Having to shave big chunks from his profit margins to be able to sell was his first wake-up call. He'd either have to become more cost conscious or differentiate from the pack. After a while he set his mind on developing equipment that would be on par with what was available in the West. Realising that for such an accomplishment outside help was required, a couple of bright professors from the Department of Electronics at a local university became part of his strategy. For a fee they developed the electronics and software required for his Widgetry Version 2. Fast forward three years and Widgetry Version 3 came out of his production hall.

During all that time he never appeared as a threat on the radar screen of his Western competitors till one day on a widget-related exhibition in Shanghai he showed off his latest range of Widgetry Version 3. The equipment contained a mix of some of the best ideas and designs from his overseas rivals. Having made a product that was sold at roughly half the price of his overseas competitors, they took notice. They had to. Suddenly Mr Zhang's equipment appeared to be a real contender for many projects. Within three years of Version 3's appearance his enterprise grew to over eight hundred employees. Foreign competitors were left only a narrow Chinese market segment where their top-of-the-line machines could be sold. Others simply disappeared from the Chinese landscape.

As Mr Zhang's company became a real risk to Western competitors, overseas companies approached him on several occasions to buy into his enterprise. The offered prices never seemed right and anyway he refused to let anyone touch his growing baby. Having seen what the bankruptcy of the SOE had done to some of the families of his old colleagues, the responsibility he felt towards his staff was too strong to ignore. Having no MBA under his belt,

gut feelings were telling him that a clash of cultures was not really
in the interest of the company.

On the one hand his instincts whispered to him 'Sweat it out
with your closely knit team of employees rather than have outsiders
interfere.' On the other hand having those esteemed companies
knock at his factory doors boosted his confidence one notch higher.
'I'm on to something big here.' The myth goes that he'd always
rebuff those investors by telling them that he'd rather buy their
company instead.

Meanwhile customers in Thailand, Indonesia and Malaysia had
shown a decent interest in the quality of his equipment. Consequently
sales spilled over into that region of the world. Encouraged by the
huge margins he could get compared to what the Chinese market
had to offer, an office was set up in Malaysia's Johor, just across the
strait from Singapore. Machinery not only ended up in Southeast
Asia but also in the hands of European end-users who discovered
to their surprise that this time the label 'Made in China' meant
'product of excellence'. As international orders poured in, a myriad
of patent infringement suits followed the company. To steer clear
of those legal confrontations, some equipment was transshipped
through a third country before reaching its final destination.
Ultimately this subterfuge failed when some of it got impounded
at customs.

Change was needed to be able to conquer the world. Cosmetic
modifications on design violations were implemented wherever
possible. As the mix of quality at unbeatable prices gained acceptance among many users, his Western competitors were facing his
products in their home market. Lulled to sleep by their past success
many of the Western managers actually thought that no customer
in his or her right mind would ever trust Chinese-made equipment.
They had underestimated the determination of Mr Zhang and his
team, their technical leapfrogs were amazing. Improvements that
had taken Western companies a decade or more to achieve were
shrunk to two years on the Mainland. The speed of innovation and
quality advances coming out of Mr Zhang's factory was for many
a total shock. As Western competitors got a taste of their own
medicine, their sales faltered in key markets and, in the case of one

German competitor, the family-run Dasdings GmbH suffered a restructuring. Among the staff made redundant were experienced R&D engineers. A fifty-eight-year-old design engineer, named Robert, was one of them. Still feeling he had something to offer to the world of widgetry, he got in contact with a government-sponsored organisation that assisted unemployed experts. The deal: they'd be sent to companies requiring their know-how; in return the government would pay salaries, while housing and travelling cost were to be covered by the applying party. Robert knew Mr Zhang very well and informed him of the opportunity available and at minimal cost.

For Mr Zhang, Dasdings' equipment was the reference in China, as during the sixties and seventies all Chinese textbooks referred to this technology as top of the line. The reason? The imported West German equipment during the fifties was a Dasdings and it was the last to enter Chinese territory before the country closed its doors to the outside world. This machine became for Chinese experts *the* reference to talk about.

Two months later Robert had signed a government-sponsored contract for ten months. In return Mr Zhang gave him free rein to develop a machine from scratch and spoiled him with a villa and car.

Having developed some bright ideas and concepts of his own on the widgetry front, this engineer was never able to fully implement them at his ex-employer. Too much red tape, a conformist company culture and lack of money had hindered putting his concepts into practice.

Now was his moment of glory to leave a legacy to the world. Overwhelmed by his newfound freedom to create and apply his lifelong experiences, he developed Widgetry Version 5. The machine that came from the drawing board had some impressive improvements; to Mr Zhang some were downright revolutionary. Version 5 used 13 percent less power, production rate increased by 9 percent, one industrial computer controlled all movements independently and resynchronised them whenever a shift cropped up, consumables' lifetime was improved dramatically while maintenance reduced to twice a year. Robert, or Luobotou (Carrot-head) as he was by now nicknamed in Chinese, became the hero of the day.

In Robert's old company everything was discussed endlessly and coming to a meaningful solution was always a painful process. When the equipment required an adaptation, a neverending cascade of meetings was required to make minor changes to the existing blueprint. Design engineers would bicker about which innovation would be most suitable and how to implement it. Often production engineers would oppose those modifications as they knew that change meant recalculations, followed by tests and a whole administrative process to evaluate the adjustments that had to be implemented. Finally top management would resist changes as it often meant gargantuan costs. Being used to having a major upgrade every eight years or so, they didn't want to write off their old development costs overnight. Their principle was to milk the cow till it dropped.

So they stubbornly stuck with their existing technology hoping that with enough persuasion power, customer training and prodding they'd be able to continue pushing their time-tested expertise onto the Asian factory floors. Apparently customers thought differently.

In a period of fifteen years some of the best in the industry had seen their technological advantage shrink considerably. The Chinese companies however were at the winning end.

Eighteen months after Carrot-head first arrived in China, the Version 5 prototype rolled out. Once the teething problems were solved, sales skyrocketed in the Asian region. Those European end-users who hadn't yet relocated their factories to cheaper pastures also thought of purchasing into Version 5. A combination of luck and gut feeling had finally propelled Mr Zhang close to the best of the best in the widgetry industry. The only thing that really eluded him was a brand name with worldwide recognition.

Mr Zhang had been in touch with me for a couple of years. My first job was to assist him with setting up a sales network in Europe and build a miniature marketing campaign. Miniature because his mindset was still stuck in the phase 'Everything that costs money but I can't see or weigh is money wasted.' On the sidelines I also assisted him with putting in place a more user-friendly maintenance and operation manual. In due course our business relationship turned into a close friendship.

So, when Robert's ex-employer Dasdings GmbH came to Mr Zhang's headquarters for business discussions, I was asked to attend. As usual with Mr Zhang, I got a call on my cell phone one day earlier requesting my presence ASAP.

'You need to come over! This company would like to discuss some business issues with me. If a barbarian is in our midst, I look more important!'

'But I'm planning to be in Taiwan two days from now!' I said, trying to rebuff him.

'You can liberate Taiwan later. I need you, so we can eat lobster and have fun with the other barbarians in the *karaoke,*' he said, trying to sweeten the deal.

'What do you expect from me there? You must tell me what I need to do. I can't just sit there for the fun of it,' I complained.

'You can listen to what they say among themselves,' he chuckled.

'But those guys speak German. I won't understand half of what they say! Why don't you ask Carrot-head?'

'I don't want him to meet them. He worked for them before. Anyway understanding half of what those barbarians say is better than us understanding nothing!'

'What do they want to talk about?' I said, still unconvinced I should go there.

'I don't know. The big boss is in China and would like to discuss some issues with me. Maybe cooperation. I really don't know.'

Sensing he was avoiding my question, I asked once again and finally got a snippet of information to build on.

'When we were in Nuremberg on a fair I happen to meet a colleague of Carrot-head, who confided to me that their business was not that good. There have been more lay offs. Actually the CFO of Dasdings GmbH has been in contact with Carrot-head to check if I would be interested to merge my operations with them.'

Taking a deep breath, I said: 'Okay I can come in tomorrow morning but at 5 PM I really will have to leave. Please promise me you'll let me go.'

'OK, OK no problem!' quickly came from the other side of line.

Arriving in his office at 9:30 AM I expected Mr Zhang to give me a quick briefing. But as could have been anticipated, there was no Mr Zhang in his office, no Mr Zhang on the work floor and no Mr Zhang anywhere in the company.

'Great!' I grumbled to myself while dialling his mobile. Two calls later he still hadn't answered the phone. Asking around if anybody had any idea where he was, the answer was a bleak no. Calling up his wife, she told me he was still in bed.

'A big customer came by and my husband had to entertain him till the wee hours. I'll tell him you're waiting for him in the office.'

Around 10:30 AM Mr Zhang was on the line. 'I just got out of the shower. Very, very sorry not to be in the office to meet up with you, but I had this urgent meeting. Let's have a coffee at Starbucks, because I have a terrible headache from yesterday. Too much alcohol with the people from Inner Mongolia.'

A bit annoyed having wasted a morning, I asked, 'When are those German barbarians arriving?'

His plain response: 'They'll reach the office around 2 PM. I just wanted to make sure you'd be in time. Let's talk later. See you at the coffee shop!' quickly ending the conversation while I heard him vomit in the background.

Around 11:30 AM Mr Zhang finally stumbled into the coffee shop, with a bewildered look dropping into the seat in front of me. The splitting headache apparently hadn't subsided yet. Slurred words mumbled out of his mouth. 'Don't talk to me now. Please. Get me some tea and coffee.'

A couple of cups later, he was ready for his first meal of the day. By now not a word had yet been exchanged about the upcoming meeting. Walking into a fast-food chain store to order his favourite dish, twice-cooked pork fat with noodles and vegetables, I tried again: 'Mr Zhang, come on, you can't just have me come over for some noodles. Let's get to the point.' A gulped bowl and a healthy burp later, his body slowly recovered from yesterday's splash.

'Jieke, I really don't know why those barbarians want to meet. Many years ago we discussed a JV, but those guys were so inflexible nothing came out of it. From Carrot-head I know they're in financial trouble, so I can't fathom what they want from me.'

We returned to the office at 1:35 PM. While Mr Zhang went off to discuss some technical issues with his production staff, I kept myself busy surfing the web.

At 2 PM sharp the receptionist, a bit nervous, came up to me: 'Jieke, Jieke, please help. There are some barbarians at the entrance who want to meet Mr Zhang. But I can't find him. I've no idea what they come to do here.'

Mr Zhang was indeed nowhere to be found, again. My DNA still reminding me that in the Western world timing meant something rather rigid, I took the decision to receive them from my end. The German delegation, consisting of five people, all in crisp European suits, stared in surprise when I walked up to them. I was not sure if the stares were because I was in jeans or because of barbarian similarities. 'Mr Zhang apologises for not being able to meet up with you. He'll be here in a minute,' I said while guiding them into the posh meeting room of the company.

'Please sit down. I'll be back in a minute.'

Seeing Mr Liu, the sales manager of the company, I gave him a wave to come over. 'Have you seen Boss Zhang? Some barbarians are in the meeting room and it's apparently important.'

Unmoved he replied, 'Oh they finally arrived. Boss Zhang told me about it and requested me to make a brief company presentation. I'll go and say hello.'

I was slowly coming to boiling point. This information sharing 'on a need to know basis' was working on my nerves.

This time dialling Mr Zhang's phone, I was really lucky. He picked up after only three rings. 'Mr Zhang where are you? The Germans have arrived!'

'You start already,' came from the other end.

'What do you mean? Where are you anyway?'

'There was a problem with the stainless-steel quality we ordered. They delivered plain steel for the price of stainless. I'm on the way to the distributor. This has to be solved straight away otherwise production might have to stop.'

'OK. When will you be back?'

'Very soon. The agent is just around the corner. Just start. Don't worry about me.' And so he hung up.

Returning to the meeting room, Mr Liu was already giving a general company presentation on his laptop. The five Germans, listening attentively to the contents, nodded in unison whenever they seemed to recognise a common company strategy. Raising some key questions to points of interest, they truly seemed to be enjoying what was being conveyed. When market numbers came up however, their faces revealed amazement. Startled by the size the company had grown to, one of the foreign managers intervened. 'Mr Liu, are you sure those figures are correct?'

'I'm really sorry,' Mr Liu replied apologetically 'these numbers are of last year. Mr Zhang only informed me yesterday of this meeting. So I had no time to update the data.'

The only thing we heard in the room was the low humming of German voices. Barely now did they come to grasps with the size of their counterpart. Having discussed years earlier the possibility of a JV or the outright acquisition of Mr Zhang's company, they already knew it was a key player in China. But at that time it wasn't considered such a giant. From a distant Europe and from their China office they had heard of Mr Zhang's growth and foray into other markets, but it was only hearsay. They had never been confronted with the facts. From their expression one could see them think 'Yes we lost market share to him, but still how could this Mr Zhang have grown so big without us realising this? A couple of years ago this company was nowhere as big as now. How did he do this? It would have taken us several decades to get there.'

After the presentation, I exchanged name cards with the five gentlemen: Mr Duering, CEO of Dasdings GmbH, Mr Schmidt H., the chairman, Mr Schmidt S., son of Mr Schmidt and vice-president of the company, Mr Sturer, the CFO and one outsider, Mr Berkmann, an attorney working for the company.

When seeing a lawyer in their midst my initial reaction was: 'Another breach of intellectual property by Mr Zhang? It might be interesting to see how this discussion evolves over the next couple of hours.'

By now it was well past 3 PM. After a couple more cups of tea, Mr Schmidt Junior decided to start his presentation. As his computer was pretty small he requested a link with the overhead projector.

While we were setting up the system, Mr Zhang finally walked in, profoundly apologising for being late and making exaggerated bows while shaking hands.

'Mr Schmidt, good to see you at long last here in my new office. I'm very honoured to have you here. Sorry for being late, but someone tried to sell me scrap metal and I had to handle this matter personally.'

While Mr Zhang was continuing to exchange pleasantries, Mr Schmidt Junior struggled to find the appropriate cables to connect the projector with his computer. None of the cables were the right one. Finally three technicians were brought in to assist with the matter.

Delving through a spaghetti heap of cables from RS232 to USB converters, they either fit in the slot of the laptop but didn't fit in the slot of projector or vice versa.

Fed up with this lousy impression, Mr Zhang ordered another projector to be brought in. In its carrying case no cables were to be found. Indifferent to the presence of his guests he shouted at Mr Liu and the others: 'Why is it that each time this equipment is used, items are missing? I'm infuriated with this situation!'

Up to that moment Mr Zhang had not yet sat down. 'Please already start your presentation, I'll be back soon.'

Slightly upset by the fact that his guests couldn't have full use of the facilities available, he stormed out of the room taking matters into his own hands. Then silence followed. The Germans, not really sure whether saying something would make matters worse, remained mute, just riffling through their papers and anxiously waiting for someone to take the lead.

After five minutes of polite inactivity while hoping Mr Zhang would return, Mr Schmidt finally decided to begin his company presentation from his small laptop.

As Mr Schmidt reached slide three we heard Mr Zhang in the background screaming in a high pitched voice: 'What the heck is happening in this company! Nobody seems to have respect for the company's property. Get me that cable right away!' On hearing this Mr Schmidt interrupted his talk and, slightly amused, looked at his colleagues. 'Shouldn't we wait for a while?' he asked, hoping Mr Liu or myself would give him a hint of how to proceed.

'Don't worry, please continue!' Mr Liu intervened.

In the middle of slide number seven, Mr Zhang returned with a couple of cables. A startled Mr Schmidt saw Mr Zhang pull away the laptop while trying to get the cable inserted into his computer. 'Sorry sorry . . . I need to connect your computer with the projector. . . .' while bowing twice in the direction of Mr Schmidt Junior.

By then the German guests were all grinning at the unusual development of this meeting. While Mr Zhang was fiddling with the cables, his phone rang. He took a look at the caller ID and decided the cables were more important. A minute later, after five more rings of a new incoming call, he finally gave in and answered. Walking out of the meeting room, he first bowed and gestured to Mr Schmidt Senior that he'd only take a minute outside of the room to discuss something.

Meanwhile the laptop's screen saver switched on. Mr Schmidt Junior, too polite to take his laptop back, decided that it might be better to wait for Mr Zhang to return.

So Mr Schmidt Senior got into a conversation with me about business in China and how it had all changed over the last twenty years.

As soon as he asked for Robert, it only confirmed my earlier feeling that this should be an intellectual property issue.

Meanwhile from behind the double-glassed meeting room I could hear Mr Zhang shout something nasty in his mobile about the caller's mother and that if the guy didn't come back ASAP to pick up the fake stainless steel, things would turn ugly.

An embarrassed Mr Liu only smirked while looking at me, not really knowing how to react in front of his guests. The cursing on the other side of the glass continued incessantly, sometimes intermingled with quiet moments while Mr Zhang paced around in wide circles.

Another fifteen minutes later a red-faced Mr Zhang returned, but with a huge smile on his face. He had found the right cable.

Connecting the two systems, Junior's laptop presentation finally came to life on the white wall of the meeting room. Mr Zhang's attention now went to the projection screen that wasn't lowered yet. Taking the remote in hand, he pressed one of the buttons to unscroll the screen. No sign of life was coming from up there on the wall. Apparently someone had taken the batteries out of the remote. . . . A pissed-off Mr Zhang looked Mr Liu straight in the eyes: 'What is all this rubbish in my company! Why is nothing working properly in this meeting room. Should I walk behind your back and make sure nothing else is missing?'

At this Mr Liu kindly offered to get some batteries while rushing out of the room.

'Sorry we're still a young company and need to learn many things from German management,' Mr Zhang apologised. A minute later Mr Liu returned.

With a reloaded remote control the screen finally came down. The discussions could again resume. However the clock by now indicated 4:35 PM and time was not on my side. I needed to head off for Taiwan.

Explaining to the German delegation that I had to leave for another commitment, I couldn't believe my ears when Mr Zhang informed me that he was personally dropping me off at the airport.

'Mr Zhang, you haven't been spending much time with your guests yet. Shouldn't you take care of them?' I protested.

'Don't you worry! You're my good friend; I can't send you off like that. Mr Liu, please take care of the guests till I return.'

As these discussions were held in Chinese the poor Germans were left out of the loop. When they saw Mr Zhang leave the room together with me I could sense Mr Schmidt Senior's displeasure with the development of the meeting. Shrugging his shoulders, twisting his hands in front of him, he gave his colleagues a ironic expression as if to say 'What the hell is this all about?'

Walking down the corridor I tried once again to convince Mr Zhang to stay.

'Don't worry. Seeing Mr Duering's face, it always reminds me how he insulted me six years ago, claiming I copied their machine. He even tried to sue me in China. The ————! Anyway I still have no idea why they want to talk to me. This German company is as good as finished. With my Widgetry v5.2 they can't compete

any longer. What did you learn from their conversations?' he finally
asked.

'Well to be honest we never went into much detail. They only
gave a very general presentation of the company. With the steady
flow of interruptions there was not much we talked about. It might
be they are looking into an IPR infringement,' came my honest reply.

'This is bullshit! Don't they have sales orders to fulfil instead of
wasting their time on this?' came the retort. 'Listen! I'll tell you why
they are here. They are on their knees and want to have a closer
cooperation. But after all the JV discussions in the past, I've no
interest. Let them sit on their asses for a while.'

'But I'm still confused why you wanted my presence?'

With a chuckle he confided to me 'Actually I had hoped you
would stay for the evening. Listen a bit more to their internal
conversations. Also I wanted to show you something new at Xiao
Wang's Karaoke, but won't insist.'

'Apparently it's now your turn to bullshit,' I hit back.

'I just wanted to make sure all the people of Dasdings GmbH
would see that my company is not that small any longer. That there
are barbarians working for me and on top of that, I did it without
any outside help.'

'So that's why he wanted to set up a perfect show of his great
company. . . . Today that part certainly wasn't very convincing,' I
thought to myself.

While walking through the front door another snippet of info
was released.

'A couple of months ago I jokingly told Carrot-head that we
should buy Dasdings GmbH so we could really go into the market
as a German company. Apparently Carrot-head took this seriously
and talked a bit too much so that's why his former bosses came over
to see me. I made sure Carrot-head would not be in town when
they arrived because I don't want another slip of the tongue.'

'So you've no interest whatsoever in Dasdings?'

'I'm actually only interested in their company name and R&D,
but this is just a far-away dream.'

Certainly such a move would enable him to project an image of
eminence in the industry and further legitimise his operations.

While walking onto the parking lot, I still felt uneasy about Mr Zhang leaving those guys behind. In a last attempt I walked up to his secretary who had just parked her cherry red mini car in front of the building.

'Maggie can you drive me to the airport? Mr Zhang needs to remain here and I don't want him to waste time by driving me to the airport.'

Ignoring Mr Zhang's pleas and arguments I got in her car.

Minutes later we were on the highway. Maggie, single and in her early thirties, was a typical product of the Chinese consumption society. Having bought a car and apartment with loans, she survived on seventy euros a month, after paying off her monthly dues. She didn't cringe under the heavy debt. The fact that her status had dramatically increased in society thanks to her valuable possessions compensated for the low disposable income. She was a happy lady enjoying her life to the fullest.

As I passed through immigration in Taipei, my phone was already ringing. Mr Zhang couldn't resist giving me the latest update: 'During dinner Mr Schmidt Senior offered to merge our companies, develop machines together, share the R&D, produce in China under the Dasdings name but split the market in different exclusive zones.'

He couldn't contain his laugh when telling me that he had said to Mr Senior: 'I'll seriously consider the proposal.' The barbarians had come from far away, so he couldn't make them lose face, but he honestly wasn't interested at all.

A couple of weeks later I received an e-mail from Mr Schmidt Junior, asking if I could assist them to bring both parties closer. This was a bit of a nasty situation to put myself into. Knowing Mr Zhang I was either with him or part of the German team. There wouldn't be a middle way. Not wanting to lose a good friend I declined the alluring offer.

Then nothing was heard from Dasdings GmbH for several months, until I got a call from Mr Zhang. 'The Germans will be back in town soon! They're in talks with some competitors to sell their company. Among them is another Chinese company. Now is the moment to rise above the rest. They might close down operations in Germany. If I can, I'll seize this opportunity. Come over so we can discuss in more detail what purchase strategy we could employ.'

One week later we got our second face-to-face meeting with the German executives.

In the posh meeting room seated at Mr Zhang's side were an old friend and financial advisor, Mr Wang, Mr Zhang's wife, and myself. Three weeks earlier, the financial statements of Dasdings GmbH had been mailed over and scrutinised at length by Mr Wang. The first shot was given by the CFO, Mr Sturer, who gave a presentation loaded with numbers, records and statistics, finally coming to the conclusion that the eighty-year-old company was worth 26.8 million euros.

Mr Wang, an experienced banker who after graduation had worked for several years in Wall Street, took up the challenge of the German CFO. Point by point he poked holes in the sales strategy of Mr Sturer. Assets were valued too high, R&D should have been written off long ago, inventory considered useless, orders on hand put into doubt, long-term debt assumed as too risky, some of the accounts receivables too old to carry along and should have been written off. And so the list went on. Finally Mr Wang claimed that the value of the company should be in the region of 3.6 million euros. Mr Schmidt Junior felt offended by the low number and walked out, only to be called back in by his father.

Mr Zhang's wife, acting as CFO, would point out some specifics to Mr Wang, who'd pick it up and use it as further ammunition to tear down Mr Sturer's presentation. A fencing match between the two ensued for hours on end. Sometimes the two Mr Schmidts would intervene to explain some of the specifics, but overall it was Mr Wang and Mr Sturer's field day.

During the whole discussion Mr Zhang remained in the background, listening in, confirming Mr Wang's points. Pinpointing how high certain valuations were compared to his operations in China, he'd inform Mr Schmidt of the mistakes in the presentation and quietly check out my opinion and exchange a few words to explain why he thought these guys were nuts. But there was actually nothing to show his burning interest in the purchase.

It all ended with a polite shake of hands, Mr Schmidt Senior expressing thanks for the open discussions followed by an offer for Mr Zhang to visit Dasdings GmbH in the next couple of weeks. Mr Zhang's suggestion for a dinner was courteously declined as the tensions built up during discussions needed some quiet private time to subside.

Once the German delegation had left the building, Mr Zhang got pretty excited. 'They're at the end of the road. I can feel it. Those barbarians are desperate to get rid of the company before it's too late. I'm sure there are not many buyers out there for this company. They need us!'

Although the Germans refused a dinner, Mr Zhang had something else up his sleeve. Mr Wang's fierce debate had to be celebrated. Calling up the sales manager, Mr Liu and some of his staff, an appointment was made at his favourite *karaoke* haunt where dinner would be consumed.

Located roughly a hundred metres from a police station, it probably was the best location for a *karaoke* lounge to run its business undisturbed.

The dinner was a quickie. Bowls of beef noodles and smoked duck heads to top it off. Mr Zhang couldn't hide his excitement when calling in his beloved mama-san to give us the premiere of a small show he had requested. Having explained in minute detail the different erotic shows he had seen overseas and noticing the eager reaction of his friends, Mr Zhang realised there would be a demand for this type of entertainment in China too.

The lights were dimmed in our private cubicle and against the backdrop of a disco beat two rather pretty ladies slowly undressed. With their contorting bodies touching each other in the right places, underwear was thrown into the goggling and giggling audience. Enthusiastic applause followed when beer bottles were swiftly opened using a bottle opener stuffed up the ladies' private parts. Ping-pong balls disappeared and reemerged with a powerful blast. Mr Liu's glasses were wiped clean with female underwear. Other performances of the kind ensued one after the other. The show finally ended with one of the beauties belting a dildo around her waist. The other naked lady, taking a seat on the lap of Mr

Wang, was softly penetrated with the rubbery appendage. With both ladies making small panting and moaning sounds of enjoyment, the crowd in the box went over the top. Mr Zhang was ecstatic. This was something people would remember!

That night alcohol was showered around freely between songs. A cocktail of red wine, ice cubes and soft drinks was poured generously in our glasses, to be topped up after every *ganbei*. We sang tipsily through the evening.

Leaving the place around 1 AM, Mr Zhang ordered me to take the front seat as he insisted on dropping me off on the way home.

It was only when he got onto Beijing's Third Ring Road that I realised Mr Zhang wasn't sober at all. Cruising at over 130 kilometres per hour on the nearly empty roads, he thought himself on the German highways.

'Mr Zhang, please slow down. This is too dangerous,' I said anxiously. In the back of the car Mr Wang and Mr Liu were quiet, either not wanting to say anything contradictory to the boss or not realising the danger.

'OK, OK, let's go to a hundred. That sounds safer, right?' But while getting down to that speed he tried another trick to frighten me.

'What do you think of this?' he asked, while veering left and right over the three lanes. Then suddenly pulling on the steering wheel way too much to the right, the heavy car started wobbling out of control. Left, right, *LEéeFT, RIíigHT,* and then a screeching sound accompanied a spin and a half while coming dangerously close to the concrete road kerb.

'We're going to make it,' the optimist in me was whispering. Then a fraction of a second later the rear left wheel hit the concrete fence with full force. After a big bang the car came to a sudden standstill. Airbags burst out, while the car slowly rolled another metre backwards, engine stalled.

Meanwhile a fully loaded twenty-ton construction truck thundering in our direction nearly hit us head on, avoiding us by a metre. Without hitting the brakes the monster roared past creating an air displacement that thoroughly shook the car. Trapped in the car against the road kerb, Mr Zhang got rid of the pressure in the airbag which had hindered his movements and insisted on making a 180-degree turn. Restarting the engine, the car limped like a fatally hurt animal, slowly making a turn on the three lanes.

The smell of burnt rubber permeated the car's interior. Huge loaded trucks were passing by left and right, ignoring the car blocking parts of the lanes.

In the back Mr Wang screamed to slow down as he saw one of the trucks flying our way at full speed. It narrowly missed the car by a few centimetres. Having seen death in the eyes, Mr Wang and Mr Liu were now looking pretty pale.

Mr Zhang, unperturbed, continued on with his manoeuvre, not realising the danger he was putting us all in. Luckily there was a lull in the truck traffic and the car could safely reach the side of the road. Getting out to assess the damage, the result was pretty clear: a twisted axle, the tyre smoking heavily from the friction against the deformed rear end. This car wasn't driving anywhere soon.

Leaving the wreckage behind we hailed a passing taxi, while Mr Zhang, on his mobile, woke up his driver and insisted he should arrange for the maintenance company to pick up the vehicle ASAP. In Mr Zhang's world anybody and everybody was available twenty-four hours a day. The following morning I got a bit of the same.

Calling me out of bed at 8:30 Mr Zhang innocently asked: 'Hey what happened last night? I only remember we hit the roadside. Did some other driver on the road make us do that?'

'Mr Zhang, don't you realise you were slaloming your car on the Third Ring Road?'

'No, no. So funny. I totally forgot. I'm blind like a bat and didn't see it coming. Doesn't matter, the driver is taking care of the car and will have it repaired soon. In case my wife asks what happened just tell her we had to avoid another car. OK?

'By the way what did you think of the show? As good as on the Reeperbahn, right?'

A month later Mr Zhang, Mr Wang and myself were heading for Frankfurt. All of us sitting in economy class, because in Mr Zhang's eyes, flying business class was a waste of company resources.

On the other hand, when renting a car in Europe, bigger and faster was the leitmotif. Driving at over 200 kilometres per hour the first stop was at Dasdings' headquarters. Located in the countryside, between undulating grassland, fields and stark woods, it was a picturesque setting. The little town could well have been the scenery for a fairy tale. With its blue sky, the April sun and the green surroundings, the area was a huge contrast to the pollution-clogged motherland. Mr Zhang declared in all honesty: 'China will also look as clean and pure sometime in the coming fifty years.' Even on the other side of the world, the relentless propaganda machine kept the Chinese mind in check.

At the entrance against the crystal-clear sky the Chinese flag was proudly waving next to the German one. The Dasdings buildings were a mix of old and new. As the business expanded over the years, the company's boom periods could easily be identified by the architectural style. Grand designs of the twenties mixed with the square steel and glass blocks of functional concrete dating from the sixties. The lawn and garden surrounding the offices were kept in pristine conditions. Most probably a gardener was assigned full time to take care of bushes, flowers and trees.

In the lobby both Schmidts met us with open arms. Bad feelings had apparently dissipated enough to project a smile. Before Mr Zhang got the grand tour of the company, an extension of an earlier negotiated confidentiality agreement was signed. Just in case. . . .

Then the gates to the forbidden fruit flew wide open. In the large production hall, only one third of the area was still in use, the rest silent and in darkness. Every five metres a couple of operators were keeping track over a battery of robots cutting metal, drilling holes, bending steel, fitting parts together. Conveyors were crisscrossing the factory floor to pick up finished items and deliver new parts. The heavy sound of buzzing electric motors, the whizzing of drills, clanking of steel against steel and the *spewshhh* of compressed air filled the cavernous hall. Everything repeated over and over again in a flawless ballet of electronic movements, the factory floor so clean one could have had a meal on it.

In the back mechanics and electricians were fitting cables and electric motors before the widgetry machine would be taken for a test spin.

Mr Zhang was impressed and couldn't get over the fact that some of the simplest actions had been automated. 'This is so high-tech ... almost no workers. I thought only the largest of companies would operate this way.'

This certainly was a far cry from the army of workers that were toiling away in his factory. More of the same was happening in the warehouse. The inventory was managed by a large robotic system that would flawlessly pick up and deliver any of the items in its registry, all operated by one person. The R&D centre was also a jewel of sophistication. With the latest software simulation systems, every part was assembled and tested in the virtual world before being manufactured.

It certainly was a pretty extraordinary experience. Mr Schmidt Senior, Junior and the CEO Mr Duering were relieved to see that their guests were overwhelmed. Hopefully it would at the very least vindicate the value of their company.

Sitting down in the plush meeting room with a view of the garden, Mr Zhang was asked if he now realised that the company had some intrinsic value. 'You have a really nice factory. I'm really very, very impressed. I can't understand why you want to sell! You're the best!'

'Thank you very much. Our family has other plans and we'd rather like to withdraw from the widgetry industry,' came the reply from Mr Schmidt. 'Well, Mr Zhang are you still interested?'

Up to now Mr Wang hadn't said a word, but talked up front for the boss. 'Why would you be interested to sell such a nice factory? There must be some problems, otherwise you wouldn't insist so much. We saw that not all the equipment was in operation. There must be something you're hiding and don't want to tell us. Maybe the long-term loans are a real drag on the future performance of the company? Also we don't see how to integrate this site in the existing facilities of Mr Zhang. Everything here is fully automated. In China we can reach the same results without those expensive machines.'

Mr Duering interfered, a bit annoyed by the way the discussion was heading. 'Yes but Mr Zhang, with our facility you could manufacture out of Europe.'

'I've no, and never had any, intention of manufacturing in Europe. My facility is big enough to handle any future production increase.'

The room went quiet, only the birds chirping away in the trees to break the silence. Mr Schmidt Junior looked tensely at Mr Schmidt Senior, before pleading: 'We have well over four hundred employees here, each one of them qualified and very experienced in our industry. All could improve your company's performance.'

'But our company doesn't need so many highly paid people,' Mr Zhang honestly confessed. 'You've the nicest factory I've ever seen, but it's useless to my operations. I thought your company was much more basic. This is too sophisticated.'

With an angry tone Junior hit back: 'So what are your intentions then? I don't understand. We've now been talking at several occasions and all the time I thought you wanted to operate out of Europe. Why did you come all the way from China if you've no interest in our company? Don't forget that we're speaking with other partners too. This is your chance to buy into our company. We had hoped to have an honest discussion here.' He threw his file on the desk to show his disdain.

Mr Zhang first talked in Chinese to me: 'Who does this barbarian think he is? I don't need this little worm. He needs me.'

Then addressing Mr Schmidt: '*It was you* who came up with the proposal to cooperate and later to sell the company to us. We never anticipated moving in this direction. We never imagined to buy such a large European operation.' Then in a slightly arrogant tone: 'The only thing that might interest me is the Dasdings brand name and the R&D department. But only at the right price. The rest of the company is of no value to me.'

Holding back his resentment, Schmidt Senior looked Mr Zhang straight in the eyes while tapping with his index finger on the table. 'No value. *No value!* As long as I'm in charge of this company no one will touch my company name. If you think this is the way to do business with me then so be it.'

Minutes later we were back in the car. Zhang, beating his chest, said: 'What the heck do those barbarians think. I'll get back at them when the opportunity arises!'

Mr Wang was dropped off at the airport. No peeping eyes allowed. The two of us continued our journey for the other part of the business we'd come to conclude.

Feeling too insecure to flaunt his money in China by driving expensive cars and living in opulent villas, Mr Zhang had developed a passion for Chinese art. This was one of the outlets where neighbours or crooks wouldn't notice his extravagances so easily.

Combining his passion for Chinese art with his business wasn't a difficult step either. Mr Zhang's talent to get from the local government what was required was well known, be it tax reductions, orders or other favours. But *karaoke* sessions, digital cameras or overseas business trips could only reach so far.

His latest scheme was offering oil paintings by famous Chinese artists to government officials. A painting was, in the eyes of the layman, often valueless or difficult to appraise. On top of that the art market was awash with copies so it became very easy for the new owners to keep it for a while, pretending it wasn't the real thing and then sell it through intermediaries for hard cash.

During auctions Mr Zhang and friends bid up the value of paintings of certain artists already in his collection. Afterwards the auction houses would report in specialty magazines and websites that this or that painter's works had been well received after intense bidding exchanges. One or two auctions later, when other buyers took the bait, he'd offload part of a particular collection knowing that prices had reached an apex.

Many of today's well-known artists had left behind a trail of paintings in Europe during some of their overseas studies a decade or so earlier.

Chinese art students or professors would come on an exchange programme for a six-month stint and often give away paintings to friends, or sell them at ludicrously low prices to make ends meet.

What twenty years ago would have been purchased for a hundred euros had in a number of cases increased in value by a factor of a thousand or more.

Mr Zhang knew many of the young artists personally, and more importantly he knew when and where they had studied abroad. The trick was to dig up the goodies before someone else did. As some of those artists' rising stars had remained unnoticed outside the confines of the Chinese art connoisseurs, the discrepancy in value perception meant money could be made.

The GPS was firmly pointing in the direction of Kassel, Berlin and Leipzig, places where Chinese artists had lived for a while. Appointments with people in possession of those art pieces had already been made a week earlier. Detailed pictures exchanged by e-mail confirmed we'd be talking about an original. Sometimes we would even authenticate with the painter in question, to avoid a mishap. Most meetings were held at private addresses where paintings often had been sitting in the attic like sleeping beauties waiting for their majestic strokes of paint to be rediscovered by Chinese art lovers. Bundles of cash were exchanged, the painting taken off its frame, rolled up and put with the rest in the back of the car.

Before leaving Europe a couple of days later, we decided to give Mr Schmidt Senior a call just to thank him and wish him well. Around 4 PM the phone rang at Dasdings GmbH.

Nobody picked up. A welcome text by the answering machine clicked in: 'Welcome to Dasdings Company. Our offices are closed from Friday 4 PM till next Monday 9 AM. For any urgent matters please leave a message after the tone.'

Mr Zhang couldn't understand. 'What do you mean already closed? It's only four in the afternoon! Try again, the receptionist might not be sitting at her desk. No wonder those guys can't compete any longer. How can a company survive if they only work so little? I really don't comprehend how Mr Schmidt could allow this to happen in his company. Holidays! That's all that seems to count here in Europe. I even heard of employees wanting to take more holidays instead of receiving more money for working a bit longer every week!'

Four months later Dasdings GmbH went into insolvency and bankruptcy proceedings followed. Under the plan, debts were to be recovered for the major creditors by liquidation of assets through public auction.

Interested parties, among those who in the past year had shown keenness to become new shareholders, were invited to register and bid for any of the listed assets, including the company's brand name.

The room was crowded with a legion of buyers. Most of them had nothing to do with the widgetry industry. A couple were frenetically bidding for the furniture, others wanted the trucks, the robots, or the computers. The sad part was the low prices at which most of those items changed hands. Mr Schmidt Senior was also in the room and for sure it must have hurt him to hear the minimal values at which his properties were sold off.

When the ownership of the Dasdings trademark came up, the auctioneer started at 110,000 euros. In the first couple of seconds nobody went for the offer. Then out of the crowd someone raised his hand.

'Shit,' Mr Zhang must have thought, 'it wasn't one of the two people I planted in the room.'

Having worked the art auction houses in China, he hoped to play the interested parties in a similar way here in Germany. His hand went up. This signalled the others to engage according to a previously discussed plan of action. I was to start bidding against Mr Zhang when only him and an outside party were fighting for the asset and at a certain price level. The hope was that with an unknown third party suddenly appearing while Mr Zhang feigned no longer having any interest, the outsider would hopefully feel unease about where the price was heading. Surprisingly, the tactic worked. As Mr Zhang was the widgetry man in the room, having him retreat caught his rival off guard and created confusion in his mind. 'Was the brand value becoming too high?' In the end the trademark was purchased for close to 320,000 euros and later transferred to Mr Zhang's Hong Kong company.

Postscript

- European and American auctions selling Chinese antiques have become a magnet for Chinese investors.
- A new Dasdings Ltd has been established in Europe, operating as a sales office for Mr Zhang's operations.
- Carrot-head has divorced the wife he married thirty years earlier and is now living in with his Chinese girlfriend.
- Maggie, Mr Zhang's secretary, in the meantime has purchased a new car, slightly bigger than the previous one.
- Beijing recently received the dismal honour of being the worst polluted capital city in Asia (according to a study sponsored by the Asian Development Bank). While more than 5.5 million cars plied Beijing roads in 2013, pollution levels in the city were the highest ever sometimes going fifty times above WHO levels that are deemed safe for health. The pollution recurrently leads to visibility in Beijing below one kilometre and results in the closure of highways, and flight delays and cancellations.
- Mr Zhang and I still enjoy a good night out. His driver is always on duty to skipper the drunken sailors to a safe haven.

CHAPTER 11

A case of mistaken identity

'In the land of the blind the one-eyed man is king', or trans-lated into MBA *lingo 'Superficial attention from investors to the day-to-day operations pushes a going concern dangerously close to a point of insolvency'.*

For some reason, many a company seems to think that without having China actively covered, their long-term future is mortgaged and the market is up for grabs by the competi-tion. Unfortunately some CEOs, *pressured by investors' demands for higher returns, enter the market ill-prepared for the pitfalls that are strewn along their path to profit. Gut feeling and even a methodical business plan alone will very often come to haunt decision makers in unpleasant ways.*

Practical HR *issues and local company laws, which are straight-forward matters in other parts of the world, might re-quire a bit more in-depth attention in China.*

The Bookworm, Beijing, Sunday July 24th, 2010 6:21 PM

While the last rays of the day are still trying to beat dusk I'm sitting on the Bookworm's rooftop bar with a couple of friends. The sweltering, clammy Beijing summer heat is omnipresent while crickets are playing their own droning concert in the background. We're enjoying an early refreshing drink before heading for one of the restaurants in San Li Tun village.

Unfortunately the buzz of my mobile disturbs the peaceful atmosphere. The caller ID is unknown, I decide what is best for my private life and switch to vibration mode. If there's one thing in

China I still can't get accustomed to, it's the business calls coming in at any time, even in the middle of the night, weekends included.

Thirty seconds later, the mobile phone rattles over the table. Same number from the Qingdao area, but I can't be bothered. The caller doesn't seem to be in the mood to stop and my phone gets another three calls. The persistence of the call tells me that if I dare to pick up, the evening will be spoiled.

Later that evening an SMS pops up: 'Please help me. My factory was stolen.'

I imagine an organised gang quietly sneaking into a factory in pitch darkness, dismantling all equipment, chairs and tables included, and vanishing into thin air before the sun comes up.

I call the mobile number around 10:30 PM and got a Ms Yang on the phone, explaining in perfect English about a certain Mr Johnny Best, who hired her for a stint of translation work . . . at the local police station.

Slightly amused by the thickening of the plot I ask, 'Any way I can talk to him?'

'Unfortunately it's late for him and Mr Best already went back to the hotel.'

It turned out that Johnny Best was a sixty-two-year-old business-man, and head of a three-generation old European company specialising in deep-frozen potato fries.

I could vividly conceive the scene that unfolded earlier that day in the police station and herewith reconstruct the events.

'My factory, they stole my factory!' Mr Johnny Best yelled in an exhausted voice still hoping that those anxious foreign grumbles would finally trickle through and convince the thirteen curious policemen gathered behind the glass counter to acknowledge 'this' as a fact.

By now, I assume he must have felt helpless, with total loss of composure and looking far from the CEO of a multi-million-dollar company.

His sagging eyes full of jetlag and bedraggled greying hair reflect back at him through the counter window. A week earlier he felt in full control of his empire and now he was begging for attention from a couple of law enforcers thousands of kilometres away from his home turf.

'What does he say again?' came from an annoyed officer while staring at Ms Yang, the translator Johnny had hurriedly hired through a small company ad found on the desk of his hotel room.

Ms Yang, a middle-school teacher by profession, signed up with a local translation company for a part-time job during the summer holidays. Her aspirations for her first assignment definitely had not included ending up in a police station trying to make a coherent story out of Johnny's confused predicament.

'He tells me that someone took away his factory. Everything including computers, safe, equipment, inventory and even staff has disappeared. Nothing is left. He urgently needs your assistance to catch the thieves.'

Thirteen faces now nodded in accord before turning into a cacophony of comments and laughs on the visitor's remarkable report. 'How stupid is that' ... 'Could only happen to really inexperienced people' ... 'But look how old he is.'

Having had enough of this commotion, the officer in charge ordered everyone to keep quiet and return to their desks. Then turning back to Ms Yang: 'Please provide us proof of company ownership, a list of assets that has disappeared from his factory and when exactly this all took place.'

Mr Best repeated his complaint once again through Ms Yang: 'There's nothing left! The premises are empty. Everything is taken away. The company stamps and legal papers were in a safe, but that has disappeared. The only person who can help is Mr Wang, the general manager of the company ... but he too is gone!' shaking his hands desperately in the air.

The official cut off Ms Yang's translation: 'If you have nothing to show except an empty factory, why would I spend time on you? You can't even clearly tell me exactly when this so-called theft took place. How can I take this seriously? Don't you think we've more urgent cases to work on? Come back with facts, not stories!'

When the officer stood up and made ready to leave, Ms Yang took the role of a destitute citizen looking for a bit of compassion and assistance and begged for support in whatever way possible.

Meanwhile Mr Best, desperately tapped on the window with his nails, trying to catch the attention of the man in charge.

Directly staring at Mr Best, the officer snarled: 'Who in your opinion, was behind the pilfering? To which Mr Best replied, 'Mr Wang, Mr Wang! The General Manager Mr Wang!'

'Fine! Give me Mr Wang's address, copy of ID card and phone number. We'll investigate from there,' while sliding a blank statement paper through the grill in the window glass.

Disconcerted by this simple question, Best replied: 'I don't know where he lives. We had a working relationship and trusted each other. There's no way I would have dared to ask him for a copy of his ID card.'

The officer had had enough of this talk. 'Case closed,' he told Ms Yang and turned around while muttering: 'Always the same with those foreigners, why can't they ever be clear and to the point?'

Johnny gave a petrified stare at Ms Yang, who shrugged her shoulders and with a sheepish smile softly whispered to him, 'You need to look for proof. In China words only are of no use,' and then they both left the police station.

While walking back to the hotel Ms Yang came up with, probably the day's most practical suggestion: 'It might be wise to check if the company's bank account still has some money and maybe try to call your embassy. They should be able to help.'

'I only have an embassy number in case of emergencies,' then he realised '. . . and I think I'm in the middle of a major one right now . . . probably it's time I use my last trump card,' came his dry reply.

It now happens that my phone number seemed to have been in his embassy's database and the staff in charge of emergencies that day must have thought, 'Theft of factory . . . mmm . . . whom should we put in the loop on this?' which resulted in the late calls on my phone.

The following day I got Johnny Best on the line and profusely apologised for not being able to pick up the phone earlier. Although I was still sceptical about the whole thing I went with the flow. A good story on a Monday morning beats the weekend blues.

Herewith Mr Best's version of events:

His China adventure started five years earlier with the decision that the time was ripe to head for China based on extensive marketing and market-entry study.

For someone used to running a business in Europe, his market findings on China were astonishing to say the least: The multi-national fast food restaurants had set up shop far ahead of him and some of those chains had hundreds of outlets spread all over the country. Young Chinese loved fries almost as much as rice. He concluded his deep-frozen fries should be in high demand.

He temporarily hired Mr Wang, a thirty-something MBA graduate, as his consultant to discover the potential of his fries in the Middle Kingdom. Quickly his forecasts far exceeded the conservative estimates Mr Best had made and it quickly became clear that selling to China was a must.

The board of directors further developed the idea and projected a return to the family shareholders far surpassing the 3–5 percent growth they saw in their customary markets. This was the boost Best had been waiting for to move his company into higher orbit and finally make a mark in the company's history.

Soon refrigerated containers of frozen fries were en route to China. Initially business boomed and month-to-month growth clearly followed the neat predictions.

Unfortunately the expensive import procedures, messy logistics to move his containers around the country, the lack of cold storage in key cities, the prohibitive cost of making small shipments from a central warehouse, quickly made him realise that to reach his buyers and keep them satisfied he had to build a production facility in China.

The board of directors went through an investment exercise and generated the customary heap of Excel predictions and graphs which indicated they build a factory at a cost of Euro 4.5 million. A location close to Qingdao in Shandong was chosen, which made sense because it looked like potato paradise. Different varieties were available within a 400 km radius and farmers were eager to sell and at very interesting prices.

Mr Wang, whom Johnny had come to trust as fully as a new-found son, was to head the operations from Day One.

Sadly many of the potatoes reaching the processing site turned out to be too starchy and were not the quality that would provide the superior French fry to which his European customers were accustomed. Production was subpar and the company was heading for a financial disaster, below the earlier worst-case scenarios of return on investment.

So Mr Wang proposed to start importing European and American potatoes instead, which could be processed into a fry which consumers would love to eat. Johnny who trusted Mr Wang's business acumen and local market knowledge, decided without too much hesitation that this should be the way forward.

Potatoes were imported in bulk and processed into the perfect fries any fast-food chain would be fighting for to get their hands on.

From then on the factory hummed along without any major glitch and the company's market share in the China grew dramatically. Mr Best visited his Asian investment at three-monthly intervals, mainly focusing on the accounting part of the business. Transactions generated enough income to break even in the second year, as was originally planned. Johnny couldn't have been happier, both for having followed his instincts and having landed the perfect local team to run his business.

The ever jovial Mr Wang never missed the opportunity to meet and greet Mr Best at the airport and on the way to the factory give him the latest update of sales figures and production costs. It seemed that from time to time the imported raw material would inexplicably rot and could no longer be used in the production process. Initially this was a little blip on the radar screen that hardly dented the profit margins. After a while however writing off inventory became more frequent to the point that growth stagnated. The general manager's responses to the many requests for in-depth explanations on the decreasing efficiency remained vague as always: goods got blocked at customs, haphazard power cuts during production, a 'negligible' amount of potatoes got spoiled during sea shipment, the insurance company wouldn't co-operate and on it went. An on-the-ground investigation became a necessity to solve this problem.

Till that fatal day in July when on Johnny Best's return to his company's most promising market, Mr Wang met him at the airport's arrival hall and handed over the keys of the car and … factory.

'Mr Best I'm really sorry to inform you that I can no longer be your general manager. My family is no longer happy with the workload I face, time spent at the factory and the extensive travel around the country. I need a break. I'm so sorry to disappoint you.'

'Couldn't you tell me earlier?' an irritated Johnny protested while walking to the car. 'Should I give you a raise? Can you return after one-month rest? Tell me what to do to retain you.' But all the objections and pleas of Mr Best were brushed aside. Mr Wang had made up his mind and left him in the middle of the airport parking lot.

Shaken by the sudden departure of his most trusted staff, he mentally replayed the way they first met, together developed the business plan, implemented it and had created a friendly bond. 'What went wrong?' kept on swirling through his head. He hadn't picked up any clues of his dissatisfaction 'Why this sudden departure? Damn you Mr Wang!' he repeated to himself while driving to the production site.

At the factory entrance, the place looked desolate, no guards at the gate, no trucks on the parking lot, no familiar smell of vegetable oil blown into the air. It even seemed that the cold storage area was missing. Wrenching himself through the half opened gateway, he rushed into the offices. Desks, computers, cabinets, tables … all had gone. The place was empty but for a couple of cardboard boxes cluttered in one corner.

He couldn't believe this was happening to him. Since he never had driven himself to the site he quietly hoped that this would be the wrong address, the wrong location in the industrial park. Rushing to the production site, he slid open the main door, only to hear the squeaking metal sound bounce off the walls of the huge workshop several times over. Where equipment once stood, awkward bareness remained. Outside where the huge cold storage units once were installed only traces on the concrete revealed that he definitely was on his company's production site.

A chill went through his spine. 'What has happened here? Where's our investment?' Anxiously calling Mr Wang's number resulted in a message informing him 'This mobile phone number is no longer in use.' Frenziedly looking in his phone's memory for the other staff's numbers only resulted in the same refrain.

Panic settled in. 'Where was his multi-million Euro investment? What to do? Where to go? Who could he talk about this?'

As if it would help, he made an overanxious call to some of his company's board members in Europe, which only stirred up more worries. Now everyone over there was in a panic as well. Since it was still the weekend, a call to the embassy went unanswered, but for a recording giving a number in case of emergency. The Chinese lawyers he used to set up the company had long vanished from his contact base as he never expected to need their services again.

His only option left was to find out where the closest police, or Public Security Bureau, was and explain what had happened.

At the end of our phone conversation I urged him to visit the bank as soon as possible, check the company's accounts and try to block any further transactions. The man at the other end of the line had sounded sharp, decisive, compassionate, intelligent and educated. Not someone you'd expect such a calamity to happen to and after hearing his story I really felt bad for him. Was it his naivety and honest trust in people that had got him into this difficult corner?

With the PSB debacle behind him, I was sincerely hoping that there would be a sparkle of feel good in this quagmire, but a trip to the bank ended in more of the same shock therapy. A kind bank employee who recognised him from his three-monthly visits informed him that the company's bank accounts were close to empty. A quick look revealed that in the last three months the company hadn't generated any revenues and a systematic depletion of cash had occurred.

When I heard this news, I had to prepare him for another possible fiasco: 'Mr Best I understand your company's chops have disappeared. As you most probably know the company chop is king here. A company seal on a document has the same value as a handwritten signature acknowledging the contents of a contract in the West and turning it into a legal paper. You might be facing unexpected UFOs.'

'UFOs? eh . . . are you sure?' came his startled remark.

'Yes UFOs, but not of the flying saucer kind. A customer of ours faced an Unidentified Financial Obligation because of sloppy handling of the company's chop. One of its employees, when she got hold of it, turned a bit entrepreneurial and chopped a couple of blank A4 sheets with the cherry red company stamp . . . "to be used at a later date". That "later date" came a couple of months later when she was let go.

'Shortly afterwards when the company owner thought everything was settled, a lawyer turned up at the company's doorsteps with a document that in short stated: "In case Ms so-and-so is fired the company has the obligation to pay her a compensation equivalent to two years' salary". The document was backdated and duly signed by the employee next to the company's red seal.

'I don't want to alarm you unnecessarily but I think it's better you are aware of this potential threat that shareholders might still have to face.'

This was the straw that broke the camel's back.

Totally frustrated, Mr Best impulsively left China that very same day to discuss further action with the company lawyer in his home country. Surprisingly enough it took many more weeks before he returned to the Middle Kingdom. But by then he knew he had lost much credibility because his organisation had still nothing that could prove goods had been illegally moved from the premises. He didn't even have copies of employment contracts or identity numbers of past employees. Those had all been kept in the factory safe. A lengthy procedure was started to get new duplicates of all legal documents and stamps of the company. It almost seemed that he had to prove to the authorities that his company really had operated in China.

A couple of lawyers and private investigators were involved in trying to reconstruct the company's activities before that fatal day of July 24th. It was discovered that the so-called 'rotten' potatoes actually were not that rotten at all but ended up in the production and the final product, using Mr Best's company brand, were sold off the books through a parallel circuit.

The equipment of Mr Best's company was officially sold to a trading company in the south of China which went bankrupt a month after the transaction. Ownership of that company could not be directly linked to Mr Wang.

Mr Wang had built a similar production site roughly 80 km away from the original location. Mr Best never succeeded at getting a court order to let him enter this copycat facility.

Mr Best, the legal representative of the Chinese company, still has outstanding tax bills for his now-defunct entity and is paying accountants and lawyers to go through bankruptcy procedures and clean up the debris. But no UFOs have appeared on Mr Best's desk.

Bringing Mr Wang to court has remained elusive because no hard proof could be provided that he had been officially hired by Mr Best's company, received a formal salary or that he was the perpetrator of the theft. The 'employment contract' between Mr Wang and the European entity was not based on local laws and regulations, but was a sloppy blend of understandings, goodwill and trust based on the initial few months when Mr Wang acted as a consultant for them. Since all went smoothly from the very beginning and there was a good working relationship, the idea of a formal Chinese labour contract never materialised.

Had Johnny Best made copies of ID cards and all vital company documents, if he had checked that the addresses of senior staff matched with their ID cards, if he had made formal procedures how and under which circumstances company stamps can be used, backed by signatures of legal representatives, chances are Chinese laws would have leant more in his favour.

Mr Wang's company has meanwhile expanded with a second production site in the south of the country. Seedling spuds are now imported into China and distributed to farmers who grow them into a potato fit for fries.

Postscript

- Many other variants of UFOs turn up on companies' desks and those alien to the significance of the company seal can easily expose themselves to the nasty legal consequences this can have for shareholders. Sadly enough those UFOs can sometimes turn out to be a real and eminent threat to the going concern of the company. Avoiding UFOs in a company can be as straightforward as specifying in the company's by-laws how 'company stamped' legal documents should be signed off and by whom.

- Chinese staff are as loyal as any other employees around the world, but give someone an open invitation to become creative and it will be taken. Don't feel sorry if your asset base has been nibbled into because of a lack of due diligence. Most probably the opportunity was created when the company was hastily created to profit from the China boom.

- In the middle of 2013 European Commission said it was ready to open negotiations with China on an investment protection agreement. 'An EU-China investment agreement will help deepen our ties and sends the signal that we are firmly committed to building a strong partnership,' said the EU trade commissioner Karel De Gucht.

- Apparently North Korea has the perfect soil quality and climate to grow fries-friendly potatoes. Large American fast food chains have played with the idea to produce in the famine-stricken country and export to China. For political or moral reasons this has never materialised.

CHAPTER 12

Good artists copy, great artists steal

Western business success in China is often the fruit of passionate understanding of the fast-changing kaleidoscope of markets and regional tastes. When combined with targeted investment adapted to local conditions and allowing deliberate learning from failure to cash in on the experience gained, China can indeed be very rewarding.

But with success follows envy and copycats are never far behind.

When accomplishments in a dynamic market gradually replace corporate obsession to succeed with complacency, lawyers make ready to feast.

Guangdong, February 27th, 2013

Weeks after the Chinese New Year holidays, the Guangzhou industrial hinterland is still coming to terms with the extended work stop. Put into overdrive, trains and long-distance buses are coming back from the furthest parts of the country, hauling in the millions of workers needed to replenish the workplaces. Some of them are first-timers escaping poverty and dullness of the countryside, while veteran migrant workers, having seen glimpses of the China dream, are reinvigorated to endure the long deprivation of kids and family staying behind in the home towns. Guangdong province is crawling back to normality, one worker at a time.

While our taxi slaloms among the packed buses cramming the highway, the dreary misty drizzle adds to the woeful after-party mood.

Off the highway and into the hinterland, human resource departments from toy factories, electronic gadget makers to mould manufactures are already working overtime. Colourful wall posters along factory fences and main bus stops display available jobs and in the largest characters of all, the benefits of joining the team: three warm meals a day, free transport, housing quarters, weekends off, remuneration for overtime, showers. . . . Already a good number of migrant workers are thronging up and finding out if this year their negotiating position has improved. Meanwhile the ever-present overnight food stalls are doing brisk business with patrons discussing, over steaming bowls of noodles, the pros and cons of a job offer.

No such activity at the gates of our destination, as if the plague was haunting the place, the surroundings remained eerily quiet. A lonely, large, official-looking placard indicated that the facility was under investigation for violating national laws. Embroiled in a legal turmoil, the factory requested its labour force to take an extended holiday and wait for further news before production would fire up once more.

A couple of years earlier our lawyers assisted Alfa Paint, a European paint manufacturer set up shop. Their product was an environmentally friendly interior paint that would release no volatile toxins in the air. Having been a success in their home turf, the search for continued growth led the company to embark on a corporate China folly. A state-of-the-art factory was built in the south with the idea to gradually expand and distribute a whole product line nationwide within five years. With the booming property market came a gazillion new owners decorating and renovating their apartments. Intertwined with the rapid economic growth were repeated health scares affecting many consumer products from children's toys containing lead paint to food contaminated with industrial chemicals and pesticides. For Alfa Paint the timing was perfect.

Business roared forward at full speed. Smart marketing strategies, specifically fine-tuned to the proud Chinese property owners, created such a buzz that distributors and Do-It-Yourself chains were almost literally fighting to get the Alfa-Paint brand on their racks.

A text book push-pull effect was created in a matter of months. Pots and cans filled with the colours of the rainbow flew off the manufacturing line.

Production couldn't keep pace with demand. Soon more staff was hired and the production lines expanded with new equipment. Although Alfa's price was at least 80 percent higher than a local products, customers still took notice. Many freshly minted home owners insisted on having Alfa Paint on the walls of their flats.

For the shareholders of Alfa Paint the Chinese Miracle was real!

But sitting in their stylish meeting room with a panoramic view of subtropical flora overgrowing the hill at the back of the factory, the China dream had abruptly and most unexpectedly evaporated. The executives sitting in front of us were all radiating doom and gloom. The contrast couldn't have been harsher compared to a year earlier when Adam and I were invited to the flashy opening of Alfa Paint's tastefully decorated office building. Between duck liver canapés and a never-ending flow of Champagne, upbeat Bossa Nova music drifted through the offices. Owners and guests mingled with Chinese artists whose contemporary art work was prominently hanging in different parts of the workplace. Alfa Paint's lucky employees would be able to alternate stressful working hours at their desk with finding solace in the abstraction on canvas. Anything was possible in the workers' paradise!

Back in today's low-spirited meeting room, Pablo, China CEO of the company, looked beyond tired, with hair that had undeniably greyed and thinned since we last met. With dark puffy eye bags one couldn't say that the recent holiday had been a time of relaxation to recharge his batteries, depleted from an intense year of China business. Instead long-haul flights back to Europe and strings of crisis meetings had hijacked this seasoned CEO's precious recovery period.

In a weary voice his slight Spanish intonation came out a bit stronger than normal: 'Our factory has now been closed for more than a month, with no end in sight. We're told our product violates the national health standard and has been taken off the shelves all over the country. We need to give an explanation for a product we've never made,' an angry Pablo gestured.

'How's that possible?' Adam queried.

'It's our competitor's fault. He copied us!' retorted Pablo.

'But you did register your trademark and got your products inspected by the General Administration of Quality Supervision, Inspection and Quarantine,' we interjected. 'You could have plastered the wall with all the certificates. You have done the conformity inspections, the company even got certificates allowing you to label it as environmentally friendly. It wouldn't be possible for a competitor to take you on from that angle. Right?'

'No!' was the irate reaction. *Joder* NO!' came out a Spanish expletive before going back to, 'No, no no! They've been envious of the success we received from the market and our Chinese counterparts got into the action too. One took a huge shortcut and decided that the best way to get a piece of the pie was to copy the packaging and brand logo while filling up the tins with their own toxic brew. They registered as Alfa Paynt and even used our address on the cans.'

'So what forced you to close down?'

'It seemed that an overzealous official did a spot check in a small DIY shop and samples of the cans labelled with Alfa Paynt were taken to a laboratory of the Bureau of Quality and Technical Supervision for testing. The results were bad all over the line. Nothing in the cans resembled, even closely, what the national directives were about.'

'In the haste to identify the wrongdoer, Alfa Paint was considered the main culprit. One letter different but it seemed nobody noticed. A couple of days after the lab test we were informed that our product was not conforming to the new regulations and the factory was ordered to stop production till further notice. On top of that the national newspapers jumped into the fray to inform the readers in graphic detail that a foreign company had acted so irresponsibly on Chinese soil and the consequences of living with a coat of Alfa Paint on the house walls. A country-wide announcement followed notifying that Alfa Paint's products were harmful to humans and anyone having purchased such goods should avoid using them with immediate effect. Stores having the products in inventory had to remove the cans from the racks and contact proper authorities for disposal. Our good name was irrevocably tarnished. Sales stopped immediately!'

Someone said that simplicity of all things is the hardest to copy. But that was before China turned into a powerhouse where ingenious copying filled the void of creativity.

Alfa Paynt was merely a local player and their products got onto the shelves in their home province but barely beyond. For the small scale of operation the piggybacking company did a brisk business, mimicking all the marketing of its superior rival. With a price half that of Alfa Paint's, shops and distributors were most happy to buy Alfa Paynt and share in the success.

But since Alfa Paint's business was growing with leaps and bounds, the marketing and sales director was way too busy or . . . didn't really care. The overseas shareholders, emboldened by the results were pushing the department to take more market share, discover new venues to sell and make Alfa Paint a household name.

Adam challenged Pablo 'Why didn't you take action earlier? And . . . why do you inform us so late? We could have investigated and hopefully stopped the perpetrators in their tracks.'

'I think we all thought this copycat would never be a real nuisance. We discussed it briefly but it didn't really pop up as a hazard to our operations. Some of us considered them an annoyance but negligible quantity, other staff were openly proud that the brand was being copied and considered it a mark of success. Our R&D managers had analyzed Alfa Paynt's product and it was found to have no resemblance with ours. The key ingredients were highly carcinogenic and volatile chemicals.

'Let me get our head of R&D to join and share some detailed info on the issue.'

Calling in his secretary over the intercom, Pablo mumbled: 'Cherry can you ask for Leader X to come over with the analysis of the competitor's paint ingredients.'

'Leader X' swirled through my mind and brought back memories of a long forgotten 'Lady X', a cold-blooded villainess who popped up in one of my favourite comic strips. A bewitching blond beauty, always dressed in tightly fitted leather pants outlining her gorgeous curved body. At the helm of a criminal empire and occasionally hired by the Soviet Union, she was the perfect weapon in the fight against the 'free' world. In her eternal early thirties she'd seduce, for the greater cause, any man of interest or jump into a fighter jet swooshing air to air missiles to my cartoon heroes.

'Sorry for the name,' Pablo apologised and summoning me back to reality. 'It's just that his real name is so hard to pronounce that the name Leader X just stuck.'

A few minutes later, the much anticipated Leader X arrived with a thin folder of facts.

In no way did he resemble the archetypal lab researcher. At one metre eighty-five, completely bald, with slim body, wearing sixties-style glasses with heavy black frames and a faint permanent smile, he reminded me of a monk in a Tibetan monastery ... with a business suit. He almost floated to one of the free seats around the meeting table. In a cartoon he'd be perfect to infiltrate Lady X's criminal network.

His serene voice proceeded through the list, as if reading a mantra. It went from dichlorobenzene to hazardous formaldehyde to scary styrene followed by a number of other unpronounceable toxins all in quantities superseding even the most lax safety standards one could find in the obscurest of countries.

'So ... isn't that good enough reason?' we all said in unison, not really understanding why no immediate action had been taken.

'We thought with the passing of time customer complaints would grow at the expense of Alfa Paynt. Therefore suppliers would no longer want to deal with the copycat product but go for the real Alfa Paint. We spent little time and energy on trying to stop Alfa Paynt while we were expecting them to wither away. It looked rather a waste of our lawyers' time. We all reasoned that the problem would solve itself.'

Aghast by this weak argument, I couldn't hold back 'Are you really that naïve? You've got a great product, a remarkable market share and you let it all slip away. This is China, a market running at lightning speed, where the competitors literally never sleep. How stupid can one be?'

Leader X took this as his cue to leave and drifted back to his research temple.

While Adam probably asked the most pertinent question of the day: 'What's the address of the Alfa Paynt facility?'

Pablo's eyes stared at Sales, who in turn looked at Production, who intensely flipped through his folder before fishing for some response from Logistics . . . who shyly responded, 'Aah . . . we never made a real effort to find out who was distributing or manufacturing. Chinese New Year wasn't the time to investigate. We only know the name of the small town, roughly 350 km north of Guangzhou.'

The dramatic end to Pablo's rising star was initiated roughly fifteen months earlier when new health and environmental regulations were drafted on the content of paint and which ingredients would be considered harmful and blacklisted by year-end. At that time the Alfa Paint factory was already running a Chinese operation with a staff of around 150. The new directives were mostly in line with those enacted in Europe, with only here and there a slight tweak of content. Alfa Paint was already committed to a 'green product' and not much needed to be done to adjust their existing product range to the new guidelines. The production process could be fine-tuned months before the government's deadline.

Meanwhile, Alfa Paynt, either ignorant of the new guidelines, not able to adapt the production process or perhaps just had total disregard for authority. No one will ever know. This corporation just continued what it had been doing best. Why change a winning formula?

A couple of weeks into January, the shit hit the fan.

The timing, just before Chinese New Year, couldn't have been worse. The immediate factory closure, the press picking up the juicy story and most government offices on leave for an extended period of time, their China dream was tossed into a nightmare.

Formulating a solution after major damage has been done is never a straightforward task and in an opaque environment going after the Lady Xs of corporate misconduct is easier said than done.

If past experiences were of any help, getting the story straight and successfully moving through a maze of government organisations was going to require coordinated work by management, investigators, lawyers, government officials and even embassy staff.

The cost of such an operation only made sense because of the market size Alfa Paint had built up and the future revenue that could still be generated if the storm would settle down.

In less sophisticated acts of corporate misconduct, the effort to straighten out the harm done is often more costly than the economic loss. The schemes are specifically conceived to relieve the honest business person from hard-earned money and name.

Everybody has most probably had a good laugh at scam letters coming out of Nigeria, promising millions of dollars for assistance to retrieve the treasures of a lost or dead relative, who happened to be the bank director or CEO of an oil company in a past regime.

More sophisticated scams are operated out of China and with a local twist. The main plot revolves around a plausible business deal which tries to suck 'only' a few thousand dollars from the credulous business man.

It often starts with a potential buyer interested in purchasing some specific goods, often with technical details directly copied from the manufacturer's website.

An alarm bell should be ringing when the order is much larger than the norm. Someone not familiar with the Chinese market might still go along with it. However the alarms should scream when one is requested to fly to China to negotiate the deal because of the size of the order. Most often the contract negotiation will take place in a small town or city far from the bright city lights. Having been wined and dined, the neophyte seller received the escort of an official-looking 'police' car that, with blaring sirens, opened the road from the airport or train station to the hotel. The impression has now settled in that the buyer must be well-connected. The excitement builds up, because the famous 'you need *guanxi*' slogan every China rookie knows and believes is unfolding in front of him.

A wide range of self-styled officials who are either assisting the buying party or purport to be the end-user are introduced. Negotiations will be firm but finally after a couple of days the contract is signed. 'Yes, yes, yes! The China dream is real,' an inner voice shouts.

But at the last minute, just before leaving . . . one is informed that there's a Lady X spoiling the fun who wants to cancel the contract in favour of a competitor. So to get the buyer to pay the full contract value, a small amount of money will first have to be paid so that Lady X doesn't spoil the goodwill of the past few days. Basically to grease the deal. But who cares, the amount asked for is only a few percentage points of the total value and shouldn't make a dent in the profit margin. One gives in, after being pressed for a while to depart with tens of thousands of dollars because in the end 'guanxi is everything'. Guess what: once this payment is made and a promise that an L/C or contractual down payment will reach the seller's bank account on his/her glorious return home, the buyer will never be heard of again.

For those buying parties who are not interested in wasting time in wining and dining, they will inform the seller that a notary fee, paid from overseas, needs to be made to make the contract official. Cost price: a couple thousand dollars. It goes without saying that once this money is paid, all actors disappear into thin air. Actually a notary fee is not required to certify or endorse a commercial contract.

Ultimately no action can really be taken, because the effort to track the culprits and rehabilitate the wronged party dwarfs the amount involved.

The deep-pocketed Pablo and his misery was another party all together. For consultants and lawyers alike those unlucky targets are good bones to feast on.

Together with Pablo's team a strategy was formulated that would request an official reaction from the ambassador and bring in a formal complaint to the relevant authorities, while tapping into the (real this time) guanxi Alfa Paint had built up on a provincial level. Managing the legal claim brought forward was as important as tracking down and identifying Lady X.

It meant juggling contacts in the Beijing based national office of the State Administration of Industry and Commerce and on a provincial level in Guangzhou. Inside this Kafka-esque labyrinth, the Trademark Office, Consumer Protection Bureau, the legal department, Foreign Enterprise Registration Office, among others, all had to get Alfa Paint's attention.

Howling like a pack of hungry wolves, the lawyers dove into action. They loved every part of it.

When the plan was put in action we discovered that Alfa Paynt was a step ahead of us. The ban forced Lady X to lay low. A quiet withdrawal from the market was a first defensive move. Distributors in Alfa Paynt's home province, Hunan, were approached but it seemed all was bought off the books; mobile phone numbers went silent or no longer answered. A breakthrough came from the logistic company who was able to provide the origin of the Alfa Paynt. The address turned out to be near a major north-south artery in an anonymous looking makeshift factory, consisting of a couple of shacks with straw roofs and hardened earth floors, covering 800 square metres. Discarded empty barrels of ingredients, traces of spilled paint and a heap of damaged Alfa Paynt cans were all that was left. Again Lady X was ahead of us. The owner of the place turned out to be an elderly grain trader who leased the property after it became more lucrative to act as a landlord. The only tidbit he could offer us was to describe a Mr Xiang in his fifties who rented the space, had paid a full year's rent in advance, and who drove a nice German car with a Jiangxi licence plate. After failed attempts to involve the local police the trail went cold. The Hunan Bureau of Industry and Commerce couldn't assist us because we couldn't identify a person or company licence. The last straw we could hold onto was the registration of 'Alfa Paynt' trademark. The news from the trademark office was negative. 'Alfa Paynt' was not a registered trademark and we were welcome to register it.

Lady X had once again escaped.

Luckily for Pablo, the gentle but persistent pressure from the embassy and more importantly the incredible assistance and understanding of local authorities were of big help to restart the operations by the middle of June.

I can only think of the words of Mexican conceptual artist Stefan Brüggeman: 'All my ideas are imported, all my products are exported, all my explanations are rubbish.'

Postscript

- If you know your product is being copied, act quickly. Inform authorities of the situation. Don't be complacent. Know what is going on in the market, because sales figures are only part of the equation to keep your operations alive and kicking. Surprises can lurk at every corner.
- A once popular scam was to offer attractively priced goods through eBay. Those could be laptop computers, carbon fibre racing bikes, antique Chinese furniture, etc. To make it look serious you were often asked to buy five to ten sets in one go from the wholesaler. Once the payment was made and the box of 'goods' arrived at your doorstep there was a good chance that the laptop computers were from the nineties, the bikes, rusted Flying Pigeon bicycles and the antique furniture . . . used IKEA cabinets.
- Another past scam Lady X kept herself busy with: A container of garlic, peanuts, vegetables or other was ordered from China but the European buyer never made the effort or spent the money to check at the shipping end what really went in the container. The buyer thought he/she was safe because 'only' a 30 percent down payment was made and the balance to be paid upon arrival of the shipment. Surprise. . . . When the goods were inspected at the destination most of the container was full of goods past consumption date.
- On several occasions have we been asked to go after these Lady X's of the industrial trade. Unfortunately the cost to follow up is often a multiple of the money lost . . . because it just takes so much time and effort to identify the parties involved. Therefore we can only suggest not to act naively and to do a bit of home-work. Don't jump at

any opportunity that seems to be too good to be true. Anyone who wants to sell or buy goods in China needs to make sure he's dealing with an honest party who's really interested in buying your goods or selling a quality product.

Afterword

I hope you enjoyed this book.

Doing business in China is often perceived as a complex puzzle with opaque rules of play that are great fun to read, talk or indeed write about. In reality the puzzle is not that hard to crack. Since the doors were timidly opened several decades ago, China has matured, and the jigsaw pieces have become fewer and much easier to put together.

From a Western perspective, certain steps along the way are indeed taken differently in this part of the world. I learned this the hard way and had to grapple with the fact that cultural sensitivity is the key to lifting the shroud of mystery. Getting rid of our own ethnocentrism, however, is easier said than done. Cross-cultural misperceptions remain the chief danger to business success. Starting the blame game can prevent a return on investment or cause you to falter in any new market.

The business basics are identical in China to anywhere else in the world. It's often the way in which the unique local culture is digested by investors that will define success. This is as valid for a Chinese businessman who wants to invest in Spain, Japan or Nigeria.

Soaking up another business culture cannot be done by merely sitting on the sidelines reading books or attending crash courses. It's in the field that you'll really be able to grasp, adjust and adapt. Having said that, don't try to be more Chinese than the Chinese – always keep in mind that your local counterparts have the home advantage.

With common sense, a good product, a bit of luck, an open mind and a level head, anyone can succeed in China.

All the best with your endeavours and enjoy the ride!